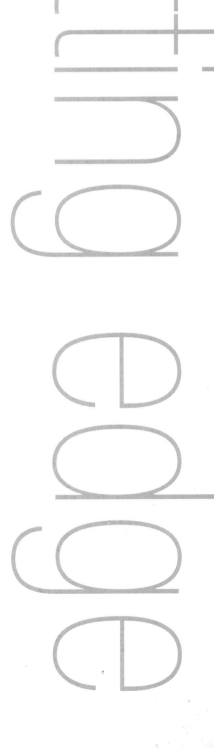
cutting edge

Japanese Swords in

Victor Harris

cutting edge

the British Museum

THE BRITISH MUSEUM PRESS

© 2004 The Trustees of the British Museum

First published in 2004 by The British Museum Press
A division of The British Museum Company Ltd
46 Bloomsbury Street, London WC1B 3QQ

A catalogue record for this book
is available from the British Library

ISBN 0 7141 2419 2

Specially commissioned sword photography
by Kishida Katsunori

Designed and typeset in Helvetica
by Harry Green

Printed in Spain
by Grafos SA, Barcelona

The Trustees of the British Museum

acknowledge with gratitude

generous support for this project from

PETER MOORES FOUNDATION

Contents

Acknowledgements 6

Preface 7

Introduction 8

The Catalogue 40

Colour Illustrations 49–64

Catalogue Illustrations 84

Glossary 154

Further Reading 159

List of Place Names
with their Present-Day Locations 160

Acknowledgements

The Peter Moores Foundation project to polish and otherwise conserve in Japan a hundred swords from the collection of the British Museum has enabled them to be properly displayed for the first time. I am most grateful to the Foundation and to Sir Peter Moores, who has been so encouraging throughout.

I owe thanks also to my long-time friend and mentor Ogawa Morihiro, who, together with his wife Sumiko, made a thorough survey of the Museum's collection in 1997 and advised on the extent of polishing necessary for each blade. The project was done with the assistance of our colleagues in the Agency for Cultural Affairs, Tokyo, and in the Japanese Sword Museum at Yoyogi in Tokyo. The late Suzuki Kanjo, Director of the Sword Museum, and his staff arranged for thirty-three expert sword polishers and a number of other craftsmen to work on the collection. These included Abe Kazunori, Aoki Mitsunobu, Dodo Takemi, Fujishiro Okisato, Hagi Yasuaki, Hakuta Osamu, Hon'ami Michihiro, Iida Masahisa, Kataoka Sumio, Kawamoto Kazuhiro, Koresawa Norimasa, Kuroda Moritoshi, Mawatari Takaaki, Mishina Kenji, Nakao Toyotsugu, Okonogi Gakushi, Onishi Nobuo, Ono Hiroshi, Oshida Yukihiro, Ozaki Akiyoshi, Saito Tsukasa, Sasaki Takuji, Shimizu Katsuyuki, Shinozaki Koki, Shundo Hideki, Sugiwara Hiroshi, Sumi Kenzo, Takaiwa Setsuo and Takayama Kazuyuki, as well as the team who worked on the mountings: Usuki Yoshihiko, Watanabe Tsunetsugu, Yanagawa Seiji and Yoshida Hideo.

The photography of the blades and mountings was done in the British Museum by Kishida Katsunori using a scanning technique developed by Tom Kishida. My friend and colleague Ogasawara Nobuo, formerly Curator of Swords in the Tokyo National Museum, attended, helped and advised with the photography, and gave of his immense expertise in the detailed cataloguing of each blade.

Members of the To-Ken Society of Great Britain made a generous donation to help with the expense of producing this catalogue, and the Toshiba International Foundation have once again helped with the costs of mounting the exhibition and producing the Gallery Guide. The catalogue has been overseen for the British Museum Press by Nina Shandloff, edited by Colin Grant, designed by Harry Green and produced by Sarah Levesley, all of whom have done a sterling and creative job in the face of various delays and complexities. My daughter Satsuki provided constant criticism and support, and made the drawings for the section on blade characteristics. My close friend and colleague Timothy Clark read through the text at every stage, and I am indebted to him for the correction of errors and a general improvement in literary style. The exhibition has been designed by Hannah Payne, Austin Barlow and Claire Edwards in the British Museum's Department of Presentation. My colleagues of the staff of the Department of Asia have been constantly supportive throughout the project.

Preface

The Japanese sword is renowned as a formidable cutting weapon and admired as a work of art the world over. It is therefore with great pleasure that we are able to present for public view for the first time this large number of Japanese swords in the exhibition *Cutting Edge*. There are eighty-nine blades alone on display here – rarely has such a number of swords been exhibited in a museum display even in Japan, and this is the first such opportunity in the United Kingdom.

There is an intrinsic mystery to the Japanese sword: its complex metallurgy and austere aesthetic are imbued with an awesome array of meanings and associations. In the exhibition of ancient Shintō art staged in the Japanese Gallery at the British Museum in 2001, for example, it was shown that swords more than a thousand years old were considered not merely the symbol of the *kami* (Shintō deities) but in some cases the actual manifestation of them.

Although the swords displayed in this exhibition were regarded first and foremost as weapons, most of them were made during that unusually peaceful time in Japanese history – the Edo period (1600–1868) – and served as symbols of the civil authority of the samurai elite. Such was the traditional appreciation for swords as works of art that they were superbly embellished with beautiful, intricate fittings made to the command of the very wealthy by the best artisans. The blades have all been recently polished to enhance the visibility of the texture of the steel down to the finest detail. We hope that this exhibition will enable an in-depth view of each blade and further the understanding of this traditional Japanese aesthetic.

The polishing project was made possible by the enthusiasm and generosity of one man, Sir Peter Moores. Sir Peter, through his charitable foundation, funded the cost of sending almost one hundred of the Museum's finest Japanese swords and their mountings back to Japan in 1998, where they were polished and otherwise conserved in the traditional manner by more than thirty specialists under the auspices of the Japanese Sword Museum in Tokyo, to which we are also most grateful. Victor Harris, Keeper Emeritus of the Japanese collections at the British Museum, has commenced his retirement by generously curating for us this special exhibition. Mr Harris is a world-respected authority on the Japanese sword and a lifelong practitioner of Kendo. For this project he has drawn copiously on the expertise of his long-time friend and colleague, Mr Nobuo Ogasawara, former Curator of Swords at the Tokyo National Museum. The To-Ken Society of Great Britain has made a generous contribution towards the costs of producing the exhibition catalogue and we are thankful also to our friends at the Toshiba International Foundation who have once again supported the costs of mounting the exhibition and producing a Gallery Guide.

Neil MacGregor
Director, British Museum

Introduction

This book is intended to be a catalogue for the exhibition in the British Museum, *Cutting Edge,* and also a guide to the study of Japanese sword blades based on that exhibition, but not a comprehensive history of the Japanese sword. It concentrates exclusively on the swords in the British Museum's collection and does not therefore cover all of the many schools of Japanese sword-making that were active over the centuries, although the Further Reading list includes references to books in English that provide that information. The catalogue itself consists of British Museum sword blades and mountings that were conserved in Japan during 1998, a project sponsored by the Peter Moores Foundation. This introduction also contains illustrations of other blades and mountings in the collection that are in perfect condition and did not need to be conserved.

The swords themselves are the curved single-edged weapons that were perfected sometime during the Heian period (794–1185) and continued to be the indispensable weapon of the samurai, the 'warrior class' of feudal Japan – and a symbol of their spirit – until the end of the nineteenth century. Other blade weapons, including daggers and pole-arms, were manufactured by the same smiths who made the long swords using the same technology. The process of manufacture originated in Chinese steel technology, which was introduced into Japan by the fifth century AD, and Chinese-style straight swords continued to be made in Japan for several hundred years until the emergence of the classic curved weapon.

As weapons, the curved swords were technically far superior to their continental prototypes, and the finely polished blades themselves revealed a characteristic beauty in the textures of the steel surface, which is unique to the Japanese sword. These attributes result from the care taken in every step of the manufacturing process, from the mining of the ore, through the initial refining of the steel and the hand-forging of the blade, to the essentially Japanese method of heat-treating to harden the steel.

As well as being a deadly weapon and a unique work of art, the sword in Japan is imbued with a spiritual essence. With the jewel and the mirror, the sword is one of the three holy objects of the ancient Japanese imperial regalia. Swords are even venerated as the resident deities of some Shintō shrines, and invocations to or representations of Shintō and other deities are found carved on some blades. Kendō (The Way of the Sword) is the spiritual study of sword-fencing, which aims beyond mere victory at war towards ultimate Buddhist awareness. The sword is also therefore considered an implement of Buddhist enlightenment and often had Buddhist emblems carved on the blade.

In traditional Japanese culture every workplace has a shrine dedicated to the deity of that particular profession, and sword-making is no exception. The concept of cleanliness is applied to man as well as material, and the smith will bathe and purify his thoughts in preparation for the job. Each process is governed by the practices of Shintō, the native religion of Japan, in which the deities of nature commune with man in his professions and other daily activities. It is often said that Shintō is not a religion but a set of

Fig.1 Katsukawa Shunshō (d.1792), Ushiwaka-maru and Benkei fighting on Gojō Bridge. About 1770s. Colour woodblock, publisher unknown, 32.0 x 22.3 cm. 1906.12-20.0141

working principles. Whereas it has no specific moral teachings, its great precepts include cleanliness, respect for materials and traditions, and an awareness of the spiritual nature of the world around us. As such, it is surely at the root of the Japanese genius for industry, and the sword is one of the enduring fruits of that industry. An appreciation of such beauty, deriving from the laws of nature, is central to the Japanese aesthetic. Like the study of ceramics, the study of the Japanese sword blade as an art form is the study of technical excellence, elegance of shape and beauty of texture.

Historical background

The changes in sword length, shape and metallurgical characteristics that occurred over the centuries make it possible to tell a sword's age and region of origin. A short review of the main historical periods in Japan will provide some background for a discussion of these blade characteristics.

Heian period (794–1185)

There was regular contact between Japan, Korea and China during the centuries of the Kofun (Ancient Mounds) period, before the introduction of Buddhism from China in the later part of the sixth century AD, and before the first written records of the early part of the eighth century AD, the *Kojiki* and *Nihongi*. Such cultural exchange continued during the early Heian period, with Japan absorbing religious, civil and literary concepts from China until AD 894, when regular diplomatic relations with China were discontinued. This event marked a turning point in Japanese cultural consciousness. From around that time Japan acquired a new confidence, and new aesthetics and native fashions gradually replaced Chinese ones. Social customs developed during the Heian period that would shape Japanese culture for the next thousand years. Native literary traditions evolved, as the angular writing of Chinese characters developed into the elegant cursive *kana* (phonetic script) of poets and women novelists. Women's hair was worn long and flowing like the sleeves of their silken kimono. Significantly, at the same time the straight Chinese sword developed into the elegantly curved Japanese sword. This was the result of no sudden rash revolution, but the fruition of centuries of absorbing and modifying the wonders of China's ancient civilization in an entirely characteristic Japanese way.

The *Engishiki* (Institutes of the Engi Era, 901–22),

Fig. 2 Katsukawa Shunzan (worked about 1780s–1790s). 'Sasaki Shirō Takatsuna'. About 1780s. Colour woodblock, published by 'Mikawa', 36.5 x 24.1 cm. 1906.12-20.0186

completed in 927, tells of the several stages involved in the special sword-polishing process, indicating the importance given to the visual appearance of blades at that period. This was probably about the time that the Japanese sword was perfected; significantly, at around the same time the natural ash glaze on hand-formed pottery was becoming established as an art form. Just as the optimum furnace conditions for the manufacture of a technically excellent pot produce a natural beauty in the glazed surface, so the conditions of forging and heat-treating a blade, so that it will not break or bend and will maintain a sharp edge, produce a natural beauty in the steel surface.

In the Heian period Japan was ruled by the imperial house in Kyoto, although imperial authority was steadily challenged by the rise of powerful provincial clans and Buddhist sects. During this period the earliest curved swords were made either in regions where there was a ready supply of iron ore (*satetsu*, or 'sand iron', washed down from mountainous areas to river estuaries) or in centres of political or religious power. There were excellent swordsmiths like Yukihira of Bungo Province in Kyūshū, Yasutsuna of Hōki and Sanjō Munechika in Kyoto. In Kibi (Bizen, Bingo, Bitchū and Mimasaka Provinces – present-day Okayama Prefecture and part of Hiroshima Prefecture) a number of groups provided the foundation for many later schools. By the Heian period certain imported esoteric Buddhists sects had been thoroughly integrated with native beliefs to form 'mountain religions' (Shugendō), in which enlightenment was sought by *yama bushi* (mountain hermits) through austere ascetic practices. Many swordsmiths were adherents and drew inspiration from the mountain deities. Smiths of the Gassan school (fig. 16), associated with Dewa Sanzan, the Three Mountains of Dewa Province (present-day Yamagata and Akita Prefectures), were active from the Kamakura period onwards.

Kamakura period (1185–1333)

During the eleventh and twelfth centuries persistent battling among the provincial clans and the increasing isolation of the aristocracy in Kyoto brought two clans, the Taira and the Minamoto, to prominence. Warfare was between heavily armoured, mounted samurai whose main weapons were the bow and sword. Infantry were also well armoured, using bow, sword and *naginata*. Rivalry between the Minamoto and Taira clans was concluded when the Minamoto under Yoritomo (1147–99) finally defeated the Taira at the battle of Dan-no-ura in 1185. From then the government of Japan was to be in the hands of a succession of military clans, although the imperial line continued to hold court at Kyoto. Yoritomo set up government several hundred kilometres east of Kyoto at Kamakura in Sagami Province (present-day Kanagawa Prefecture), until his clan was superseded by the Hōjō in 1219.

The Kamakura period was a time of the flowering of the martial arts and rapid development of sword-making technology. Samurai were required to rigorously study horsemanship, archery, swordsmanship and other military matters, and looked to Zen Buddhism for the spiritual frame of mind necessary for combat. At the same time 'Pure Land' Buddhism was brought to the general populace with the Kamakura government sponsoring the building of temples in the provinces.

After a failed attempt to overthrow the Hōjō at Kamakura in 1221, Retired Emperor Gotoba-In (1180–1239) was exiled to the island of Oki where he spent the remaining years of his life. He was permitted to pursue a passion for sword-making there, and was attended in rotation by smiths from the main schools, particularly those of Bitchū, Bizen and Yamashiro Provinces (present-day Kyoto Prefecture). Many of the early smiths from established provincial schools were thus able to study each other's technologies, due to the emperor's interest. Blades made at the emperor's forge often have the imperial *mon* (crest) of a chrysanthemum engraved on the tang. It was the emperor who gave the name Ichimonji to the school of Norimune of Bizen Province, signifying that they were the 'first under the heavens'. The use of the character *ichi* (one), which they accordingly signed on the tangs of their swords, and the imperial chrysanthemum *mon*, was

Fig. 3 Utagawa Kuniyoshi (1797–1861). 'Satō Shirobei Tadanobu', from the series 'One of the Eight Hundred Heroes of the *Water Margins* of Japan' (*Honchō Suikoden gōketsu happyaku nin no hitori*). About 1831. Colour woodblock, published by Kagaya Kichibei, 37.6 x 25.0 cm. 1906.12-20.01309

continued by later smiths during the Edo period, particularly those of Bizen Province.

Throughout the Kamakura period swordsmiths moved from provincial centres to Kamakura itself to supply the demand for weapons there; notable among them were Saburō Kunimune and Sukezane of Bizen Province. Around the end of the thirteenth century sword-making further evolved with the coming together at Kamakura of diverse styles, and the Sōshū (Sagami Province, present-day Kanagawa Prefecture) tradition became established. Shintōgo Kunimitsu, whose name is linked in the *Kanchi-in bon mei zukushi* (List of Swordsmiths' Names from the Kanchi-in Hall of the Tōji Temple, 1423) with both Sukezane and Kunimune of Bizen Province, is recognized as the originator of the Sōshū tradition, which was further perfected by his pupils Masamune and Yukimitsu, and subsequently by the so-called 'Ten Pupils of Masamune' in the fourteenth century. The Hōjō clan continued to govern at Kamakura until the town was taken in 1333 by an army of discontented provincial samurai, ostensibly under the banner of the Emperor Godaigo (1288–1339).

Fig. 5 (above) Utagawa Kuniyoshi (1797–1861). 'Moor at the Foot of Mt Fuji: Picture of the Soga Brothers Achieving their Avowed Wish' (*Fuji no susono, Soga kyōdai hommō o togeru zu*). About 1843–7. Colour woodblock triptych, published by Yamaguchiya Tōbei, 37.0 x 74.9 cm (3 sheets together). 1915.8-23.0919(1-3)

Fig. 4 (left) Utagawa Kunisada (1786–1864). 'Musashibō Benkei'. About 1830s. Colour woodblock, published by Daikokuya, 38.1 x 26.2 cm. 1906.12-20.01054

Nambokuchō period (1336–92)

Following the fall of Kamakura, Emperor Godaigo ruled from Kyoto for three years before the Ashikaga clan under Takeuji set up a rival imperial house in the north of the city in 1336. This act sparked off sixty years of civil war between the supporters of the northern and southern courts, which was to end with victory for the northern faction under Ashikaga Yoshimitsu in 1392. This sixty-year struggle is known as the Yoshino period, after the place outside Kyoto where a number of battles were fought, or alternatively as the Nambokuchō period (North and South Courts period). During this time smiths again migrated, some returning from Kamakura to their original provinces, others moving to new ones (see 'Changing Traditions' below, pp. 32–3).

Muromachi period (1392–1573)

In 1392 victorious shogun Ashikaga Yoshimitsu (1358–1408) re-established military government at Muromachi in Kyoto. The Ashikaga renewed contacts with China, and sponsored arts and crafts inspired by Zen Buddhist concepts, in tune with the martial spirit of the samurai class. But in time, just as the Kamakura government had become too inward-looking during the early fourteenth century, so the Ashikaga came to neglect the country at large, and civil war erupted in 1467 that was to last for a century – the Period of the Warring Provinces (*sengoku jidai*). Huge armies of *ashigaru* (light foot-soldiers), drawn from the non-samurai population, fought on foot, led by far smaller numbers of mounted samurai. In 1543 guns were taken from a Portuguese ship grounded at the island of Tanegashima, and within a few decades Japan was

Fig. 6 (Kano?) Ichigyokusai Eisen (worked about mid-19th century). Minamoto no Yoshiie (Hachiman Tarō) on horseback (detail). About mid-19th century. Hanging scroll; ink and colour on silk, 144.0 x 49.0 cm. Japanese Painting 988 (1881.12-10.01375)

fully armed with the new weapons. The gun was the decisive factor in bringing the Period of the Warring Provinces to an end, with the victory of a force of 3,000 musketeers under Oda Nobunaga (1534–82) at the battle of Nagashino in 1575. This event heralded the end of the sword as a major weapon of warfare. Nobunaga ruled from a castle he raised at Momoyama in Kyoto until his death, when he was succeeded by Toyotomi Hideyoshi.

Momoyama period (1573–1600)

Toyotomi Hideyoshi (1537–98) inherited a unified Japan and in 1594 set up his headquarters at Fushimi in Momoyama. As part of a strategy aimed at enforcing the stabilization of the nation, he forbade the possession of swords, bows and arrows, spears and guns by the agrarian populace. Hideyoshi's 'sword hunt' of 1588, as it was known, effectively stopped large-scale production in Mino and Bizen

Provinces, and the better smiths dispersed elsewhere. For the sword-making industry new technologies associated with gun-making were introduced, and steel, largely from Izumo, was centrally distributed from the port of Sakai in the Kansai region. Smiths left the regions that had been controlled by temples and powerful clans before Hideyoshi's time, and moved to large cities and new castle towns in the provinces.

At around this time the practice started whereby swordsmiths, like bronze mirror-makers, were granted titular honours that had previously defined the ranks of samurai officials. One of the earliest recorded examples is Mutsu no kami Kanemichi, who moved from Mino Province to Kyoto during the Momoyama period and established the Sampin school there. There were usually four ranks available to swordsmiths, from the highest *kami*, through *suke* and *jō*, to (rarely) the lowest *sakan*. There were subdivisions in some ranks, but in the inscriptions on swords one finds a higher version only of *jō*, called *daijō*. From the Nara period (AD 710–94) onwards these ranks were the real titles of persons in provincial government service so that, for example, Etchū no kami would actually have been an official with the rank *kami* working in Etchū Province. In the Edo period the award of such ranks was controlled by early generations of the family of the swordsmith Iga no kami Kimmichi, through whom monetary contributions were made to the imperial household. It was usual for a smith to start at the bottom of the hierarchy, raising his contribution periodically until he reached the rank of *kami*, equivalent to fifth court rank.

During the relatively peaceful Momoyama period the arts, centred on the society of Kyoto, flourished on a grand scale, ranging from colourful fashions and paintings to the interior decorations of castles and mansions. The new fashions applied also to sword mountings. Hideyoshi himself wore a pair of swords with bright vermilion scabbards decorated with a broad helix of gold and gilt hilt fittings. The best old swords were sought after by the wealthier of the warrior class almost as fashion accessories. The custom of wearing swords thrust through the belt edge-uppermost became widespread, and many long *tachi* of the Kamakura and Nambokuchō periods were shortened for this purpose.

Hideyoshi built a fortress at Osaka, not far from Kyoto, and further castles were built by powerful clans in the provinces. Swordsmiths moved from the traditional centres of production during the civil wars to the new castle towns. The migration of smiths from the regions of high production in Bizen and Mino Provinces was particularly influential on the budding new styles. After his victory over the Toyotomi forces at the battle of Sekigahara in 1600, Tokugawa Ieyasu (1542–1616) was in 1603 pronounced shogun, the military ruler of Japan.

Edo period (1600–1868)

Tokugawa Ieyasu raised a castle at Edo (modern Tokyo). The last violent act of unification was the sacking of Osaka castle and the overthrow of Hideyoshi's son, Hideyori, in 1615. Under the Tokugawa regime, which was to last until the imperial restoration in 1868, Japan was ruled by *daimyō* (literally 'great names', feudal lords), each of whom built castles in the provinces they were entrusted with. Towns sprang up around these castles, to become centres of industry and commerce. The demand for swords had fallen with the cessation of civil war, so that only the best smiths were able to continue in business, and the best of these were retained by the provincial *daimyō*.

The fall of Osaka castle and the suppression of the Shimabara rebellion in 1637 confirmed the position of the Tokugawa, and they were able to impose peaceful rule over Japan for over two hundred years. Strict legislation was introduced to ensure that there could never again be armies conscripted on the scale seen during the Period of the Warring Provinces. This included the *sankin kōtai* system of alternate periods of residence in Edo, whereby the *daimyō* had to leave their families hostage in their Edo estates when they returned to their home province. The size of castle garrisons was limited, the possession of firearms strictly regulated, and a system of local government inspection was set up. Foreign exchange was limited from the 1630s to contact with Dutch and Chinese traders at the port of Nagasaki, on the west of Kyūshū. A descending social hierarchy of samurai, farmers, artisans and merchants (*shi nō kō shō*) was rigidly enforced. Regulations were made limiting the possession of swords and specifying the type and length allowed to the various classes of people. In 1626, for example, the length of swords was limited to 2 *shaku* and 8 or 9 *sun* (around 80 cm). The use of vermilion scabbards, which had been popular in the Momoyama period, was prohibited. Under the *sankin kōtai* system, the large retinues accompanying annual *daimyō* processions to and from Edo had to wear uniform clothing bearing the *mon* (crest) of their clan, keep their hair dressed in the standard *chommage* style (i.e. with a dressed top-knot), and carry matching pairs of swords. The demand for swords declined in the final decades of the seventeenth and early decades of the eighteenth century, however, probably because of restrictions placed on ownership and because there were

Fig. 7 Sumiyoshi Hirotsura (Hirosada, 1793–1863). Yoshitsune at the battle of Yashima. Mid-19th century. Unmounted hanging scroll; ink, colour and gold on silk, 49.1 x 66.6 cm. Japanese Painting 326 (1881.12-10.0435)

Fig. 8 ?Morimasu. Battle of Ogaki. About 1832? Section
of a handscroll; ink, colour and gold on paper, 39.8 x 97.8 cm.
Japanese Painting 295 (1881.12-10.0261)

already enough blades in existence. But during this same
period schools of decorative metalwork flourished as never
before, indicating a tendency to treat the sword as a fashion
accessory rather than primarily as a weapon.

During the second half of the eighteenth century the renewed
maritime activity of the Western powers around Japan caused
tensions within the country, and factions for and against the
ending of the isolation emerged. A movement to instil new
military vigour into a country now accustomed to nearly two

centuries of peace brought about a return to ancient styles of
sword-making. During the 1850s and 1860s there was
sporadic insurrection against the Tokugawa by groups in favour
of modernization and a return to imperial rule, and foreign
residents were also occasionally attacked. In 1868 the old
feudal regime was toppled and a new government was formed
under Emperor Meiji. The emperor moved from the ancient
imperial palace in Kyoto to Edo and ruled until 1912 in a period
of rapid change that saw Japan established as a modern
nation state. Western customs, technologies, thinking and
fashions were adopted. Military, police and dress swords were
now put into Western-style sabre mountings, and although
many old blades were adapted, shorter and poor quality blades
were also made for this use.

Structure of the blade

Manufacture

During the manufacturing process steels of different quality are combined in a number of ways to make a blade with a hard skin and a relatively soft core. The steels are first treated to obtain the required purity and carbon content, and then made into a block that is repeatedly heated and folded to produce a laminate structure. After several or as many as twenty folds the block is beaten out into the final shape of the blade. It is then further shaped with scrapers and files, and prepared for heat treatment. The grain on the blade results from the folding process during the early stages of manufacture, after which

hammering and filing form the final shape. The most important part of the process then takes place: the heating and quenching of the blade to harden it.

The blade is first coated with a thick slurry of clay, charcoal and the fine mixture of steel and stone dust obtained as a by-product of the polishing process. This is partially scraped off along the cutting edge, and when it has dried hard, the blade is heated until it is red hot and quenched by plunging it into a bath of cold water. The effect of the different thicknesses of clay is to vary the rate of cooling and consequently the degree of growth of the various crystalline structures formed in the steel. The most extreme conditions in the metallurgic transformation of the steel occur along the junction of the thicker layer of the clay mixture with the thinner band along the edge. This forms the *hamon* (badge of the blade), where the most prominent crystal structures are seen. This is visible as a whitish continuous line from a few millimetres to about a centimetre in from the cutting edge. At the same time the slower rate of cooling under the thicker layer of clay produces further structures on the *hira* (flat) of the blade, whereby the *jihada* (ground skin) is produced. The mechanical properties of the sword, and hence the beauty, depend upon the skill with which the quenching process is done.

The polishing process is no less important than the initial manufacturing process. This often involves the use of more than twenty grades of stone, from the coarsest down to the finest. It is the unique nature of the Japanese polish that it reveals all the varied textures in the blade. Above all the polisher ensures that the lines of the curved blade are smooth and continuous and that the angles of the planes are clearly defined. He must maintain the sectional form of the *ji* (ground), which might be perfectly flat or slightly convex (*hamaguri-ba*, literally 'clam blade'). The polisher produces a completely even surface, which not only renders the textures of the blade clearly visible but also helps to preserve it against corrosion. The final stages of polishing involve the use of various powders, including stone dust and iron oxides. Microscopic examination of traditionally polished blades shows that the minute traces of abrasion lie in haphazard directions, whereas an examination of modern polished metallographic specimens shows the polishing lines all lying in one direction, so that the surface is uniform. The final stages of Japanese polishing are thus intended to produce a surface that reveals microscopic variations in both grain contour and crystalline formations.

Reading the blade

JIHADA

The quenching process that decides the texture of the *jihada* (ground skin) is primarily intended to form the *hamon*. A metallurgically well-made sword will exhibit harmony between the *jihada* and the *hamon*. It is not possible to have a sword with a good *hamon* and a poor *jihada*, or vice versa. Indeed, the beauty of the sword lies largely in the form of, and harmony between, the two. Both the *jihada* and *hamon* will give indications of when the sword was made, the school that made it and often the individual smith.

The laminations produced by the folding process during the manufacture of the blade result in a visible grain on the surface. This grain in the *jigane* (metal of the ground) can be one of several types, or a mixture of them. The most widely found resembles the grain of a cut and planed piece of timber and is called *itame* (plank grain). A similar grain consisting of closed concentric rings is called *mokume* (wood grain). *Mokume* is not found alone, but is always mixed into *itame hada*. The patterns are classified as large (*ōitame*) or small (*koitame* and *komokume*). A very fine grain found on Hizen (present-day Nagasaki Prefecture) swords is called *konuka hada* (rice bran), intimating the skin of a beautiful woman's face, since in the Edo period women used small bags of bran to wash their faces. One of the finest *hada* is called *nashiji* (pearskin), and the very finest of all, being virtually invisible to the naked eye, is called *muji hada* (groundless).

A grain consisting of straight, or almost straight, parallel lines – like the appearance of a log cut down the centre – is called *masame* (true grain). A wavy, sinusoidal pattern called *ayasugi hada* (cryptomeria twill) is found on the work of the Naminohira school of Satsuma Province, the Gassan school of Dewa Province from the Kamakura period onwards (fig. 16), and on some later eighteenth- and nineteenth-century swords. A blade will often have more than one kind of grain mixed together. Many swords, although not with perfectly straight *masame*, will have a *nagare* (flowing) grain.

Crystalline structures called *nioi* and *nie*, which form the *hamon*, are also frequently found to a greater or lesser extent on the *ji* (ground) of the blade. *Nioi* is described as a martensitic structure in which the crystals of steel are not individually visible to the naked eye. It has been likened to the appearance of the Milky Way on an autumn night, to layers of a morning mist, or to the aspect of blossoms on distant trees. *Nie* may be likened to frost on leaves, to silvery grains of sand, or to expanses of clearly visible stars. *Nie* on the *ji* is called *jinie*, and it may occur in a number of formations. *Jinie* might be evenly spread over the whole blade (e.g. Hizen school blades, nos 53–6), occur in patches called *jifu* (ground spots) or create long dark formations called *chikei* (ground shadow) conforming roughly to the flow of the grain. In work of the Aoe school during the Nambokuchō period dark patches of steel with a sunken appearance are known as *sumi hada* (black ink skin), and larger patches with indistinct profile are called *namazu hada* (catfish skin). A similar *sumi hada* is also found on blades by Tadayoshi I of Hizen Province in the early Edo period.

A longitudinal white shadow of *nioi* on the *ji* is called *utsuri* (reflection, or transfer), since it is removed from the *hamon*. *Utsuri* is found especially on Bizen Province swords of the middle Kamakura period, when it appears as a continuous wavy line known as *midare utsuri* (wild *utsuri*) or *chōji utsuri*

(*utsuri* resembling a row of clove buds). A straight form of *utsuri* called *bō utsuri* (bar *utsuri*) is found on work of the Aoe school of Bitchū Province during the Nambokuchō period, and on Bizen work of the early fifteenth century. Less visible, indistinct, shadowy-pale forms of *utsuri* are found on swords of many other schools and by individual smiths. Seki (in Mino Province, southern part of present-day Gifu Prefecture) work, in particular, often has a white sheen less clearly defined than *utsuri*, known as *shirake* (whiteness).

Other formations occur that follow the boundaries between different kinds of steel. Darker lines on the steel of swords by Norishige, the pupil of Masamune of Sōshū who worked in Etchū, is sometimes called *matsukawa hada* (pine bark *hada*) or *hijiki hada* (*hijiki* is a stringy kind of edible seaweed). Some later, Edo-period smiths deliberately mixed different quality steels in order to produce vivid effects, like the alternate bright and dark layers of the *itame* on the *wakizashi* blade by the smith Naotane (no. 62).

HAMON

The *hamon*, or 'badge of the blade' – the line defining the hardened edge and the crystalline structures within it – will be mainly composed of either *nioi* or *nie*, or a combination of the two. The line defining the boundary between the *ha* (the hardened steel along the cutting edge) and *ji* is known as the *nioi-guchi*. Its quality is described as tight, if the line is clearly defined, or deep, if it gradually becomes less distinct towards the cutting edge. It may also be described more subjectively as 'hard' or 'moist', respectively.

Lines falling within the *hamon* towards the cutting edge are called *ashi* (legs), and separate small patches are named *yō* (leaves). Longitudinal stretches of *nie* within the *ha* are called *sunagashi* (flowing sand). Finer bright lines of *nie* within the *nioiguchi*, sometimes extending erratically into the *ha*, form *kinsuji* (metal lines) or *inazuma* (lightning), found on fine early swords, particularly those of Sōshū. *Nijū-ba* describes a line parallel with the *hamon* forming a kind of double *hamon*, while shorter upturned crescent formations are called *uchinoke* (struck-off).

The most common *hamon*, which is found on swords of all periods, is *suguha* (straight *hamon*). This might be perfectly parallel with the cutting edge of the blade or it might have variations. A *hamon* with extreme variations is called *midare* (wild). During the early Kamakura period smiths of Bizen and Bitchū Provinces made blades with a *hamon* called *chōji* (cloves) since it resembles a row of clove buds. During the later Kamakura period this style spread to other provinces, and in

Yamashiro Province swords were produced with *chōjiba* in *nie* – as opposed to those of Bizen, which were predominantly in *nioi*. *Gunome hamon* (reciprocating *hamon*) was also made during this period. During the late Kamakura and Nambokuchō periods the Sōshū school at Kamakura, established by Shintōgo Kunimitsu and his pupils Yukimitsu and Masamune, produced blades with *jihada* and *hamon* rich in activity. Their complex *hamon* included *notare* (undulating) *hamon* with *gunome*, *midare*, *sunagashi* and *kinsuji*, and in the *jihada*, *chikei* and other formations of *jinie*.

In the work of Masamune's pupils, Hiromitsu and Akihiro, and later smiths the *hamon* activity becomes more extreme, breaking into distinct patches of *tobiyaki* (jumping) in the *jihada*. A large patch of steel of the same quality as the *hamon* in distinct areas over the whole blade is called *hitatsura*. During the Muromachi period the variety of *hamon* increased further, and various forms of *gunome* were contrived into interesting shapes. Kanesada of Seki made a *hako gunome* (box *gunome*) or *umanoha gunome* (horses' teeth *gunome*). Kanemoto of Seki, for example, made *sambon sugi* (triple cryptomeria), a row of peaks resembling the profile of cryptomeria trees, with every third peak higher than the others. During the Edo period *hamon* became even more contrived, with, among others, the *tōramba* (billowing *hamon*) of Sukehiro of Osaka; the *sudare-ba* (reed curtain *hamon*) of Tamba no kami Yoshimichi; the *kobushigata chōji* (fist-shaped *chōji*) of Kawachi no kami Kunisuke; and the *juzuba* (rosary *hamon*) of Nagasone Kōtetsu.

The *bōshi* (cap) is the most important part of the *hamon* to inspect when judging the quality of a blade. It refers to the part of the *hamon* that follows the line of the *kissaki* section and terminates on the back of the blade. It must be clearly terminated, either with a return along the back of the blade or with an abrupt stop at a harmonious angle. The quality and shape of the *bōshi* is a further indication of date, school and smith. The most usual form of *bōshi* is rounded, either *ōmaru* (large round) or *komaru* (small round), and is found on blades of all periods. A *bōshi* with small irregular reciprocations is called *midare-komi*, while one with a gentle undulation away from the cutting edge is called *notare-komi*. The *bōshi* is described as *hakikake* (swept) in cases where lines of *nie* separate away from its round form and drift towards the *kissaki*. A *yakitsume bōshi* stops abruptly on the back of the sword with no return. A number of *bōshi* are peculiar to particular smiths or schools, like the *Jizō bōshi* on blades by Kanefusa of Seki, which is named after its perceived resemblance to the rounded shaven head of the Bodhisattva Jizō.

Some characteristic blade features

Shown with cutting edge to left unless otherwise indicated

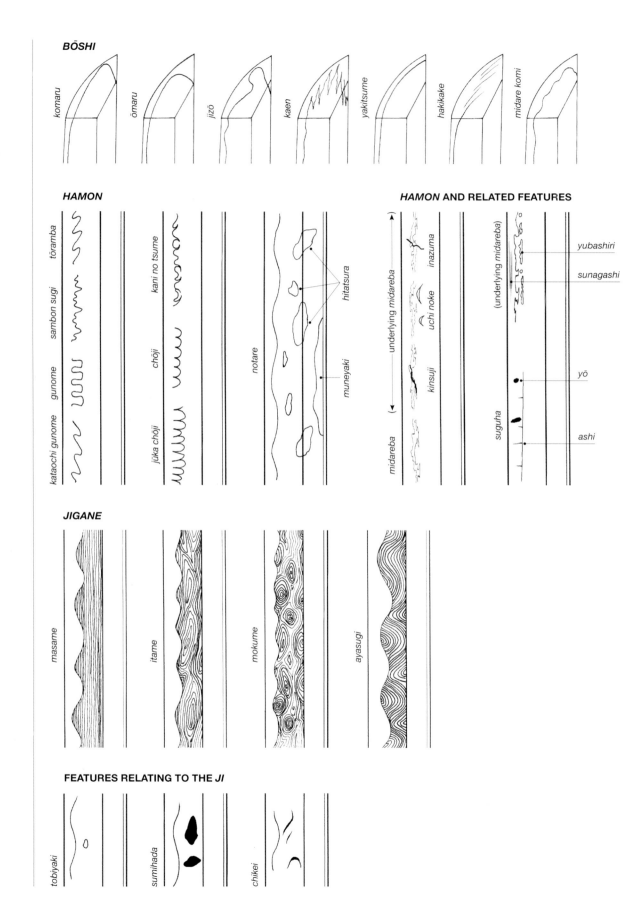

BŌSHI

komaru — ōmaru — jizō — kaen — yakitsume — hakikake — midare komi

HAMON

tōramba — sambon sugi — kani no tsume — gunome — chōji — kataochi gunome — jūka chōji — notare — hitatsura — muneyaki

HAMON AND RELATED FEATURES

inazuma — uchi noke — kinsuji — underlying midareba — midareba — (underlying midareba) — suguha — yubashiri — sunagashi — yō — ashi

JIGANE

masame — itame — mokume — ayasugi

FEATURES RELATING TO THE JI

tobiyaki — sumihada — chikei

BLADE CROSS SECTIONS *shown with cutting edge lowermost*

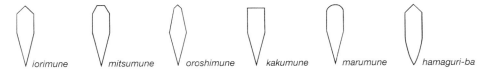

iorimune *mitsumune* *oroshimune* *kakumune* *marumune* *hamaguri-ba*

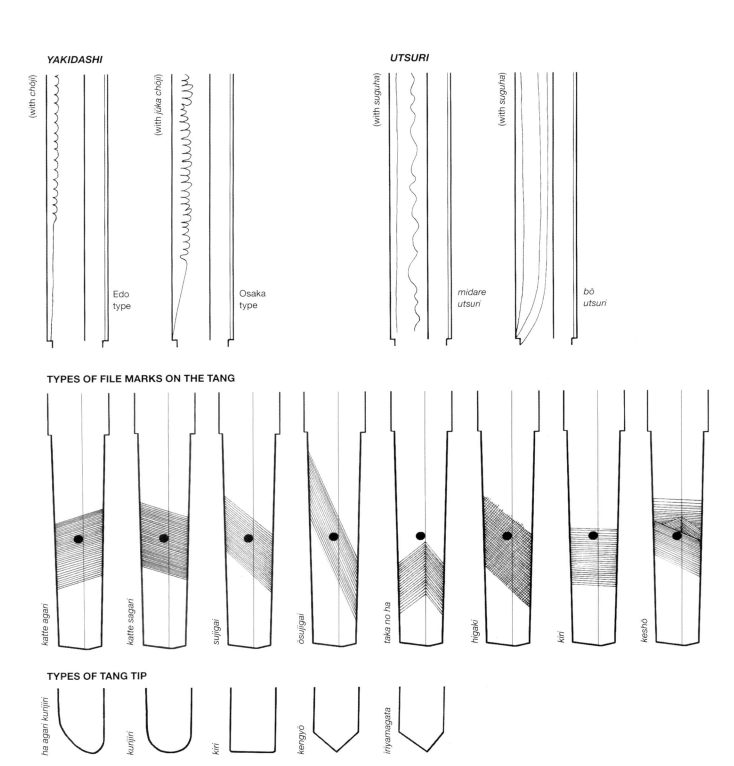

YAKIDASHI

(with *chōji*)

(with *jūka chōji*)

Edo type

Osaka type

UTSURI

(with *suguha*)

(with *suguha*)

midare utsuri

bō utsuri

TYPES OF FILE MARKS ON THE TANG

katte agari *katte sagari* *sujigai* *ōsujigai* *taka no ha* *higaki* *kiri* *keshō*

TYPES OF TANG TIP

ha agari kurijiri *kurijiri* *kiri* *kengyō* *iriyamagata*

Types of swords

By convention blades are divided into four types according to their length, measured from the boundary between the tang and the beginning of the back of the blade (*mune machi*) to the tip of the point (*kissaki*). *Tachi* (great sword) and *katana* (sword) are more than two *shaku* (about 60 cm) in length. *Wakizashi* (companion sword) are between one and two *shaku* (about 30–60 cm). *Tantō* (short sword, or dagger) are under one *shaku* (about 30 cm). *Tantō* that are considerably less than one *shaku* in length are sometimes called *suntsume tantō* (foreshortened *tantō*) and those over one *shaku* are sometimes called *sunnobi tantō* (extended length *tantō*).

These length conventions were established during the Edo period (1600–1868) and are still used in Japanese government sword-registration documents under the terms of the Law to Control the Possession of Firearms and Swords (*Jūhōtōkenrui shochi tō torishimari hō*) introduced in 1958. But nomenclature has changed over the centuries, and it is not always possible to tell what kind of sword an old document refers to. For example, during the Heian period (794–1185) *katana* or *koshigatana* (waist sword) referred to swords worn through the belt, as opposed to *tachi* which were carried slung by cords, and included what are now called *tantō*. *Tantō* worn on the right were sometimes called *mete zashi* (horse-hand sword), since the right hand held the reins while the left carried the bow. The word *wakizashi* has sometimes been used to describe any sword worn through the belt under armour, irrespective of its length. The situation is further confused by the writings of Kendō schools in which *katana* are often referred to as *tachi*, and *wakizashi* as *kodachi* (small *tachi*).

Tachi

Tachi were the long swords used by armoured samurai on horseback from the Heian period onwards. They were carried loosely suspended from the belt by two cords or chains attached to metal bands encircling the scabbard about 20 cm apart at the point of balance, with further metal bands to strengthen the scabbard. Some, called *ito maki no tachi* (cord-bound *tachi*), were bound partway along the scabbard with cord, like the hilt, to protect the scabbard from rubbing against the armour.

Katana

Katana swords, used from the Muromachi period (1392–1573) onwards, were worn through the belt edge-

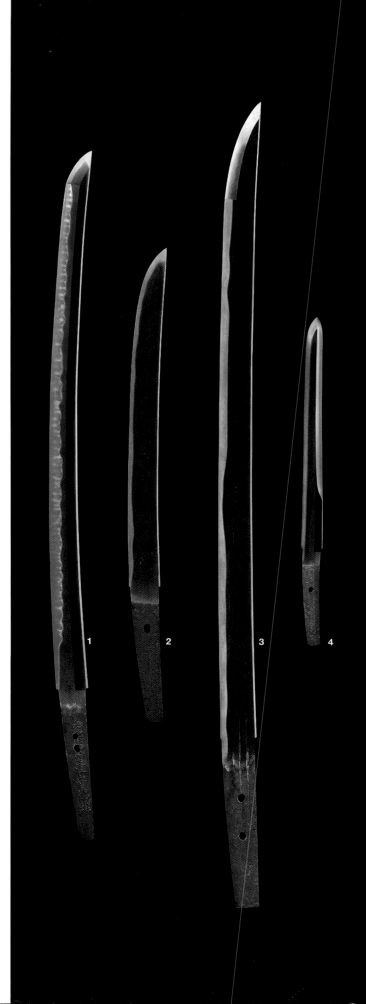

1   2   3   4

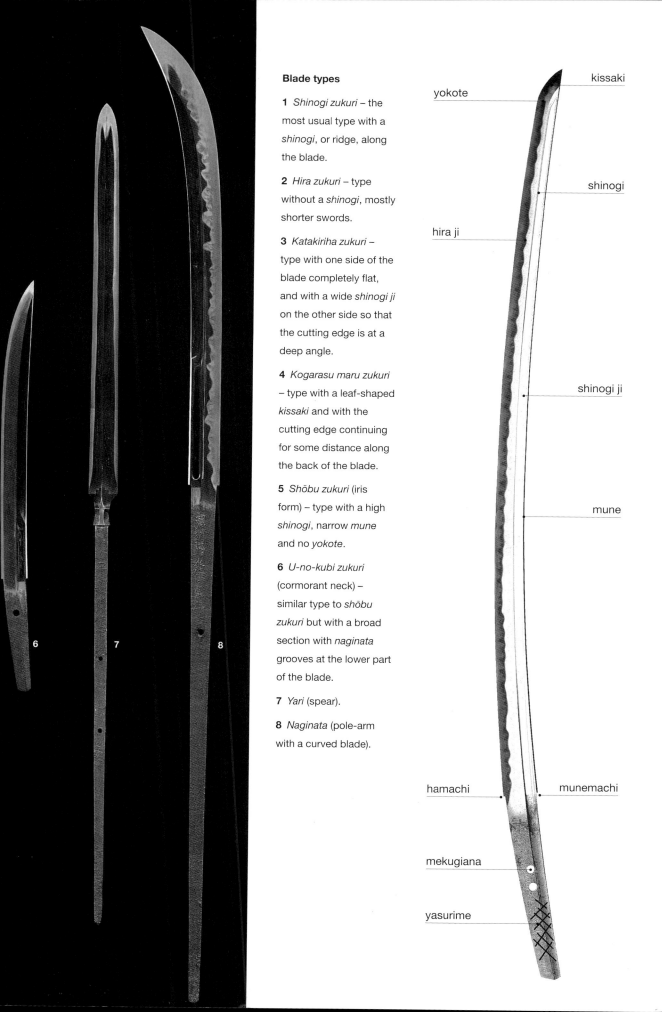

Blade types

1 *Shinogi zukuri* – the most usual type with a *shinogi*, or ridge, along the blade.

2 *Hira zukuri* – type without a *shinogi*, mostly shorter swords.

3 *Katakiriha zukuri* – type with one side of the blade completely flat, and with a wide *shinogi ji* on the other side so that the cutting edge is at a deep angle.

4 *Kogarasu maru zukuri* – type with a leaf-shaped *kissaki* and with the cutting edge continuing for some distance along the back of the blade.

5 *Shōbu zukuri* (iris form) – type with a high *shinogi*, narrow *mune* and no *yokote*.

6 *U-no-kubi zukuri* (cormorant neck) – similar type to *shōbu zukuri* but with a broad section with *naginata* grooves at the lower part of the blade.

7 *Yari* (spear).

8 *Naginata* (pole-arm with a curved blade).

yokote

kissaki

shinogi

hira ji

shinogi ji

mune

hamachi

munemachi

mekugiana

yasurime

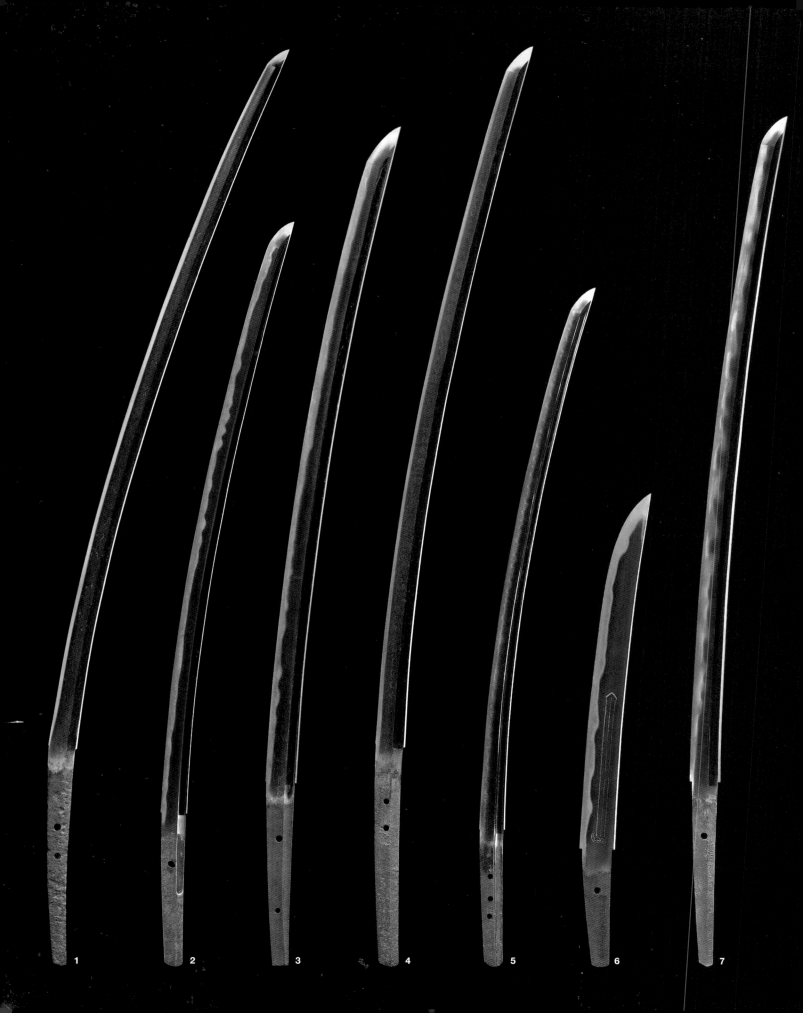

1   2   3   4   5   6   7

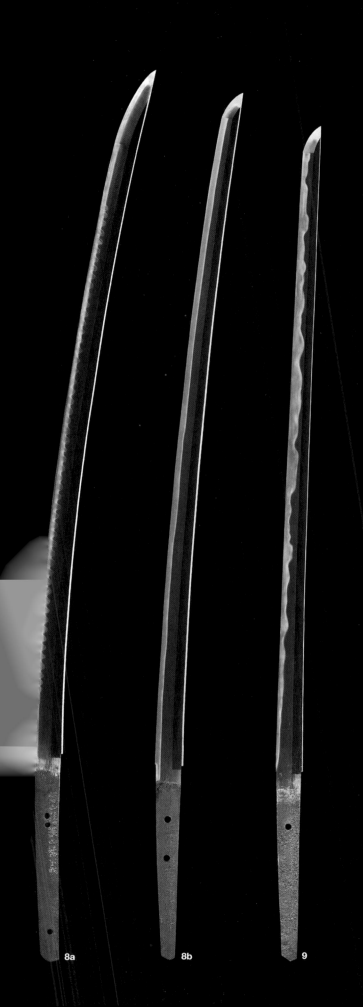

uppermost. This was due to the changing style of warfare during the Period of the Warring Provinces when battles between well-armed horsemen gradually gave way to large-scale warfare between great armies of infantry. Many such swords, known as *uchigatana* (hitting swords), were correspondingly shorter than the *tachi* made for use on horseback, typically around 60 cm long or even shorter. Some intended for use in one hand have very short tangs.

The tangs of swords are in general signed by the smith on the *omote* (face), the surface that faces outwards when the sword is worn. *Katana* are also usually signed on the *omote*, but as they are worn through the belt with the edge uppermost, this is the opposite side to the *omote* of *tachi*. Date of manufacture is usually inscribed on the *ura* (underside). Sometimes *tachi* blades were mounted as *katana*, and vice versa. There was no absolute rule regarding the length of swords until the passing of a number of edicts during the Edo period, and many *uchigatana* of the period were about 70 or even 80 cm long.

Change in blade shapes
from the Heian to late Edo periods

1 Heian and early Kamakura periods – deep *koshizori* (curve in the waist of the blade), a low curve in the upper part of the blade, and small *kissaki*.

2 Late Kamakura period – robust blades with substantial *kissaki* and a deep, more even curve than (1).

3 Nambokuchō period – long, broad blades of great length, with even curve and extended *kissaki*; frequently cut down as with this example.

4 Early Muromachi period – emulating early to middle Kamakura period with *koshizori* and low curve in the upper part of the blade.

5 Middle to late Muromachi period – *sakizori*, deep curve in the upper part of the blade.

6 Momoyama and early Edo periods – emulating the shape of cut-down swords of the late Kamakura and Nambokuchō periods, but thicker.

7 Middle Edo period – Kambun-era *shintō*, low curve and blade narrowing considerably towards the point.

8 Late Edo period – *shinshintō*: (a) emulating the shapes and styles of cut-down late Kamakura- and Nambokucho-period swords, (b) emulating the shapes of Kambun-era blades.

9 *Chokutō*, straight blades from the Kofun to the Heian periods and occasionally later, like this one from the Edo period.

8a 8b 9

Wakizashi

The *wakizashi* (side or companion sword) was the shorter of the two swords, worn at all times by the samurai, whereas the *katana* was usually only carried out of doors in a pair with the *wakizashi*. In accordance with the *Buke Shohatto* (Laws of the Military Houses) edict of 1629 defining the duties of a warrior, samurai were required to wear matching swords when on official duty. The manufacture of matching sets of mountings for the paired *katana* and *wakizashi* (or *daishō*, large and small) increased from this time.

Tantō

Most *tantō* from the Heian period onwards are *hira zukuri* (flat make), without a *shinogi* (ridge line) defining the angled portion of the blade. The curve on Heian and Kamakura period work is usually *uchizori* (inner curve), with a slight curve downwards towards the cutting edge. Some had no curve at all, and the *mune* (back) is correspondingly straight. From the Nambokuchō period (1336–92) *tantō*, like the *tachi*, became longer, with broad blades having extended points. In the Muromachi period (1392–1573) some daggers were made in the middle Kamakura-period (1185–1333) style with *uchizori*; some were quite straight; but most had slightly curved blades. There were also double-edged *tantō* with a slight curve.

Yari

The *yari* is a spear with a blade for cutting and thrusting. Most were double-edged straight blades, but a variety of shapes were used, some with one or more extra blades at right angles to the main blade. The straight *yari* was either of shallow triangular or regular diamond-shape section (no. 38). Most *yari* blades are straight edged, but there are also leaf-shaped blades. The blades may be just a few centimetres in length or as much as 60 cm or more, while the poles are typically 2 or 3 metres long.

Naginata

The *naginata* is a glaive-like pole-arm with a curved, single-edged blade that broadens out towards the point. It is usually of characteristic shape (no. 23) with a narrow *mune* (back section) between the *kissaki* and a point about one-third along the blade where it broadens, up to where standard *naginata* grooves are carved. Long-bladed *naginata*, in particular, were mounted on relatively short poles, sometimes with hilts partially wrapped with silk braid, similar to sword hilts. During the Muromachi period they were known as *nagamaki* (long wrapping) after the style of mounting. They might be either of *naginata* shape or similar to *tachi* with extra long tangs.

Other aspects of the blade

Suriage: the shortening of swords

Long swords of the late Kamakura and Nambokuchō periods were often shortened in later times due to changing methods of warfare. Some swords of the Nambokuchō period might be as long as 2 metres and, as their name (*nodachi*, moor swords) suggests, were essentially for outdoor use. They are also known as *seoi dachi* (swords carried over the back). Such long swords are said to have been particularly useful against horsemen, especially when fighting at night. Apart from dedicated swords kept in shrines and temples, most *nodachi* were shortened, often during the Momoyama period, so that they could be carried normally.

Since it is necessary to retain the hardened *bōshi* at the point, swords were shortened by cutting away a length from the lower end, thereby losing all or part of the original tang. In such a case an inscription might be wholly or partially lost. Sometimes a portion of the original tang bearing the inscription was carefully cut out on a thin panel and inlaid into the new tang. Alternatively, the portion of the tang bearing the inscription might be folded over into a recess cut into the opposite side of the tang. The name of the smith might be simply inscribed anew on the new tang, or, in the case of very fine swords shortened by specialists like the Hon'ami family, an attribution to the swordsmith might be inscribed and inlaid in gold (no. 15). During the Edo period swords were also cut down in accordance with legislation restricting length, or to make the blade suitable for a particular type of mounting.

Shape of the mune

The cross-section of the *mune* (back of the sword) has four basic types: the triangular *iorimune* (roof-shaped *mune*), the truncated triangular *mitsumune* (three *mune*), *kakumune* (flat *mune*) or *marumune* (rounded *mune*). Most swords have the triangular *iorimune* shape. On swords of the Yamato school, its *shintō* derivatives and by some Echizen smiths the *shinogi* is high and the *mune* makes a relatively shallow angle, whereas the *mune* is steepest and the *shinogi* correspondingly low on Bizen work. During the late Muromachi period blades with a narrow *mune*, called *mune-*

oroshi (lowered *mune*), were reputed to be effective against lightly armoured combatants, and were made in Bizen, Mino and, to some extent, Sōshū. The next most universal type, *mitsumune*, is found frequently on Sōshū school work of the *kotō* era, and on the work of smiths who emulated Sōshū swords during the *shintō* era, for example Horikawa Kunihiro (no. 18) and Echizen smiths (no. 22). The less common *marumune* shape can be seen on some *kotō* blades such as those of the Takada school of Bungo Province and the Heianjō (Kyoto) school.

Tangs

Unlike the curved swords of any other nation, the tang of a Japanese sword is an integral part of the whole sword, and its shape and size influence the cutting efficacy of the weapon. Indeed, Japanese swords are practically the only curved swords whose tang line is an elegant continuation of the curve of the blade. Since the Heian period when it was customary for smiths to sign their work, the tangs of swords have been an invaluable guide to the whole history of sword-making in Japan. Name of smith, and place and date of manufacture are found on many swords of the earlier periods. From the late Muromachi period honorific titles of smiths are also included (p. 14), sometimes with the name of the person who commissioned the sword, sometimes also with religious or auspicious phrases. From about the middle of the seventeenth century swords were sometimes tested on the bodies of condemned criminals, and the results of such tests were inscribed on the tangs.

The position of the *mekugi ana* (peg hole or holes), through which a wooden peg passes to retain the blade in the hilt, also indicates the period. In the Heian and Kamakura periods they are generally positioned low on the tang (i.e. closer to the tang tip) and in the Muromachi period roughly halfway along the tang. *Mekugi ana* on *shintō* are higher up the tang, as are those on swords that were cut down during the Momoyama period. There may be more than one hole in a tang depending on how many times it has been shortened or re-mounted. The holes on early blades are often irregular, even square in shape, having been made with a special chisel or awl. The openings are made either side of the tang, so that the sizes of the holes differ and the two holes do not meet smoothly inside the tang, but it has been said that this helps to grip the bamboo *mekugi* (peg) in place; *mekugi ana* on Edo-period blades are drilled perfectly round. On some blades of the Heian period onwards, particularly the longer ones, there may be an additional hole, or *shinobi ana* (hidden

hole), near the tip of the tang (no. 72). *Kambun shintō* and *shinshintō* blades often have such *shinobi ana*, but they are rarely put to use in later mountings.

The shape of the tang, particularly of the tip, and the file marks will also indicate the period and the school of a swordsmith. Tangs of the Heian and early Kamakura period tend to be deeply curved and slender, narrowing considerably towards the tip. Late Kamakura- and Nambokuchō-period tangs are larger and sturdier, commensurate with the increasing size of the blades. In the Muromachi period some *tachi* were made close to the Kamakura-period style, but the shorter *uchigatana* had short and broad tangs. *Shintō* blades generally have tangs that are well balanced in relation to the overall blade shape.

Before the sword blade is polished with stones, its final shape is produced using files. However, the tang itself was never polished, and the file marks used to give it its final finish are also indicative of the period and school of the blade, as is the shape of the tip. Some typical tang shapes and file mark arrangements seen on swords in the catalogue are shown on p. 21.

Horimono: carvings on blades

Various forms of groove may be carved either partially or wholly along the length of the finished blade, for both structural and aesthetic reasons. Pictorial carvings and inscriptions on the blades of swords made since the Heian period have often been religious or martial, commonly with depictions of Shintō or Buddhist deities, or invocations to them. Inscriptions may be formed of Chinese characters or Japanese *kana* (phonetic script), or they might be stylized Sanskrit; although actual Sanskrit characters can rarely be identified with accuracy. The early pictorial *horimono* (carvings) found on Heian-period blades are simple and austere, and reflect the religious sensibilities of the samurai. During the Muromachi period more obviously martial themes were used; for example, the deity Daikokuten appears clad in armour as a god of war (whereas in the peaceful later Edo period he appears as a jovial member of the traditional Shichifukujin group of Seven Lucky Gods). From the Momoyama period purely decorative motifs appear on some blades, often the three auspicious plants: pine, bamboo and plum. The *horimono* on a sword by the smith Horikawa Kunihiro (no. 18) are indicative of the transition from the Period of the Warring Provinces to the peace and stability of the Edo period. On one side of the blade is engraved the figure of Fudō Myō-ō (the Unmoving King of Light – Acala in Sanskrit) and on the other a sprig of plum blossom.

The deity Fudō Myō-ō is frequently found on swords. Of ferocious aspect with bared fangs, he sits in flames holding the attributes of a sword in his right hand and a rope in his left. The rope is to snare the enemies of Buddhism, such as worldly delusion, and the sword to cut through delusion to reach the ultimate reality, the *Kongōtai* (diamond world) of Shingon Buddhism. Fudō Myō-ō's unmoving aspect represents the aspiration of the samurai to remain calm and unmoved during the heat of combat and even at the instant of impending death. The sword and rope are often depicted together as the *kurikara* (a double-edged sword entwined by a dragon – in Sanskrit *kulika*) and are carved in three varying degrees of stylization: *shin-no-kurikara*, roundly and realistically (no. 20); *gyō-no-kurikara*, largely in outline with cuts of varying depth and angle; and *sō-no-kurikara*, in negative silhouette (no. 29). The conventional stylistic division, *shin* (true), *gyō* (going) and *sō* (grass), is also observed in brush calligraphy.

From the Momoyama period the dragon is often depicted alone – usually with a Buddhist *hōshu* (jewel of enlightenment) clenched in its jaws or in pursuit of it – or in pairs, with one beast ascending on one side of the blade and one descending on the other. A sword depicted in the tail of a dragon derives from the creation myth in which the deity Susano-ō-no-mikoto obtains a sword from the tail of the dragon Yamata-no-orochi. Known as Kusanagi no tsurugi (Grass-Cutter Sword) or Ama no kumo no tsurugi (Heavenly Clouds Sword), this sword is established as the deity resident in the Isonokami Shrine. A further allusion to Fudō Myō-ō is the carving of two narrow parallel grooves on the lower part of a blade. Known as *goma-bashi* in the *goma-e* ritual of Shingon Buddhism, these represent the ritual tongs with which charcoal fuel is supplied to a fire, in the flames of which Fudō Myō-ō materializes.

Fig. 9 (below) *Tachi* (early thirteeenth century) signed by Yoshikane with a distinctive *koshi zori* curve lowering towards the point and with the *fumbari* (stability) typical of the Heian and early Kamakura periods. This blade has *itame hada* with *utsuri* and *jinie*. The *hamon* is *suguha* in *nie* with many variations of *komidare* and with *uchinoke*, *sunagashi* and *kinsuji*. Yoshikane was a representative smith of the early Bizen (Ko Bizen) school. 1992.05-23.1

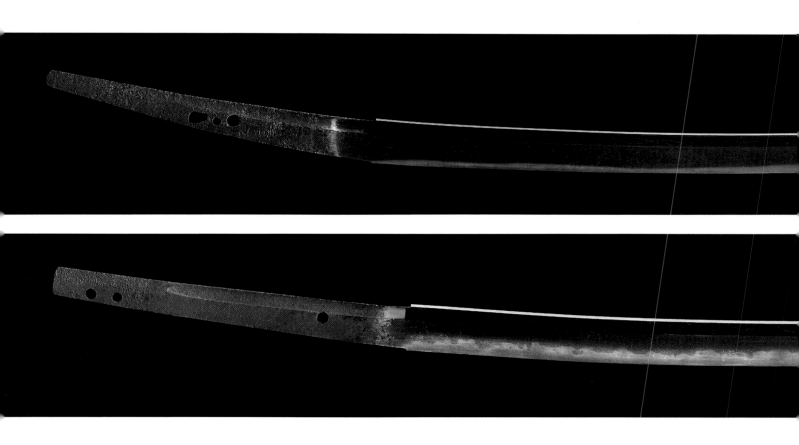

Changing traditions

Kotō and shintō

Swords are classified as *kotō* (old swords) or *shintō* (new swords) depending on whether they were made before or after radical changes in manufacturing technology and fashion that occurred in a relatively short period at the end of the civil wars in the sixteenth century. Until that time sword-making traditions had been regional, and styles had continued basically unchanged for centuries at a time. The date of transition between *kotō* and *shintō* is not precise, but by convention the *shintō* era is counted from the beginning of the Edo period, with all swords before then said to be *kotō*. Three dates are variously used: 1596, the first year of

the Keichō era; 1600, the date of Ieyasu's victory at the battle of Sekigahara; and either 1603 or 1604, when Ieyasu's shogunate was established at Edo (the date is disputed).

The use of the *kotō/shintō* terminology dates from the early seventeenth century when a number of directories of contemporary smiths were published, such as *Kotō meijin taizen* (Compendium of *Kotō* Smiths, 1611) by Takeya Rian. But the word *shintō* was first widely used during the Edo period, predominantly to refer to seventeenth-century smiths who had made names for themselves. *Arami meijin* (List of New Sword Signatures, 1712) by Kanda Hakuryūshi was the first of a number of books listing contemporary swordsmiths. *Shintō bengi* (Discussion of *Shintō*, 1777) by Kamada Natae was a detailed and comprehensive study of contemporary blade characteristics. Since *shintō* are frequently inscribed with makers' names, place names and dates, the important dates of activity of the earliest *shintō* smiths are well known.

Whereas swords of other cultures that date from the sixteenth century and earlier will usually be in poor condition, Japanese swords have generally been carefully preserved and old blades can look as new. It is therefore not always immediately apparent whether a blade is a *shintō* or a *kotō*, particularly as many *shintō* smiths emulated *kotō* traditions and some made very close copies of *kotō* blades. But there

Fig. 10 (bottom) Slightly shortened *tachi* signed 'Bishū Osafune Moro[kage]', with the last character of the inscription missing. The deep curve and shape found in early Kamakura-period work is also a characteristic of blades of the Ōei era (1394–1428; see also no. 2). The *hada* has a fine *itame* with *mokume* and vivid *utsuri*. The *hamon* is *gunome chōji* with many *ashi* and *yō*. 1979.07-30.2

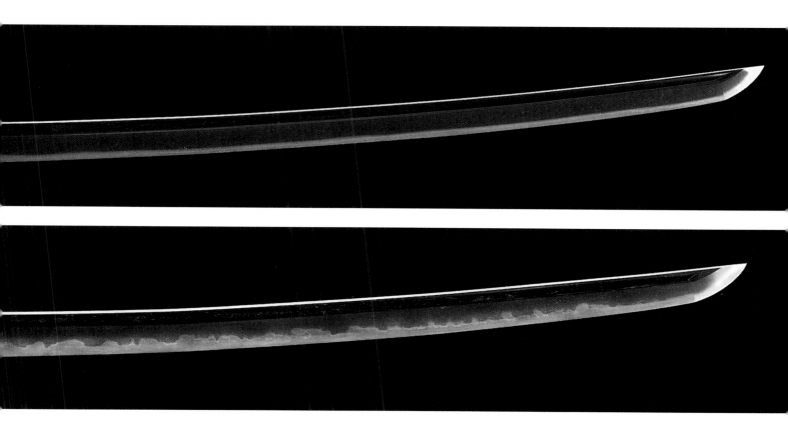

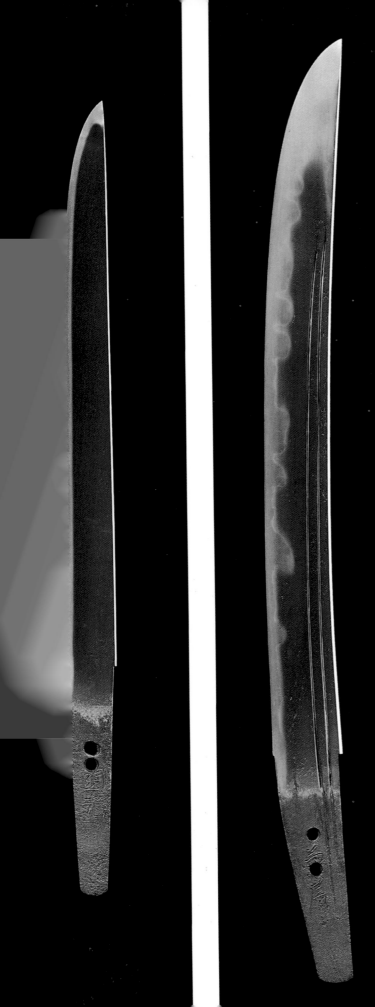

are considerable differences between *kotō* and *shintō*, and these differences are the first things to consider when appraising a blade. In general, *shintō* appear younger than *kotō* and the textures of the blades are less complex owing to simplified manufacturing methods. They are likely to be heavier, thicker and of lower curvature than *kotō*. On the other hand, *kotō* are generally of more elegant proportions, feel lighter and better balanced in the hand, and are altogether easier to wield than *shintō*. Differences in blade texture have been discussed in 'Reading the blade' above, pp. 18–19, but the *hamon* of *shintō* tend to be more precisely contrived than those of *kotō*, and they are usually poor in activity in the upper part (i.e. towards the *kissaki*) of the blade. However energetic the *hamon* appears on a *shintō*, the *bōshi*, as a rule, is comparatively featureless and harsh.

Kotō are divided into five main traditions, although there were a number of sword-making provinces that fell outside these, particularly in Kyūshū and the San'indō region. The five traditions were associated with Bizen Province (present-day Okayama Prefecture), Yamashiro Province (Kyoto), Yamato Province (Nara and environs), Sōshū (Sagami Province, present-day Kanagawa Prefecture, around Kamakura) and Mino Province (present-day Gifu Prefecture). Few collections outside Japan are comprehensive and early works – Heian- and Kamakura-period blades, and Yamashiro and Sōshū examples in general – are rarely encountered.

Fig. 11 (far left) *Hira zukuri tantō* blade with the slight *uchizori* curve of the late Kamakura period. The blade has *itame* with *mokume* grain with *jifu utsuri* and much *chikei*. The *suguha hamon* is of fine *nie* with *kinsuji*. The maker, Shintōgo Kunimitsu, is fêted as the founder of the Sōshū tradition at Kamakura in the late Kamakura period. 1992.05-23.2

Fig. 12 (left) *Hira zukuri tantō* with a slight *saki zori* curve of the late Muromachi period. The grain is a bright *itame* with some *nie utsuri* close to the groove. The *hamon* is predominantly *hako gunome* with copious *sunagashi* in *nie*. The blade is characteristic of the work of Kanefusa of the sixteenth-century Seki group in the Mino tradition. This example was given by the Emperor Meiji to Lord Redesdale, who witnessed the act of *seppuku* (ritual suicide) carried out by two convicted samurai of the Shimazu clan who had assassinated the Englishman Richardson in 1862 during the unstable years preceding the imperial restoration in 1868 (col. pl. 23). OA+3792

Heian and early Kamakura periods

Schools of the Heian period continued into the early Kamakura period, and for the most part there is little clear definition between twelfth- and early thirteenth-century blades. The shape of these *tachi* is unmistakably elegant. The blades are broad at the base, becoming slender towards the upper part, giving a feeling of stability (described as *fumbari*, 'bottom'). The curve is deep at the base, and the blade straightens slightly as it approaches the *kissaki* section. The length of around 2 *shaku* and 4 or 6 *sun* (approximately 72–8 cm) and the ease of use in one hand show that they were intended for heavily armoured samurai on horseback, while the infantry had altogether poorer quality weapons (these *uchigatana* described in the fourteenth-century *Masu kagami* have not survived, since they were not of a quality worth preserving). In addition, a number of *kodachi* (small *tachi*) were made by some of the important smiths and are highly prized today. Many *tachi* of the period survive because they were dedicated to the deities of Shintō shrines or Buddhist temples in gratitude for military successes, or preserved in family collections.

Some early swords were so damaged in combat that they could not be further used. The most frequent injury was the loss of the point, including the hardened section (the *bōshi*). In such cases the *kissaki* might be re-shaped and the appearance of the missing *bōshi* artificially suggested by cunning polishing. Chipping of the cutting edge was another frequent occurrence, but the efficacy of the weapon was little impaired. Rather than re-polishing the blade to remove such a chip and thereby making it narrower overall, the injury was often left as a reminder of the battle in which it had occurred. Severely damaged blades could be completely heat-treated so as to restore the *hamon*, although the original characteristics of the sword would thereby be lost.

The *hada* and *hamon* on swords of this period are generally uncontrived with much variation of *nie*; exceptionally, blades by Tomonari and other early Bizen Province makers have beautifully ordered *chōji hamon* and closely packed, clear *jigane*. Although not included in the five traditions, there was a school active in neighbouring Bitchū Province called the Aoe, whose work is characterized by a fine, bright, distinctive *hada* called *chirimen* (crêpe).

Middle to late Kamakura period

In the middle Kamakura period the schools of Bizen, Yamato and Yamashiro Provinces produced more robust blades – broader, and with a more even curve than before. The *kissaki* of these broad swords remained short in proportion to the increased breadth of the blades, probably owing to an inherent conservatism among the smiths, leading to the term *inokubi kissaki* (wild boar neck *kissaki*). The defect of such a configuration is that even a small chip broken off the point renders it impossible to re-shape the *kissaki* without losing the *bōshi*. It is said that this was first realized during the two abortive invasion attempts of the Mongols in 1274 and 1281, when swords proved inadequate against the leather and iron armour of the enemy. The solution was to extend the length of the *kissaki* and most swords of the late Kamakura and Nambokuchō periods have this characteristic.

Bizen smiths made swords with *chōji hamon* in *nioi*, with vivid undulating *utsuri*, and the group at Osafune continued the tradition, which was to last for several hundred years. The Ichimonji school, in particular, thrived during the Kamakura period and into the early Nambokuchō period in several branches. Their work includes the most grandiose *chōji* and vibrant *midare utsuri* of any school or period. The *chōji hamon* was also favoured, in a more subdued form, by the Yamashiro-school smiths of the time – in particular the Rai school – whose work was in *konie* rather than the *nioi* of their Bizen Province contemporaries. The Yamato tradition was formed by groups of smiths who supplied the great Buddhist temples of Nara, which retained brigades of armed priests (*sōhei*) to protect their land and other interests. Chief among them were the Hōshō, Shikkake and Senjuin schools who supplied Kōfukuji Temple, the Tegai school of Tōdaiji Temple, and the Taemadera Temple school. Their work is characterized by a straight longitudinal *masame* grain with *jinie*; *hamon* that are basically straight *suguha* with *gunome*; and longitudinal effects along the grain like *hotsure* ('fraying', lines of *nie* straying above and below the *hamon* resembling frayed thread), *uchinoke* and *yubashiri* (hot water run). It was perhaps due to Buddhist propriety that few Yamato tradition blades were signed, although this can be hard to judge as many long *tachi* of the middle and late Kamakura period were later cut down, thus losing their original tangs.

The Sōshū school started with the arrival at Kamakura of smiths from Bizen, Yamashiro and elsewhere during the early to middle Kamakura period. By the late Kamakura period smiths like Saburō Kunimune and Ichimonji Sukezane of Bizen, and Kunitsuna of Awataguchi in Yamashiro were working for the Kamakura government in Sagami Province, though in the styles of their own native provinces. The inevitable cross-fertilization of ideas resulted in great improvements in technology, largely

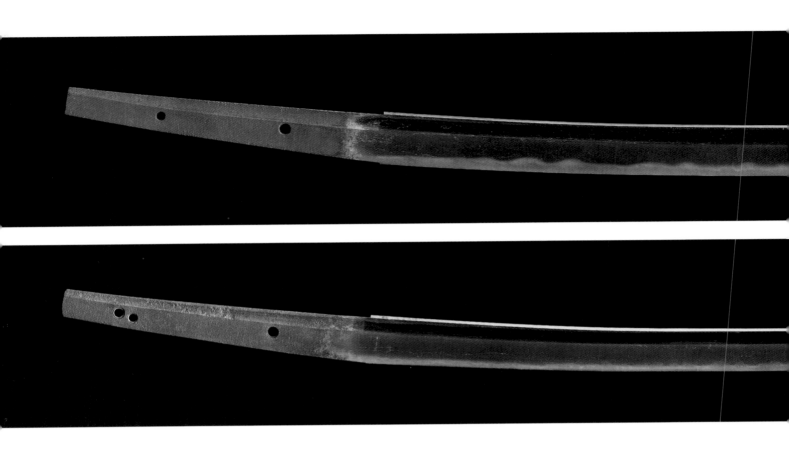

through the endeavours of Shintōgo Kunimitsu, who is associated with the Awataguchi school of Yamashiro and the Yamato school. Kunimitsu specialized in making *tantō*, although a number of *tachi* by him also survive. His work is characterized by a close-grained *itame* of a somewhat helical form with rich and even *jinie*, and by a *suguha hamon* with delicate *kinsen* (metal lines). The technical exchanges, which coincided with the requirement for more robust blades, resulted in further improvements in sword-making, as evinced by the work of Kunimitsu's pupils Yukimitsu and Masamune, and of later groups of smiths including those known as the 'Ten Pupils of Masamune'. Masamune perfected the Sōshū tradition, which was to influence the whole of later sword-making. His steel shows an intimate yet discrete mixture of steels of differing quality, with abundant *jinie*. The Sōshū-tradition *hamon* is wide, with *midare* impressed on *gunome*, and *notare*. The activity in both *ji* and *ha* is wildly variable, with *jinie*, *chikei* and *jifu* in the ground, and a *hamon* with copious *inazuma*, *sunagashi* and *kinsen* more violent than that of Kunimitsu. Abundant *nie* and complex *hamon* characterize the work of Masamune's school, exemplified by his Ten Pupils, who spread the style throughout Japan during the subsequent Nambokuchō period.

Nambokuchō period (1336–92)

Swords of this period were long and broad, and of even curve with extended *kissaki* – many were considerably over a metre in length. Few survive in their original length, however, having been cut down to a size suitable for everyday wear during the late Muromachi and Momoyama periods. Further innovations were introduced by the Sōshū smiths. Sadamune, said to be Masamune's son, is noted for blades with a finer *hada* than that of Masamune, and an undulating *hamon* with even *nie*. Two of Masamune's pupils, Hiromitsu and Akimitsu, specialized in *hitatsura*, a type of *hamon* that separates into discrete patches throughout the surface of the blade. These styles of *hamon* spread to many other schools during the Muromachi and Edo periods.

Technological innovations also occurred within the Bizen tradition. Kanemitsu of Bizen continued the Bizen-style *hamon*, favouring *gunome*, but characteristically these were in *konie*, in contrast to the *nioi* of earlier Bizen swords. Elsewhere, Norishige of Etchū Province, a contemporary of Masamune at Sōshū, made a characteristic *hada* with a flowing grain and bands of alternating light and dark steel known as *matsukawa hada* (pine bark *hada*) or *hijiki hada* (seaweed *hada*). Dark steel similar to *jifu* characterizes swords of the Hokkoku region

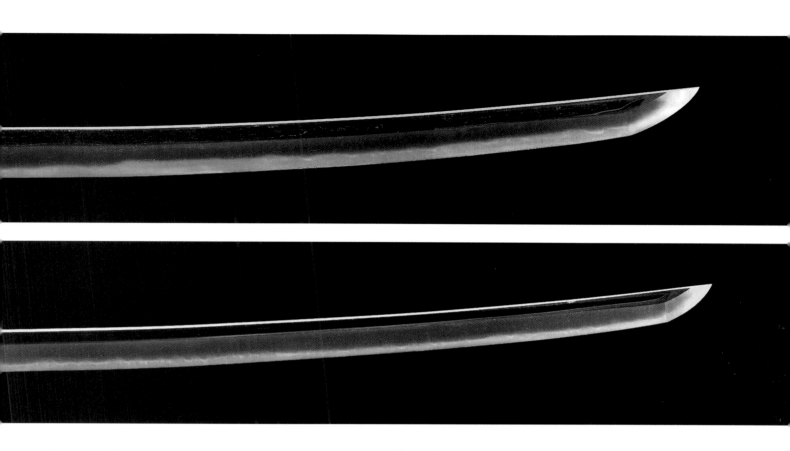

Fig. 13 (top) Greatly shortened *tachi* with the broad shape, even curve and extended *kissaki* typical of the Nambokuchō period. The blade has *itame* with *komokume hada* and vivid *utsuri* with *sumihada* in places. The *hamon* is *saka gunome chōji* in *nioi* with deep *ashi*. Although this blade is attributable to Motoshige of Bizen Province, any original signature has been lost through the shortening process. The blade characteristics are similar to those of the Aoe school of Bitchū Province, which thrived during the same period. 1979.07-30.2

Fig. 14 (above) *Tachi* blade with the even breadth and curve of the Nambokuchō period. The blade has *itame hada* with *mokume* and a *hamon* of small *gunome* with *togariba* and many *ashi*. Although the blade is slightly shortened, the remaining signature 'Osafune Masamitsu' identifies it as work of Masamitsu, pupil of Kanemitsu of Bizen in the late Nambokuchō period, who was still active during the early fifteenth century. 1958.07-30.68

(the northern provinces, including Etchū Province). The sword attributed to Tametsugu (no. 1), who was a pupil of Norishige, is a good example of just such a blade made at this time, incorporating *jifu*.

Greater mobility in the Nambokuchō period resulted in a confluence of different styles that brought about the foundation of the last of the five traditions, the Mino school. Saburō Kaneuji, a pupil of Masamune who is believed originally to have been of the Yamato Tegai school, migrated to Shizu in Mino Province, where swords had been made since the Kamakura period, and is considered the founder of the Mino tradition.

Although the Yamashiro tradition was by now dying out, swords continued to be made at Yamato (no. 17) and Sōshū on a reduced scale throughout the following Muromachi period. By the close of the Nambokuchō period, of the original five *kotō* traditions, two, Mino and Bizen, were the main suppliers of swords.

Muromachi period (1392–1573)

The early Muromachi period saw a return to the styles and proportions of the *tachi* of the early and middle Kamakura period, although there was altogether less *fumbari*. Bizen swords followed the early style closely, with *suguha*, *gunome*

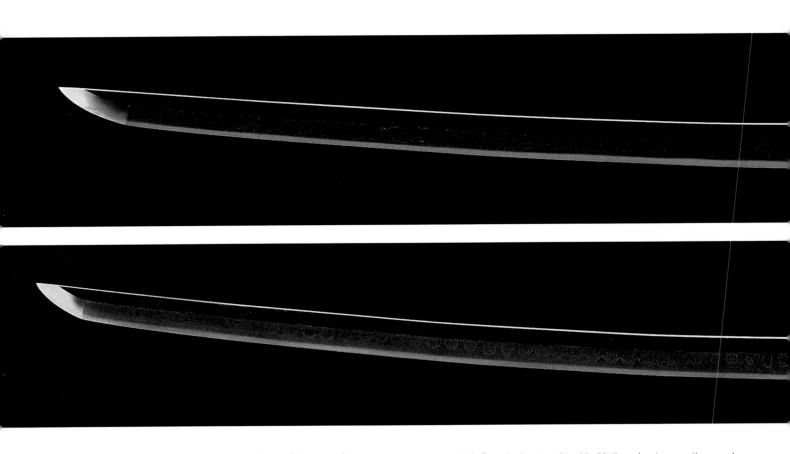

and *chōji hamon*, and a distinctive form of *bō-utsuri*. Representative Bizen smiths of the early fifteenth century include Yasumitsu (no. 2).

The large-scale demand for swords during the Period of the Warring Provinces led to the virtual mass production of poorer quality blades for the *ashigaru* foot-soldiers. Swords of this time are characterized by a *sakizori* curve, where the deepest part of the curve is in the upper part of the blade. Swords were made in great quantities, and these so-called *kazu uchi mono* (swords made in quantity) or *sokutō* (bundle swords) were made by several workshops of smiths signing the same name. In Osafune village several dozen smiths of widely varying skill are known to have used the names 'Norimitsu' and 'Sukesada'. Whereas it was usual in the first half of the Muromachi period to sign using the formula seen in 'Osafune jū Sukesada', meaning 'Sukesada, resident of Osafune', now the smiths signed using the simpler formula 'Osafune Sukesada' (nos 5–8). The name of the village Osafune was treated like a surname.

In the latter half of the Muromachi period the traditional *chōji hamon* continued, but with added picturesque variations like *kani-no-tsume* (crab's claws) *chōji*. The *nioi* of the early work changed into *nie*; *utsuri*, even though sometimes present on the later blades, became indistinct and weak.

Fig. 15 (top) Greatly shortened *tachi* with the robust proportions and medium-extended *kissaki* of the late Kamakura or early Nambokuchō periods. The low curve is indicative of the Yamato tradition. The grain is a prominent flowing *itame* rich in *jinie* with *chikei* and the hamon is *suguha* with *nijūba*, *uchi no ke* and *kogunome* with *ashi*. The tang bears a vermilion lacquer attribution to Norinaga (of the Tegai group) but the blade characteristics are altogether more typical of the Ryūmon school of the Yamato tradition. 1958.07-30.1

Fig. 16 (above) *Katana* blade of the early Muromachi period with *ayasugi hada* and a *suguha hamon* with *gunome* and *uchi no ke* blending into the grain. This distinct sinusoidal grain characterizes the work of the Gassan school of Dewa Province, devotees of the 'mountain religion' surrounding the Dewa Sanzan (the Three Mountains of Dewa Province), from the Heian or Kamakura periods onwards. 1958.07-30.70

The village of Seki in Mino Province was as prominent during the middle and late Muromachi period as Osafune in Bizen Province. Descendants of the Nambokuchō-period smiths, many using the identical character 'kane' in their names, made blades with a whitish *shirake utsuri*, and a variety of *suguha* and *gunome hamon*. Among them Kanemoto (no. 35) and his descendants are noted for their *sambon sugi* (triple cryptomeria) *hamon*, Kanefusa for his *hako-gunome,* and Kanesada and his school (no. 15) for varied *gunome* and *suguha*.

Momoyama and Edo periods (1573–1868)

Swords made during the Momoyama period were similar in shape to the shortened swords of the Kamakura and Nambokuchō periods, and the *hamon* of those periods were also emulated. In particular, smiths made swords with large *nie*, similar to the work of Masamune and his school of Sōshū. The fashion continued through the Keichō (1596–1614) and Kan'ei (1624–44) eras. Among those who specialized in shortening swords and preparing the blades for re-mounting was Hon'ami Kōtoku (1554–1619). The Hon'ami family continue as sword appraisers and polishers to the present day. Kōtoku would have known the smith Umetada Myōju in Kyoto, who is fêted as the founder of the

shintō tradition. Umetada Myōju is also said to have introduced new technologies, and his many pupils spread these methods throughout Japan. The work of some of these smiths and their descendants is catalogued here. They include Umetada Yoshinobu (no. 41), Horikawa Kunihiro (no.18) and Hizen kuni Tadayoshi (nos 54–6).

The city of Osaka grew quickly around Hideyoshi's original castle, so that by the end of the seventeenth century both Edo and Osaka rivalled London and Paris in terms of population. Many smiths worked in Osaka, such as Ōmi no kami Tadatsuna (no. 44). In Edo there were Yasutsugu of Echizen (nos 24–5) and a branch of the Ishidō school (nos 42–5). Smiths who had worked in Mino Province spread all over Japan and were very influential in promoting the new *shintō* technology. For example, whatever the grain might be on the *hira ji*, most *shintō* blades have *masame* on the *shinogi ji*, which had been a defining characteristic of *kotō* blades of Mino tradition. Many *shintō* smiths followed the old traditions, and some made close copies of earlier swords: in Hizen the family of Tadayoshi worked in the Yamashiro style; in Bizen the Ishidō group emulated the Kamakura-period Bizen style; Horikawa Kunihiro and the Echizen smiths worked in the Sōshū style; and there were many branches of the Mino tradition.

The length and curve of swords were gradually standardized, although in provinces distant from Edo earlier shapes persisted. Both *katana* and *wakizashi* of this period are of shallow curve, narrowing somewhat towards the point in the so-called 'Kambun *shintō*' shape (*shintō* of the Kambun era, 1661–73). Such swords feel light in the hands, almost like *kotō* blades, and were shown to be very effective in the cutting tests that were fashionable at the time. Their shape possibly owed something to the rise of Kendō schools that taught formalized systems of cutting and counter-cutting with large circling cuts using wooden swords.

Towards the end of the eighteenth century a revival of old styles was instigated by a swordsmith called Suishinshi Masahide (1750–1825), who advocated the revival in the climate of growing nationalism that was a reaction to increased foreign shipping activity in Japanese waters. From around the beginning of the nineteenth century this nationalistic spirit evolved into the stirrings of a movement to restore imperial rule, with the cry *sonnō jōi* (revere the emperor and expel the barabarians). The time was ripe for large-scale armament of Japan, albeit in the anachronistic form of a reversion to longer swords.

Masahide studied the early traditions and strived to emulate them. His writings on the subject, like *Kenkō hiden shi* (Secret Traditions of Swordsmiths), which he gave to his pupil Koyama Mutsu no suke Hiromoto, and *Tōken jitsuyō ron* (A Practical Treatise on Swords), tell of his exhaustive experimentation with different steels and manufacturing methods. He taught over a hundred pupils, and influenced all but the smiths retained by the remotest and most conservative of the *daimyō*. His close successor was the smith Hōji Taikei Naotane (nos 62–3) who travelled and taught throughout Japan. These *shinshintō* (new, new swords) smiths revived long swords, particularly those of the Sōshū and Bizen styles of the Kamakura and Nambokuchō periods, and also several of the styles established by the Kambun *shintō* smiths.

Mountings

Although sword blades have been treasured and carefully preserved in some cases for more than a thousand years, the same has not always been the case with their mountings. Fashions changed, and the same blade might be re-mounted with a new wooden scabbard and hilt many times. Even so, certain types of ceremonial mounting used by samurai and the aristocracy at court have remained unchanged. Early mountings have rarely survived intact, except for collections in Shintō shrines and Buddhist temples, and those in collections of the great samurai families amassed during the Edo period (1600–1868).

Tachi mountings

Tachi were typically between 75 and 80 cm in length, although during the late Kamakura and Nambokuchō periods they could be as much as a metre or more. There are a number of styles of *tachi* mounting. The *ito maki no tachi* (cord-bound *tachi*) is for battle or, during the Edo period, parade use. In addition, various styles of mountings were required for formal occasions, including the *efu-dachi* (*tachi* mounting designated for palace guards; no. 42), and the *hoso-dachi* (slender *tachi*; nos 3, 69).

The materials of the hilt and scabbard of a *tachi* are the same as those for the *katana* and *wakizashi*, but there are more metal fittings to the scabbard, and the hilt fittings have different names. The equivalent of the pommel (known as a *kashira*) is called the *kabuto-gane* (helmet metal), and a swivelling metal loop passes through the *kabuto-gane*, to which a cord may be attached for retaining the sword in the hand during use. This metal loop, or *saru-te* (monkey hands), is sometimes in the form of clasped hands. The chape of a *tachi* scabbard, which is called the *ishizuki* (stone piercer), is, like the *kabuto-gane*, longer than its equivalent on a *katana* mounting and is pierced with a decoratively shaped opening on either side. There are usually three *semegane*, metal reinforcing bands around the scabbard, and metal strips that extend for several centimetres above the *ishizuki* on the back and edge of the scabbard, called *shiba-hiki* (grass-pullers), which originally served to prevent damage if the sword was dragged along the ground. Two further metal bands, *ashi kanamono* (foot metal), form the points of suspension for wearing the sword. Leather loops, with metal fittings called *obitori* fitted to the *ashi kanamono*, provide passage for the carrying cord. They have between one and four metal pieces, *kawasaki kanamono*, which keep the loop of leather stiff. Traditionally there was one fewer metal piece in the upper *obitori* so that the *tachi* would hang down at an angle. When it became fashionable in the late Edo period to wear *tachi* at a lower angle, the upper *obitori* was either replaced or simply bent over to make the upper loop shorter than the lower.

Efu-dachi were carried since the Nara and Heian periods by imperial palace guards (*efu*) when on formal duty. They are distinguished by the stylized, long tweezer motif of the *menuki*, which derived from the Heian-period *kenuki gata tachi* (tweezer-shape sword); this had the tang in the shape of the hilt and was pierced with a long oblong to resemble tweezers. The first *efu* on the establishment of the guard system in AD 811 carried business-like blades, but during the Heian period the posts became filled by the aristocracy, and their swords were often of poor quality but with highly decorative mountings. The *hosodachi* was a similar type of *tachi* mounting with an unbound hilt that had rows of non-functional rivets called *tawara-byō* ('rice bale pins', after their shape), and was carried by high-ranking samurai and aristocracy on formal occasions.

Katana, wakizashi and *tantō* mountings

Blades are mounted with scabbards of magnolia wood, which does not exude any fluid that might damage the steel. The scabbard is made in two halves glued together along the edge and back, and usually lacquered. The hilts are of wood, also made in two halves, with an opening of the same shape as the tang, so that it can be fitted over the tang and kept in place with a bamboo peg that passes through holes either side of the hilt and through the *mekugi ana* hole in the tang itself. The hilt is usually wrapped with the skin of the ray fish, which is strong and long-lasting. Metal pieces known on *katana, wakizashi* and *tantō* as *kashira* (head) and *fuchi* (surround) are fitted over the butt and open end of the hilt respectively. The *kashira* is fixed to the hilt most often by silk braid, which is bound around from just above the *fuchi* and passes through slits in the *kashira. Fuchi* and *kashira* usually had the same design.

Under the binding of the hilt there will be two *menuki* (eye drawers, ornamental metal pieces that originated as *mekugi*, pegs, on ancient *tachi* mountings). The *menuki* are made in pairs, one each side of the hilt, and they are arranged slightly offset along the length. Some styles place the *menuki* within the palm when the sword is wielded, and some place them either side of the hand. *Menuki* were made in pairs by sculpting pieces of metal held still in a block of pitch. That used on the *omote* of the hilt would often represent the Yang principle, and that on the *ura* the Yin. Thus the male of a pair of *shishi* (lion-like beasts) with an open mouth would be placed on the *omote*, and the female with a closed mouth on the *ura*. The blade is kept tight in the scabbard by means of a *habaki*, a copper collar that slides over the tang to rest on the *machi*, where the tang widens to form the blade.

Between the *habaki* and the *fuchi* is placed the *tsuba*, or sword guard, which prevents the hands from slipping onto the blade during combat. It is a roughly disc-shaped metal component with a central aperture in the shape of the cross-section of the tang, and the tang passes through it. *Tsuba* were usually round, oval or a rounded rectangular shape with inverted cusps at the corners called *mokkō*, said to derive from the shape of the Japanese flowering quince. Large square *tsuba* were fashionable among a lawless brotherhood of ex-samurai called *kabukimono* (swaggerers) in the early Edo period, but their use was prohibited by an edict of 1645. Foliate, eccentric, many-sided or decoratively outlined *tsuba* were especially popular during the late Edo period, and iron *tsuba* were often pierced with designs in positive or negative silhouette. The *tsuba* is further supported in position by metal spacers, *seppa*, on either side. The mouth of the scabbard might be rimmed with horn, sometimes metal. The *kojiri* (chape) might also have a horn or metal fitting. On the *omote* of the scabbard several centimetres down from the mouth there is a projection called a *kurikata* (chestnut shape) with an aperture through which can be passed a *sageo*, the cord used to tie the scabbard into the belt. The *kaerizuno* (return horn – the horn-shaped projection about 10 cm below the *kurikata*) serves to prevent the scabbard from being pulled inadvertently upwards through the belt. Both *kurikata* and *kaerizuno* may be of horn or metal.

Some mountings are equipped with a *kozuka* (small hilt, a small slim-bladed utility knife) and/or a *kōgai*, a kind of bodkin that has a number of uses such as dressing the hair and cleaning the ears using a small protrusion on the end. A more robust, double-edged steel implement called an *umabari* (horse needle) is found on some mountings in place of the *kōgai*. This was especially used in Higo Province to relieve blood congestion in horses' legs, and for other minor surgery to their leg injuries. These items are kept in pockets in the scabbard and may be drawn through *hitsu-ana*, holes provided in the *tsuba*. The same assemblage is used for *wakizashi. Tantō* may be of similar form, but most do not have a *tsuba*, in which case the mounting is called *ai-kuchi* (meeting mouths). This form of mounting was also sometimes used on longer swords in the Muromachi Period.

Lacquerwork

Lacquer for coating wooden scabbards was used both for its mechanical properties and for its decorative effect. Lacquer is tree sap, which in its raw state is an almost colourless pale yellow. Colouring agents or fillers were added to make coatings, which, when set hard, could be polished to give smooth, durable and beautiful surfaces that were wholly waterproof and corrosion-resistant. Since the hardening reaction requires a damp environment, only thin layers of lacquer could be hardened. When a thick coating was required, it had to be built up using several layers, allowing each to dry before the next is applied. The most widely used colours were black, made by mixing finely powdered charcoal into the liquid lacquer, and vermilion, made by adding cinnabar.

Gold, silver or other metallic particles or filings could be used to decorate the surface in several ways. The most important technique was *makie* (sprinkled illustration), by which gold or other metallic particles were sprinkled onto a tacky lacquer surface; when hardened, this could be left as it was, polished smooth or given a further layer of lacquer. If a lot of gold was used, a matt gold surface, *ikakeji*, could be obtained. When polished smooth, the work might appear to be solid gold. The use of less gold produced a speckled ground, *nashiji* (pear ground). This could be done evenly or in patches called *mura nashiji* (thicket pear ground). Sparsely sprinkled gold particles covered with further layers of transparent lacquer gave a sparkling effect within the lacquer, similar to the appearance of the stars at night. Particles of mother-of-pearl or other shells were often used to give a similar effect (*raden*). Pictorial motifs could also be applied using coloured lacquers. This could be done either under the surface, which would be wholly or partially revealed by polishing, a process called *togidashi* (polishing out), or by applying layers of varying depth over the finished surface. Several layers of lacquer could be applied to build up areas that could then be sculpted and polished into three-dimensional motifs. This is similar to high-relief coloured metal inlay (*iro-e taka zōgan*) and is called *taka makie* (high sprinkled pictures).

Metalwork

Copper was plentiful in Japan and was a principal export during the Edo period. The most important characteristic of the metal is its ease of working, and it is also the main constituent in a range of alloys used in sword fittings. A low-purity form of copper known as *yamagane* (mountain metal), which patinated naturally to a brown colour, was appreciated for its air of rusticity. The impurities in *yamagane* – antimony, arsenic and traces of lead – contributed to the colour of its main decorative alloys, *shakudō* and *shibuichi*.

Shakudō (red copper), also known as *ukin* (cormorant metal), is an alloy of (usually) 1 or 2 per cent gold in copper, although the best quality might have up to 5 per cent. It can be patinated by the use of various fruit vinegars to give a rich black colour. *Shibuichi* (one part in four), also known as *oborogin* (hazy silver), is an alloy of copper with 25 per cent silver. It patinates to give a range of colours from silver-white to greys and browns. *Sentoku* is a form of brass containing copper, tin and zinc. The word is written with the characters of the Xuande Chinese era (1426–35), since it first appeared in Japan in the form of brass vessels exported from China bearing the mark of that reign during the Muromachi period.

These were the principal alloys used on sword fittings, together with bronze, iron, leather and lacquer. The metals in all their various colours were sculpted and inlaid to form three-dimensional pictures on the various components of the sword mounting.

METHODS OF DECORATION

Iron was one of the most favoured metals for *tsuba*, certainly up to the seventeenth century when memory of earlier civil wars still lingered. The metal surface to be decorated was invariably patinated with the black oxide of iron, which was aesthetically pleasing as well as preventing further rusting. But in fact all the metals and their alloys could be used as a ground, upon which further decorative work was done. The surface might be polished smooth (*migakiji*) or it might be roughened with hammer or chisel to create a broken effect called *tsuchimeji* (hammered ground). A similar rough surface called *ishimeji* (stone ground) was also produced by hammering with special chisels (and the effect was sometimes imitated by the lacquerers who made scabbards). *Nanakoji* (fish roe ground) is a regular array of minute raised circular nodules made with a hollow punch, similar to, but far more precise than, the surfaces on some Sassanian or Chinese Tang-dynasty silverware. This was the favoured ground used by the Gotō family, who originated in Mino province and were retained as chief metalworkers to a succession of military governments from the time of Gotō Yūjō (1440–1512).

Itobori (hairline engraving) was the most basic method of decorating a plain surface, using a chisel to engrave a linear outline. *Keribori* (kick carving) was the use of hammer and chisel to make lines with distinct cuts, each retaining a visible triangular cross-section. *Katakiri-bori* (oblique-cut carving) was the use of a chisel held obliquely to produce cuts at varying angles and depths, giving the appearance of ink brush-strokes. *Sukidashi-bori* was a method whereby the ground was cut away to leave a raised design. *Shishiai-bori* was a form of *sukidashi-bori* using a chisel to cut away the metal so as to leave the design in relief, with the highest point level with the original ground. *Takabori* (carving in high relief) was a sculpted design raised above the ground. This could be done by *uchidashi* (hitting out), hammering the ground metal into raised sections, or by *zōgan* (inlay).

Sukashi-bori (pierced carving) was a method whereby the ground was cut through to leave a pierced design. This could be in either negative or positive silhouette – *in* (yin) or *yō* (yang) *sukashi*. With *in-sukashi* (negative piercing) the design was formed by the space cut out. With *yo-sukashi* (positive piercing) the design was formed by the remaining metal whose profile was defined by the metal cut out. Positive piercing was often carved in the round rather than just left as a flat profile.

There were several forms of *zōgan* (inlay), each involving the mechanical joining of a metal that might be similar or dissimilar to the metal of the ground. The piece to be inlaid was roughly shaped, then set into a cavity made in the ground. It could be set firmly in place by hammering so that it deformed into the sides of the cavity. The work was *taka zōgan* (high inlay), when it stood out in high relief above the level of the ground, or *hira zōgan* (level inlay), when it was made level with the ground.

Nunome zōgan (textile weave inlay) was a method by which the decorative metal, usually gold foil, was pressed onto a surface which had been prepared by filing in two directions to make a hatched, textile-like pattern. The foil stayed just by virtue of mechanical adhesion in the hatching. The hatched pattern was often visible through the foil or in places where foil had become detached. A similar method of gilding was by *suritsuke zōgan* (rub-fixed inlay) whereby a piece of gold or silver was rubbed over a roughened surface (usually iron) so that small particles adhered forming an indistinct layer. *Kaga zōgan* (Kaga province inlay) was a form of level inlay in which a thin sheet of gold or silver was laid flat on the ground and hammered into an engraved profile. The method was widely used on sword fittings, guns and horse equipment during the Edo period. *Uttori* was a form of overlay in which a sheet of gold was fixed over a piece of high-relief inlay, and tamped into place at the edges. It was widely used by the Gotō school until the seventeenth century, after which soldering became more prevalent.

SCHOOLS OF METALWORK

There were many distinctive regional schools of metalworking that specialized in sword fittings from the mid-Muromachi period onwards, particularly of iron *tsuba*. Although a detailed discussion of the many schools of sword-fittings makers is far beyond the scope of the present book, it is worth looking at the origins of the highly decorative soft metalwork that is found on most of the mountings in the collection.

Metal fittings for swords became increasingly decorative during the Muromachi period, and one of the most thriving groups of makers was to be found in Mino. Their work was decorated with the same sort of designs found on old armour, typically with high-relief carvings of chrysanthemums, autumnal plants, deer and other animals in high-relief gold inlay on a *yamagane* or *shakudō* ground. Gotō Yūjō (1440–1512) from the Mino school found permanent employment in the household of the ruling Ashikaga shogun. His family continued in this position of trust for seventeen generations until the last master, Gotō Ichijō (1791–1876), in the Meiji era. Since the early Muromachi period the Gotō family of metalworkers specialized in making matching *midokoromono* (things of three places), meaning *menuki*, *kozuka* and *kōgai*, with a common design motif. Since they were employed by the ruling houses of Japan, first the Ashikaga and then the Tokugawa, Gotō-school work is known as *iebori* (house carving). The Gotō specialized in Chinese-influenced decoration, which had been fashionable during the Ashikaga rule. From the seventeenth century, however, both samurai and townspeople required more varied subject matter. Yokoya Sōmin (1660–1733), a resident of Edo who had been schooled in the Gotō tradition, set up an independent workshop to make metal fittings with popular motifs. He specialized in *katakiri-bori* and, using this technique and high-relief inlay, was able to convert imagery from the paintings of the Kano school and by his close friend Hanabusa Itchō (1652–1724) into metal pictures.

A similar development occurred in Kyoto, represented by the Nara Sansaku (Three Makers of Nara): Toshinaga, who specialized in soft metal inlay onto iron; Sugiura Jōi , who carved subjects in *shishiai-bori* on *shibuichi;* and Tsuchiya Yasuchika, who worked in high-relief inlay. A pupil of Toshinaga, Hamano Shōsui, established an enduring studio that made high-relief inlay representations of themes from the Chinese novel *Sanguoshi* (Japanese: *Sangokushi*) depicting the 'Three Heroes of Han'. Whereas the paintings of Hanabusa Itchō inspired the Edo-period metalworkers, Ichinomiya Nagatsune (1727–70) and others in Kyoto were profoundly influenced by the paintings of Maruyama Ōkyo (1733–95). Schools multiplied and diversified, until the Haitōrei (law prohibiting the wearing of swords in public) of 1876, after which most of the metalworkers took to making small personal accessories, although some continued to make lavish sword fittings for export to the West.

The Catalogue

The blades of the swords in this catalogue are listed in roughly chronological order, within which they have been grouped, as far as is possible given the nature of the collection, into schools or provinces. Chronological divisions are by no means rigidly defined, since a regional tradition might continue relatively unchanged throughout the Edo period or even longer; examples include the Mino style, which evolved from the fifteenth century and exists to the present day, the school of Tadayoshi of Hizen and the school of the Yokoyama smiths of the province of Bizen.

The mountings are mostly described and illustrated (pp. 84–149, unless indicated otherwise) together with their blades, but ten mountings whose blades were not conserved for this project (apart from that for no. 99) are covered separately at the end of the catalogue. Some of the blades are kept in *shirasaya*, which are not catalogued because they are merely plain wood preservation scabbards, and are of limited relevance except for the ink inscriptions on some of them. The mountings of blades might be changed a number of times over the centuries, and almost all the mountings of the swords in the collection date to the eighteenth or nineteenth centuries, even though in some cases the blade is much older. For example, the first sword in the catalogue is a fourteenth-century blade, but the mounting is nineteenth century and is illustrated (col. pl. 2) together with the nineteenth-century *wakizashi* (no. 2), with which it forms a *daishō*.

Blade measurements are given in the following form: the length (L) is measured from the boundary between the tang and the beginning of the back of the blade (*mune*) to the tip of the point (*kissaki*), while the curvature (C), where applicable, is measured as the perpendicular distance from the straight line that defines the length of the blade to its back at the point of deepest curve. Some blades, particularly *tantō* of the Kamakura period, only have a very slight downwards curve (*uchi zori*), which is so small as not to be measurable.

Kotō (nos 1–17)

Bizen tradition (nos 1–8)

Swords have been made in the province of Bizen (present-day Okayama Prefecture) since the Heian period (794–1185). Swords of Bizen Province were prominent among the 'Five Traditions' of kotō blades – Bizen, Sōshū, Yamashiro, Yamato and Mino. From the Kamakura period (1185–1333), and throughout the kotō and shintō periods, there were many family lineages of swordsmiths living in the village of Osafune in Bizen Province that continued unbroken. The Kamakura period saw the flowering of the Bizen tradition. Retired Emperor Gotoba-In gave the appellation 'Ichimonji' (literally the character 'one', since they were 'the first under heaven') to a group of smiths known thereafter by this name.

Bizen work is associated with the chōji hamon and midare utsuri (no. 1). During the Muromachi period (1392–1573) the smiths of Bizen Province produced large numbers of swords to supply the armies who fought in the continuous civil wars. During the early fifteenth century smiths such as Yasumitsu of Osafune village strove to emulate the work of the middle Kamakura-period (thirteenth century) Bizen smiths and produced swords with a similar shape (no. 2). The curve at the bottom part of the blade was deep and became straighter towards the top of the blade. This was an almost universal shape during the early and middle Kamakura period but has become popularly known as Bizen zori (literally 'Bizen curve'). The hamon also changed, with more togariba and yō in addition to ashi within the ha itself. But the most evident difference was the lack of vivid midare utsuri on the blades. By the middle of the Muromachi period utsuri became less frequent and the traditional nioi structure of the hamon gave way to nie. The straight form of utsuri known as bō utsuri characterized the early Muromachi-period Bizen Province blades, but utsuri is less frequently found on late Muromachi-period work. Many swords of the fifteenth and sixteenth centuries were not made for use by hereditary bushi (i.e. samurai), but intended for armies of conscript and non-professional soldiers.

Many poor quality swords were also made at this time, the so-called kazu-uchi mono (literally 'swords made in quantity'), otherwise called sokutō (literally 'bundle swords').

1 Katana blade and mounting

Unsigned, attributed to Yoshioka Ichimonji (early 14th century)
L 65.2 cm, C 1.8 cm
1952.10-28.16, given by Mrs Margaret Plass

This blade is shinogi zukuri, with a medium kissaki. The curve is deep, particularly in the lower part of the blade, and the upper part straightens slightly towards the point. The blade has been shortened at some time, and it can be seen from the position of the rounded ends of the grooves either side of the blade on the re-shaped tang that its original length was about 75–6 cm. The tang has been over-zealously cleaned sometime before the sword came into the collection, and the details cannot clearly be seen.

The grain of the jigane is itame with extensive midare utsuri throughout the length of the blade. The hamon is of small chōji mixed with small compacted togariba and with many small ashi in nioi. The bōshi is midare komi with an almost ōmaru return and some haki.

Both the shape of the blade and the beautiful appearance of the midare utsuri identify it as work of the Bizen school, probably dating from the closing years of the Kamakura period. It may be attributed to the Yoshioka Ichimonji group, who moved from Fukuoka to Yoshioka in Bizen at the end of the Kamakura period (early fourteenth century). The accompanying single-piece habaki is gilded.

The uchigatana-style mounting (col. pl. 2) for this sword forms a daishō with the following sword (no. 2). The scabbards of both swords were lacquered in the style popular during the late seventeenth century known as 'Wakasa nuri', after the old province of Wakasa (forming the western part of present-day Fukui Prefecture). This style was achieved by carving an irregular pattern into the base of black lacquer, which was then filled with gold leaf, coloured lacquers and other material such as crushed eggshell; a transparent lacquer layer was then applied overall. The fuchi and kashira have bird and flower motifs in high-relief coloured metal inlay on *shibuichi*, and the *menuki* are gilt copper dragons.

The *tsuba* (col. pl. 3) is of patinated iron pierced and roundly carved with battle scenes, the details set in gold inlay, and is signed 'Hikone jū Nyūdō Sōten sei' (made by monk Sōten, resident of Hikone). According to the book entitled *Sōken kishō* (by Inaba Tsūryū, published in 1796), Kitagawa Sōten (also known as 'Kitagawa Shūten') moved from Kyoto to Hikone in Ōmi Province around 1750. There were several later generations all doing similar work of varying quality, as well as many pupils and imitators. This *tsuba* dates from the Edo period (eighteenth or nineteenth century).

2 *Wakizashi* blade and mounting

Yasumitsu (early 15th century)
Signed on the *omote* 'Yasumitsu'
L 48.2 cm, C 1.0 cm
1952.10-28.17, given by Mrs Margaret Plass

This blade is *shinogi zukuri* with square-ended *bōhi* and a small *kissaki*. The shape of the blade is typical of early Muromachi-period small *wakizashi*, with a graceful deep curve and narrowing towards the point. The fine *jigane* has close-packed *itame*, with the vivid *bō utsuri* characteristic of early fifteenth-century Bizen blades. The *hamon* is *suguha* with many small *ashi* and small *gunome*, lending vigour to the appearance of the cutting edge, and has a *komaru bōshi*. This is very fine and pretty steel for work of the Bizen school in the Ōei era (1394–1428).

The *wakizashi* mounting (col. pl. 2) forms a *daishō* with the blade attributed to Yoshioka Ichimonji (no. 1), and differs only in being equipped with a *kozuka* of copper with inlaid paulownia *mon* of *shakudō*.

3 *Wakizashi* blade (1449) and *hosodachi* mounting

Osafune Norimitsu
Signed on the *omote* 'Bishū Osafune Norimitsu' and dated on the *ura* 'Bunnan roku nen ni gatsu jitsu' (a day in the second month in the sixth year of the Bunnan era), in accordance with 1449
L 52.7 cm, C 1.9 cm
OA+3790

This blade is *shinogi zukuri*, has *saki zori* and a medium *kissaki*. The *mune* is slender, so that the *shinogi* is high and the *shinogi ji* broad. There are engraved *kurikara* on both sides of the blade. The tang has two holes, one of which has been plugged with steel. The file marks are a rather shallow version of *sujigai*, although there are also more recent, deeper file marks, which were made over the portion of the tang that was originally part of the blade. The tang tip is *kurijiri*. The grain is closely packed *itame* with *utsuri*. The *hamon* is a rather open *gunome*, with *yō* in places, and it has a tight *nioiguchi*, with a *midare komi*-style *bōshi*.

This blade has been modified by moving the *machi* forward to shorten the cutting edge. It is possible that this was done so that the retaining peg should be in the required position on the newly made hilt when the blade was mounted as a *tachi*. The original length of the tang was thus shorter in relation to the length of the entire piece, although the re-shaped tang does not seem disproportionately long. The original peg-hole in the tang has been plugged with steel and filed over so that it is barely visible.

The *hosodachi* mounting (col. pl. 5) is lacquered in gold *nashiji makie*, with paulownia and stylized plum *mon* in gold leaf. The metal fittings are all gold. The *tsuba* (col. pl. 4) of Kara style is signed on the *omote* 'Kashū jū Mizuno Mitsunobu' (Mizuno Mitsunobu, resident of Kaga Province) and 'Suzuki Mitsuhiro', with *kaō* (written seals); it is dated on the *ura* 'Bunsei go nen jūichi gatsu kichi jitsu' (An auspicious day in the eleventh month

of the fifth year of the Bunsei era), in accordance with 1822. The *mekugi* are of the screw-in type, with the traditional anticlockwise thread. There are five *tawara byō* (rivets in the shape of rice bales) on the *omote* of the hilt and four on the *ura*, but these are decorative and non-functional. This fine quality mounting was evidently commissioned by the ruling clan of Kaga Province, doubtless especially for use in court ceremonial.

4 *Katana* blade (1512)

Osafune Norimitsu
Signed on the *omote* 'Bishū Osafune Norimitsu' (Osafune Norimitsu of Bizen Province) and dated on the *ura* 'Eishō kyū nen ni gatsu jitsu' (a day in the second month in the ninth year of the Eishō era), in accordance with 1512
L 62.5 cm, C 2.1 cm
1958.07-30.14, bequeathed by R W Lloyd Esq.

This blade is *shinogi zukuri* and has the *saki zori* curve and short tang that characterize the shorter *uchigatana* of the Muromachi period. There are square-ended *bōhi* with *soehi* on both sides of the blade. The unmodified tang has one hole and the file marks are a shallow version of *katte sagari*. The tang tip is *kurijiri*. The grain is *itame*, with intermittent *utsuri*. The *hamon* is small *chōji* intermixed with *gunome* and *togariba* and the *bōshi* is *midare komi* style. The single-piece gold-covered *habaki* bears a finely incised triple *tomoe* design.

5 *Tantō* blade (1574) and mounting

Sukesada
Signed on the *omote* 'Bizen kuni jū Osafune Sukesada' (Osafune Sukesada, resident of Bizen Province) and dated on the *ura* 'Tenshō ni nen hachigatsu jitsu' (a day in the eighth month in the second year of the Tenshō era), in accordance with 1574
L 22.1 cm
1958.07-30.104, bequeathed by R W Lloyd Esq.

This blade is *hira zukuri*. The unmodified tang has one hole and the file marks are *kiri*. The tang tip is rather severe *kurijiri*. The prominent grain is *itame* mixed with mokume. The hamon is gunome with a tight nioiguchi and clusters of nie in the valleys of the undulations. The bōshi is komaru with hakikake. The blade is typical of late Bizen-school work, although the quality is not the highest.

The scabbard of the mounting is wrapped with wrinkled leather. The metal fittings all have motifs of auspicious treasures in coloured enamels set in iron. The menuki are of a rat on a rice bale and a mallet, both attributes of Daikoku-Ten, the popular deity of plenty, whose mallet showers the 'Seven Treasures'. The tsuba is signed 'Jukō' (or 'Toshiyoshi') and elsewhere the mounting is signed 'Matsushiro Jukō'. The mounting was assembled in the Meiji era.

6 Tantō blade (1562) and mounting

Shinjurō Sukesada

Signed on the omote 'Bizen kuni jū Osafune Sukesada' (Osafune Sukesada, resident of Bizen Province) and dated on the ura 'Eiroku go nen hachi gatsu jitsu' (a day in the eighth month in the fifth year of the Eiroku era), in accordance with 1562

L 21.3 cm

1958.07-30.58, bequeathed by R W Lloyd Esq.

This blade is hira zukuri. The unmodified tang has one hole and the file marks are shallow sujigai. The tang tip is kurijiri. There is a koshihi on the omote and gomabashi on the ura. The grain is prominent itame. The hamon is suguha and is comprised of konie with a tight nioiguchi. The bōshi is somewhat pointed komaru with haki on the return.

Of the large number of recorded smiths who signed the name 'Sukesada', three used signatures similar to that on this blade during the Eiroku era (1558–70): Gembei, Tōhei and Shinjurō. In this case the chisel marks in the signature identify it as the work of Shinjurō. This short tantō blade, with its sturdily shaped tang, has the thick-bodied triangular cross-section of a yoroi dōshi (literally 'armour piercer', a thick-bladed hira zukuri dagger).

The scabbard of the mounting is lacquered and carved in simulation of wood grain. The menuki are silver in the form of dragonflies, and there are silver pieces in the form of a wasp and a praying mantis applied to the scabbard. The other metal fittings are silver, carved with chrysanthemums and signed 'Bishū Uguisudani jū Katsuaki kore (o) tsukuru' (made by Katsuaki, resident of Uguisudani in Owari Province). Hasegawa Katsuaki (1837–1913) was a specialist sword-fittings maker who was retained by the Owari Tokugawa clan during the Edo period. After the Meiji Restoration in 1868 he made smoking pipes and other metal accessories.

7 Tantō blade (1582) and mounting

Sukesada

Signed on the omote 'Bishū Osafune Sukesada' (Osafune Sukesada of Bizen Province) and dated on the ura 'Tenshō jū nen hachi gatsu jitsu' (a day in the eighth month in the tenth year of the Tenshō era), in accordance with 1582

L 22.2 cm, C (uchi zori)

1958.07-30.48, bequeathed by R W Lloyd Esq.

This tantō is a straight hira zukuri blade with bōhi grooves. The tang has two holes and the file marks are katte sagari. The tang tip is kurijiri. The grain is flowing itame with bō utsuri. The hamon is suguha with a tight nioiguchi and a moist yakidashi, and the bōshi is komaru with a long return.

The scabbard is of black lacquer with applied silver chrysanthemums and foliage in gold makie. The metal fittings are of shibuichi with an ishime ground with floral designs, and the menuki are in the form of morning glories. The hilt is bound with 'whale's beard' (extracted from the fringe coating found on whales' baleen). The mounting was assembled in the Meiji era.

8 Tantō blade and mounting

Sukesada (16th century)

Signed on the omote 'Bishū Osafune Sukesada' (Osafune Sukesada of Bizen Province)

L 20.5 cm, C (uchi zori)

1948.07-30.60

This small tantō is a hira zukuri blade and has uchi zori. The tang has one hole and the file marks are katte sagari. The tang tip is kurijiri. The grain is a flowing itame with jinie. The hamon is overall suguha and comprises gunome with ashi, sunagashi and uchi noke. The bōshi has haki and is in yakitsume style (i.e. the hamon ends at the mune without turning back). Although this is a well-made blade, it is a kazu-uchi mono and has not been attributed to any of the recorded Sukesadas.

The black-lacquered scabbard has been sparsely sprinkled with gold powder, then decorated with maple leaves formed by first embedding real leaves in the lacquer before it is fully set, removing them and filling the impressions with pigment. The metal fittings have leaves and insects in high-relief coloured inlay on silver. The menuki are in the form of paulownia blossoms. Both kozuka and kōgai are signed 'Masayoshi'. The ensemble dates from the Meiji era.

Blades of other provinces
(nos 9–17)

9 Tachi blade and mounting

Unsigned, attributed to Esshū Tametsugu (14th century)

L 71.7 cm, C 1.7 cm

OA+3808

This shinogi zukuri blade with a large kissaki has been considerably shortened from its original length. On both sides of the blade are carvings of suken, made after the blade was shortened. The tang has two holes and the file marks are kiri. The tang tip is kurijiri.

The grain is prominent itame mixed with mokume and flowing hada. There is *jinie*, some of which agglomerates to form *tobiyaki*. The *hamon* is *suguha* overall and contains *midareba* with dense *nie*, *gunome*, *ashi*, *yō* and much *sunagashi*. The *bōshi* is *midare komi* and has *haki* on the return. The *hamon* seems to stop at the reshaped *hamachi* (whereas it might be expected to continue into the rust on the new tang), but this is probably due to the blade having been partially heated to soften the tang and reshape it.

The shape of the blade if extrapolated to its original length dates it to the Nambokuchō period (1336–92). The dark and vivid forging as well as the prominent *mokume* distinguishes it as a *Hokkoku mono* (work of the northern provinces). The *jigane* is somewhat similar to that found on the work of Etchū Norishige (a pupil of Masamune), who is associated with the early Uda school of Etchū. It is therefore not unreasonable to suggest that this blade was by Tametsugu who was a contemporary of Norishige and is believed to have been his direct pupil.

The *tachi* mounting of this sword forms a *daishō* together with the mounting of a nineteenth-century *tantō* by Masafusa of Satsuma Province (no. 61).

10 *Tantō* blade and mounting

Unsigned, attributed to Tsukushi Nobukuni (Ōei era, 1394–1428)

L 32.5 cm, C (*uchi zori*)

OA+3809

This straight *sunnobi tantō* blade is *hira zukuri* and has a *marumune*. On the *omote* there are *gomabashi* that taper off on the tang and on the *ura* there is a *bōhi* with an inset *ukibori* carving of five characters reading 'Hachiman Dai Bosatsu' (Great Bodhisattva Hachiman). The unmodified, deeply angled tang has one hole and the file marks are *sujigai*. The tang tip is *kiri*. The grain is *koitame* with some large *hada*, and the steel is bright and gentle. Very little of the straight *hamon* of small *nie* remains, save for some patches along the edge and on the *kissaki*, due to repeated and severe

polishing over the ages. What little remains of the *bōshi* reveals it as *komaru*.

Despite the poor survival of the *hamon*, the shape of the blade and tang identifies it as the work of Tsukushi Nobukuni, made during the Ōei era (1394–1428). Three generations of a family who signed 'Nobukuni' are said to have worked in the Yamashiro tradition in Kyoto during the fourteenth century, as well as a certain 'Shikibu no jō Nobukuni' who produced *tantō* in the early fifteenth century. Records tell of smiths signing 'Nobukuni' in different provinces thereafter. But the name is particularly associated with the smith to whom this blade is ascribed – who worked in Tsukushi (Chikuzen and Chikugo Provinces) in the early fifteenth century – and with his successors during the Muromachi period (1392–1573). 'Nobukuni' became virtually a family name, and was used as such during the ensuing centuries and into the Edo period.

The *wakizashi* mounting for this *tantō* has a vermilion- and black-lacquered ribbed scabbard, with bamboo and paulownia in *makie*, which appear to have been added at a later date. The *fuchi* and *kashira* are of iron with stylized grasses in gold *nunome zōgan*. The *menuki* are of fruits and wasps sculpted in coloured metals. The small *tsuba* is patinated iron with a plum tree carved in *ukibori*. The *umabari* is of iron with paulownia and grasses in gold *nunome zōgan*. This mounting was assembled either in the late Edo period or Meiji era.

11 *Wakizashi* blade

Kuninaga (15th century)

Signed on the *omote* 'Kuninaga'

L 50.9 cm, C 1.7 cm

1958.07-30.08, bequeathed by R W Lloyd Esq.

This blade is *shinogi zukuri* and has a medium *kissaki*. The unmodified tang has two holes and the file marks are *kiri*. The tang tip is *kurijiri*. The grain is *itame* with *jinie*. The *hamon* is *gunome* with *nie* and faint *sunagashi* throughout, with a *midare komi bōshi*.

It is recorded that two smiths used the name 'Kuninaga' during the *kotō* era. One was related to the Uda school and was active during the Bummei era (1469–87), and the other was in the Akasaka Senjuin school and active during the Kakitsu era (1441–4). The slightly dark visual quality of this steel is suggestive of the Uda school. In addition, Senjuin work usually involves *taka no ha* file marks, quite unlike the *kiri* marks on the tang of this sword. Although Uda work of the period usually has the name 'Uda' incorporated into the inscription, and this is just a two-character signature, the Uda attribution is nevertheless reasonable.

12 *Tantō* blade

Unsigned, attributed to Muramasa (16th century)

L 27.6 cm, C 0.2 cm

1958.07-30.103, bequeathed by R W Lloyd Esq.

This blade is *hira zukuri*. There is a *koshihi* on the *omote*, and *gomabashi* on the *ura*. The tang has two holes and the file marks are shallow *sujigai*. The tang narrows markedly so that it becomes particularly slender at the tang tip in the so-called 'tanagobara' (literally 'bitterling fish belly') form that characterizes the work of Muramasa. The tang tip is *iriyamagata*. The bold and prominent *hada* is comprised of *itame* and a flowing grain with *jinie*. The *hamon* is small *notare* with *gunome* and *hako gunome* in *nie*, with *sunagashi* throughout. The *bōshi* is a swelling form of *komaru* slightly dropping towards the cutting edge.

With its distinctive tang and *hamon*, this blade is unmistakably Muramasa's work. The silver inlaid inscription of the smith's name is of poor quality and was probably added much later. Although such silver inlay is quite rare, interestingly a similar *tantō* by Muramasa in the collection of Chiddingstone Castle in Kent also has a crude silver attribution on the tang.

After Masamune the name of Muramasa

is probably the best known of all swordsmiths. He was a native of Kuwana in Ise Province who worked in the early sixteenth century. His earliest recorded dated blade is marked 1501, and there are signed blades dating to the 1530s and 1570s believed to be by the second and third generations, whose works are very similar. There are later blades bearing the name 'Muramasa', but their relation to the first generation is not clear.

Muramasa's swords were of ill repute during the Edo period, having been used several times in incidents in which members of the Tokugawa family were injured or died. It is said that both Tokugawa Ieyasu's father Hirotada and his grandfather Kiyoyasu were injured by means of Muramasa's swords, and Ieyasu himself was accidentally cut on the hand by a spear made by him. But the most awful episode was when Ieyasu's son Nobuyasu, having fallen foul of Oda Nobunaga, was ordered to commit *seppuku* (ritual suicide by cutting open the abdomen, vulgarly 'hara-kiri'). In *seppuku* a second, often a close friend, beheads the principal at a convenient time after the wound is afflicted to the abdomen, and the sword used in this case was also by Muramasa. Subsequently, Ieyasu ordered that all swords made by Muramasa were to be destroyed. Possibly owing to resentment against the shogun's family, however, many blades by the smith have in fact been carefully preserved. The practice during the late Edo period of spuriously incising blades with the name 'Muramasa' doubtless reflects the unpopularity of the Tokugawa house in certain parts of Japan.

13 *Tantō* blade and mounting

Kaga Katsuie (16th century)
Signed on the *omote* 'Katsuie'
L 26.2 cm, C (*uchi zori*)
1952.10-28.18

This *tantō* blade is *hira zukuri*, and has *uchi zori*. The unmodified tang has one hole and the file marks are *kiri*. The tang tip is *kurijiri*. The coarse, prominent grain is flowing *itame* mixed with *masame*. A whitish hue near the *mune* forms *bō utsuri*. The *hamon* is *suguha* overall with shallow *notare* in *nie* and with *uchi noke*. The *bōshi* is *komaru* with a deep return. The steel is coarse, with many faults, but it is nevertheless a Muromachi-period blade of character made by one of the several generations of Kaga Province signing 'Katsuie'.

The scabbard has stylized clouds sculpted and filled with *makie* and gold leaf. The *fuchi* and *kashira* have clematis in coloured enamels on an iron ground, and the *menuki* are clematis in gold. The *tsuba* is of *shakudō* with cherry blossoms in coloured enamels, and the *kozuka* also has clematis in enamels on copper.

14 *Tantō* blade and mounting

Unsigned, attributed to Kongōbei (16th century)
L 23.9 cm, C (none)
1958.07-30.33, bequeathed by R W Lloyd Esq.

This *tantō* blade is *hira zukuri*. There is a *koshihi* on the *omote* and *gomabashi* on the *ura*. The unmodified tang has two holes and the file marks are *kiri*. The tang broadens slightly at the base and the tang tip is *kengyō*. The grain is *itame* mixed with *mokume* and there is *bō utsuri*. The *hamon* is *suguha* with *konie* and *hotsure*. The *bōshi* is *komaru* on the *omote* and *ōmaru* with *haki* on the *ura*. The characteristic shape of the tip of the tang, *suguha* and the *utsuri* indicate the work of one of the smiths of the Kongōbei (or Kongōhyōe) school of Chikuzen Province, originally established by Kongōbei Moritaka during the Kamakura period.

The black-lacquered scabbard has thickets of gold powder forming cherry blossoms. All the metal fittings have bird and flower designs in coloured metal inlays on *shakudō*. The *menuki* are of acorns in gold and *shakudō*. This fine quality Meiji-era decorative work was probably from the school of Gotō Ichijō.

15 *Katana* blade and mounting

Unsigned, attributed to Kanesada (16th century)
L 65.2 cm, C 1.6 cm
1958.07-30.123, bequeathed by R W Lloyd Esq.

This blade is *shinogi zukuri*, has undergone *ōsuriage*, and has a medium *kissaki*. The tang has two holes and the file marks are *kiri*. The tang tip is *kiri*. The grain is flowing *itame* mixed with *mokume* with much *jinie* and *chikei*. The *hamon* is a deep valleyed *gunome* with *togariba* in *nie*, and there are many *ashi* and *yō*. The *nioiguchi* is tight. The *bōshi* is *komaru* on the *omote*, and *notare* with *komaru* on the *ura*.

The tang has a gold inlay attribution reading 'Kanesada ake' (cut-down Kanesada), implying that the original signature was of the early sixteenth-century smith Kanesada, known as 'Nosada'. Although the blade might not be the work of Kanesada, it is a fine quality piece of the same Seki school in Mino Province.

The *uchigatana*-style mounting has a scabbard of gold *ikakeji* with a *kurikara* in high-relief gold *makie* and gold leaf on the *omote* and seven *mon* of five different types on the *ura*. The metal collar at the mouth of the scabbard has the deity Marishi-ten in high-relief coloured metal inlay on *shibuichi* on the *omote*, and an inscription in Chinese meaning 'If you persevere, you will always accomplish' on the *ura*. The *fuchi* and *kashira* have a priest's fly whisk, a Buddhist sutra scroll and an incense burner, with *menuki* in the form of Buddhist gongs, all in coloured metals. The *fuchi* is signed 'Yumeiken Masahiro', a metalworker of Kai Province. The *tsuba* has scenes from the Chinese story *Saiyūki* (The Water Margin) in high-relief coloured metal inlay. It bears the spurious signature of the important eighteenth-century maker Shōjūken Nobuyuki, but is actually export work of the Meiji era, albeit of outstandingly high quality.

16 *Naginata* blade

Kanetsuji (16th century)

Signed on the *omote* 'Nōshū Shimizu jū Kanetsuji' (Kanetsuji, resident of Shimizu, Mino Province).

L 45.6 cm, C 3.0 cm

JA+11

The blade has the pronounced *saki zori* and broadening towards the point typical of Muromachi-period work. It has round-ended *naginata hi* with *soehi*. The unmodified tang has one hole and the file marks are *ōsujigai*. The tang tip is *kurijiri*. The grain is a somewhat distinct, flowing *itame* with *jinie*. The *hamon* is *gunome* with *chōji*, *togariba* and *tobiyaki* resembling *hitatsura*. The *bōshi* is somewhat pointed *komaru*.

17 *Katana* blade

Kanabō Masazane (late 16th century)

Signed on the *omote* 'Nanto jū Kanabō Hayato [no] jō Masazane' (Kanabō Hayato no jō Masazane, resident of the southern capital [i.e. Nara])

L 64.8 cm, C 1.5 cm

1958.07-30.84, bequeathed by R W Lloyd Esq.

This blade is *shinogi zukuri* with *saki zori*, and has a *mitsumune*. On either side there is a *bōhi* with a *soehi*. On the *omote* there is an *ukibori* carving of Fudō Myō-ō under a waterfall set within a wide *bōhi*. On the *ura* there is an inscribed invocation 'Namu Amida Butsu' (In the name of Amitabha Buddha) on the flat of the blade. The unmodified tang has one hole and the file marks are *katte sagari*. The tang tip is a shallow form of *iriyamagata*. It is notable that although the engraving of the religious invocation on the *ura* of the blade has evidently

been worn down through polishing in the past, the carving of Fudō Myō-ō on the *omote* remains in its original unworn state.

The grain is a closely packed *koitame* with *jinie* and very occasional patches of *tobiyaki*. The *hamon* is a broad, somewhat languid *suguha* in small *nie* crystals and with a hint of *hotsure*. The *yakidashi* rises up from below the *machi*, rather like *mizukage*, to form into *utsuri*. The *bōshi* is *komaru* with some *haki*.

The group of Yamato School smiths who originated in the city of Nara, probably in the earliest days of sword-making during the Nara period (AD 710–94), later spread through the auspices of the Kasuga Shrine of Nara to other parts of Japan. They were influential in the refinement of technology, which led to the Mino tradition. The name 'Masazane' occurs on work from both Yamato (centred on Nara) and Mino during the early to middle sixteenth century, and the first generation is said to have been associated with the smith Muramasa (no. 12). The smith of this blade, Kanabō Masazane, worked in Nara.

Blades of the Momoyama and early Edo periods (nos 18–22)

18 *Wakizashi* blade and mounting

Horikawa Kunihiro (early Keichō era 1596–1615)

Signed on the *omote* 'Kunihiro'

L 50.6 cm, C 1.0 cm

1958.07-30.128, bequeathed by R W Lloyd Esq.

This blade is *shinogi zukuri* with a narrow *mitsumune* and a medium *kissaki*. The blade has been slightly shortened and the re-shaped tang has three holes, two of which have been filled with a lead alloy; the file marks are *sujigai*, and the tang tip is *kiri*. There is a carving depicting Fudō Myō-ō in flames on the *omote*, and a carving of a flowering plum bough on the *ura*.

The grain is *itame* with *jifu utsuri*, *chikei* and much *jinie*. The *hamon* is essentially *notare* rich in *nie* and has intermixed *gunome*, with violent *kuichigaiba*; some of the *nie* continues onto the *ji* forming into *jifu utsuri*. The *bōshi* is *komaru* with *haki*. This extravagant *hamon,* with its plentiful nie and grandiose texture, conveys well the aesthetic of the Momoyama period. There are two slight sword-cut marks on the *mune*, possibly indicating that the sword has been used in combat.

Horikawa Kunihiro was foremost among the pupils of Umetada Myōju of Kyoto, who is often regarded as the first and greatest of the *shintō*-era smiths. Kunihiro was originally retained by the *daimyō* of the Itō clan in Hyūga Province in the very south of Kyūshū, after whose fall he travelled throughout Japan in order to broaden his study. According to the record *Hyūga Shishi*, he was living at Furuya in Hyūga in 1576 at the age of forty-six, and his earliest-known dated work was made at that time. He was at some time granted the honorific title 'Shinano no kami'. From 1599 he lived for a period at Horikawa in Kyoto, where he taught many pupils.

Kunihiro's blades are frequently of even curve and breadth with the extended point typical of the Momoyama and early Edo periods. This slender blade is more in keeping with the late Momoyama period (1573–96) and Kunihiro's early days, though the style of the signature suggests a Keichō-era date. The incongruity of the ferocious deity Fudō Myō-ō on the omote sharing space with the flowering prunus on the ura is representative of the transitional exuberance of the Momoyama decorative style.

The steel texture of Kunihiro's work is often described as 'gravelly', in contrast to the rather pretty steel of his teacher Umetada Myōju and that of Myōju's other pupils like Etchū no kami Masatoshi (no. 19). Kunihiro's hamon are often, like that of this sword, in large bright nie crystals, with copious variations in activity, similar to the work of the fourteenth-century Sōshū school, which Kunihiro emulated.

The scabbard is lacquered black with a spiral of ishime ground giving a grey appearance. The fittings are of shakudō with mushrooms and eggplants in high-relief inlay. The tsuba is signed 'Bushū jū Masayoshi' (Masayoshi of Musashi Province) and the fuchi is signed 'Buzen', probably by Yoshioka Buzen who was active in Edo during the 1860s.

19   Wakizashi blade and mounting

Sampin Masatoshi (early 17th century)

Signed on the omote 'Etchū [no] kami Masatoshi'

L 30.7 cm, C (uchi zori)

1958.07-30.46, bequeathed by R W Lloyd Esq.

This blade is kawarigata zukuri (literally 'of unusual shape'). The omote is hira zukuri, and on the ura the shinogi ji slopes down to the centre of the mune from the upper part of the blade, so that the shape resembles a naginata. The blade has been very slightly shortened and the almost unmodified tang has two holes with katte sagari file marks and a kurijiri tip. On the omote there is a carving of a suken located within a bōhi, and on the ura there is a vajra with a soehi. The grain is delicate itame with jinie. The hamon is irregular gunome in nie with ashi and some gentle sunagashi. The bōshi is notare and returns somewhat sharply in the style known as sampin bōshi.

Masatoshi was the fourth son of Kanemichi of Seki, with whom he moved to Kyoto sometime in the early 1590s. His elder brother Kimmichi worked in the original Mino style after the work of the fourteenth-century Shizu smiths, and his descendants continued in Kyoto for several generations. The third brother Tamba no kami Yoshimichi worked variously in the Shizu, Yamato and Sōshū styles, and developed the characteristic sudareba (a type of layered hamon resembling sudare, i.e. hanging bamboo curtain), which is found on the work of his descendants. Masatoshi was given the title 'Etchū no kami', probably after arriving in Kyoto, and his son received the title a few decades later. Although the signatures of the first two generations are not dissimilar, this blade is very much in the Momoyama shape, confirming that it is by the first Masatoshi.

The ribbed scabbard (also col. pls 19–20) is lacquered black. The fine matching metal fittings have chrysanthemums and other autumn flowers in gold high-relief inlay on a shakudō nanako ground. The kozuka and wari-kōgai have chrysanthemums in trellises. These are of seventeenth- or eighteenth-century Mino-school work.

20   Tantō blade

Shimosaka (early 17th century)

Signed on the omote 'Echizen kuni Shimosaka'

L 29.9 cm, C (uchi zori)

1958.07-30.24, bequeathed by R W Lloyd Esq.

This straight tantō blade is hira zukuri, and has a mitsumune. The unmodified tang has one hole and the file marks are katte sagari. The tang tip is iriyamagata. The blade is pierced through with a carving of a kurikara. The grain is flowing itame with jinie. The hamon is a small notare with gunome in nie with a komaru bōshi. The sword is not actually by Yasutsugu, who signed 'Shimosaka' in his early days, but this blade nevertheless is a good example of typical Momoyama-period Echizen work.

21   Wakizashi blade

Harima daijō Fujiwara Shigetaka (17th century)

Signed on the omote 'Harima daijō Fujiwara Shigetaka' and continued on the ura 'Echizen jū' (resident of Echizen Province)

L 39.4 cm, C 0.6 cm

1958.07-30.25, bequeathed by R W Lloyd Esq.

This blade is hira zukuri, broad, thick and evenly curved. The tang bears slightly angled kiri file marks and a kurijiri tip. On the omote is a carving of a vajra-hilted sword and on the ura an engraving of a flowering plum tree. The grain is prominent itame intermingled with komokume, with jinie. The hamon is notare mixed with gunome and rich in nie. The bōshi is a deep komaru.

This wakizashi blade is longer than one shaku, so it might be described as a sunnobi tantō. It might have been a copy of, or inspired by the work of, the fourteenth-century smith Sadamune of Sagami Province.

22   Wakizashi blade and mounting

Harima daijō Fujiwara Shigetaka (17th century)

Signed on the omote 'Harima daijō Fujiwara Shigetaka' and continued on the ura 'Echizen jū' (resident of Echizen Province)

L 31.5 cm, C 0.4 cm

1951.07-24.02, given by Henry N Ridley Esq.

This curved blade is hira zukuri, of sunnobi tantō proportions, and has a mitsumune. The unmodified tang has one hole and the file marks are kiri. The tang tip is kurijiri. The grain is prominent itame with jinie. The hamon is shallow notare in nie, with much sunagashi and kinsuji. The bōshi is komaru.

Shigetaka I worked during the Kan'ei era (1624–44). The shape of the blade and the hamon are similar to the work of Sadamune of Sagami Province, although the hada is coarse in places.

The wakizashi mounting has a black-lacquered scabbard with shibuichi fittings depicting a boy riding an ox beneath the moon. The tsuba has coloured metal inlay of a traveller before pavilions. The fuchi is signed 'Toshinori'.

Blades of the middle Edo period (nos 23–56)

Blades of Echizen and Edo Echizen (nos 23-8)

Echizen (the eastern part of modern Fukui Prefecture) became a major centre of sword-making during the Edo period. Smiths migrated there from other provinces, notably Mino and Ōmi. The family of Yasutsugu is probably the best known of the Echizen groups. The first Yasutsugu came from a family of swordsmiths in the village of Shimosaka in Ōmi Province. He was known as 'Shimosaka Ichizaemon', and is believed to have travelled around Japan in his youth, working in both Mino Province and Kyoto. His early work was sometimes signed 'Shimosaka'. He moved to Echizen sometime in the 1590s, by which time he had acquired the title 'Higo daijō', and entered the service of the *daimyō* Matsudaira Hideyasu, the third son of Tokugawa Ieyasu. He was later retained by the first and second Tokugawa shoguns Ieyasu and Hidetada, receiving from Ieyasu the first character 'Yasu' of his name and the privilege of carving the triple-hollyhock *mon* on his work. This was around 1605 when, with a high income and shogunal sponsorship, he was able to live alternately in his Echizen home and in the Tokugawa estate in Edo. His son continued this practice of alternate residence, but from the third generation the family divided into Echizen and Edo branches. The Edo branch is said to have continued for eleven generations into the Meiji era, and the Echizen branch for nine generations. Both the *katana* (no. 24) and the *wakizashi* (no. 25) were made by the third-generation Yasutsugu in Edo.

A succession of smiths signing 'Shigetaka' worked in Echizen and also in Edo from the early Edo period, and two swords by Shigetaka I (nos 21 and 22) have been catalogued in the previous section on Momoyama and early Edo-period work.

23 *Naginata* blade

Echizen Shigetaka (17th century)

Signed on the *omote* 'Echizen jū Harima daijō Fujiwara Shigetaka' (Harima daijō Fujiwara Shigetaka, resident of Echizen Province)

L 45.3 cm (length of tang 48.9 cm), C 2.5 cm

JA+56

The blade has marked *saki zori* and a *mitsumune*. There are round-ended *koshihi* with *soehi* in traditional *naginata* style on either side of the blade. The unmodified tang bears one hole and the file marks are *katte sagari* and, from halfway down the tang, *sensuki* (i.e. chiselled). The tang tip is *kurijiri*. The grain is closely packed *itame* with *jinie*. The *hamon* is *gunome* with *nie* and many thick *ashi*. The *bōshi* is *komaru* that returns into a long *muneyaki*.

This blade is by Shigetaka II, who flourished during the Kambun era (1661–73). The *jigane* and *hamon* of this *naginata* are very similar to the work of the Edo smith Kotetsu, leading to conjecture that Shigetaka II might have worked closely with that smith in Edo.

24 *Katana* blade and mounting

Edo Yasutsugu III (mid-17th century)

Signed on the *omote* 'Yasutsugu namban tetsu o motte Bushū Edo [ni] oite kore [o] tsukuru' (Yasutsugu made this using imported steel in Edo, Musashi Province), with a carved triple-hollyhock *mon*

L 74.3 cm, C 1.3 cm

1958.07-30.136, bequeathed by R W Lloyd Esq.

This blade is *shinogi zukuri*, with the shape and shallow curve typical of Kambun-era (1661–73) *shintō*, and a medium *kissaki*. The unmodified tang has one hole and the file marks are *katte sagari*. The tang tip is *iriyamagata*. The grain is closely packed *itame* with much *jinie*, blending into *masame* on the *shinogi ji* region. The *hamon* is a particularly well-contrived bright *suguha* with much *nie*. The *bōshi* is *komaru* with a deep and broad return.

This is a healthy blade, which remains much in its original condition. The inscription tells that the blade was made in Edo by the smith Yasutsugu using *namban tetsu* (literally 'barbarian iron', imported steel). It was made by the third generation of the Yasutsugu family.

The *uchigatana* mounting has a black-lacquered ribbed scabbard with the Seven Lucky Gods depicted in high-relief coloured metal inlay on *shakudō*. The *fuchi* and *kashira* are signed 'Kikuchi Noritaka' and the *tsuba* is signed 'Kankyū'. The *fuchi* and *kashira* are by Naotaka, who established a branch of the Yokoya school in Edo, and was active during the second half of the eighteenth century. The *tsuba* maker Tani Kankyū, later called Yokoya and probably related to the Yokoya school of Naotaka, took to painting with the fall in demand for sword fittings after the Meiji Restoration in 1868. He lived in Matsue, Shimane Prefecture, until his death in 1915 at the age of eighty-two.

25 *Wakizashi* blade and mounting

Edo Yasutsugu III (mid-17th century)

Signed on the *omote* 'Yasutsugu namban tetsu [o] motte' (Yasutsugu, using imported steel), with a triple-hollyhock *mon*, and continued on the *ura* 'Bushū Edo [ni] oite kore [o] tsukuru' ([Yasutsugu] made this at Edo in Musashi Province)

L 36.9 cm, C 0.3 cm

1958.07-30.120, bequeathed by R W Lloyd Esq.

This blade is katakiriha *zukuri*. There is a broad *bōhi* on the *ura* of the blade. The unmodified tang has two holes and the file marks are *katte sagari*. The tang tip is *iriyamagata*. The blade narrows above the *monouchi*, giving a rather pointed effect. The grain is small *itame* mixed with small *mokume*, with *jinie*. The *hamon* on the *omote* is overall *suguha* with shallow *notare* in *nie* and with many

1 Anon. Portrait of Minamoto no Yoritomo. Kamakura Period (early 14th century) or later. Hanging scroll; ink, colour and gold on silk, 145.0 x 88.3 cm. Japanese Painting ADD 10 (1920.7-13.01), purchased with the assistance of George Eumorfopoulos and the National Art Collections Fund

2 Scabbards of a *daishō* (nos 1–2)
lacquered in the *Wakasa nuri* style using
layers of coloured lacquers, gold leaf and
materials such as crushed eggshell.
The *fuchi* and *kashira* have bird and flower
motifs in high-relief colour inlay, and the
menuki are gilt copper dragons.
1952.10-28.16–17

3 Pair of *tsuba* for the above
daishō (nos 1–2). Iron, roundly
carved with battle scenes and
with details in gold inlay.
Signed 'Gōshū Hikone jū nyūdō
Sōten sei' (made by the monk
Sōten, resident of Hikone, Ōmi
Province). Edo period, 18th or
19th century. 1952.10-28.16–17

4 *Tsuba* of the *hosodachi* mounting below (col. pl. 5). Gilt copper of the standard 'Chinese' style used on formal *hosodachi* mountings. Signed 'Kashū jū / Suzuki Mitsuhiro / Mizuno Mitsunobu' (Suzuki Mitsuhiro and Mizuno Mitsunobu, residents of Kaga Province), signifying that the metal fittings were a joint work by the two metalworkers. Dated on the reverse in accordance with 1822. OA+3790

住刎加

水野光信等

鈴木光弘沿

5 Mounting of a formal-wear *hosodachi* (no. 3), which carries the *mon* of the Maeda *daimyō* of Kaga province during the Edo period. OA+3790

6 (opposite) Anon. The battles of Ichinotani and Yashima from
the *Tale of Heike* (detail). About early 17th century. Pair of six-fold
screens; ink, colour, gold and gold-leaf on paper, each about
155.3 x 365.5 cm. Japanese Paintings ADD 324, 325
(1950.11-1.022, 023), given by the Trustees of James Martin White

7 (above) Hishikawa Moronobu (d. 1694). Sword polisher,
from 'Scenes of Craftsmen'. About 1680. One from a pair of
handscrolls; ink, colour and gold on silk, 27.5 x 843.0 cm.
Japanese Painting ADD 26 (1923.11-14.02, 2)

8 (right) Artist unidentified. Portrait of a retired warrior of the
Nabeshima clan. Late 18th–early 19th century. Hanging scroll
(mounted); ink and colour on silk, about 57.5 x 43.8 cm.
Japanese Painting ADD 869 (1988.5-17.01)

11 (above) *Tantō* mounting with metal fittings by Gotō Ichijō. Late 19th century (see fig. 11, p. 30, *tantō* blade by Shintōgō Kunimitsu, early 14th century). 1992.05-23.2.

12 *Kozuka* with a crane in high-relief coloured metal inlay on a silver ground by Gotō Ichijō (detail from *tantō* above, col. pl. 11).

9 (left) *Kozuka* from the mounting of a *wakizashi* (no. 51). Bamboo with a nest of fledglings in high-relief coloured metal inlay on a *shibuichi* ground. Signed Hosono Sōzaemon Masamori. Early 18th century. 1981.08-08.72

10 (below) *Wakizashi* mounting for a blade by Taikei Naotane (no. 63). Black-lacquered scabbard and metal fittings with paulownia and chrysanthemums in gold inlay on a *shakudō* ground. Gotō school, 19th century. 1952.10-28.19

13 (below) Utagawa Toyoharu (1735–1814). 'Perspective View: Picture of a Feudal Lord's Procession' (*Uki-e, On daimyō gyōretsu no zu*). About early 1770s. Colour woodblock, published by Nishimuraya Yohachi, 24.3 x 37.7 cm. 1906.12-20.0116

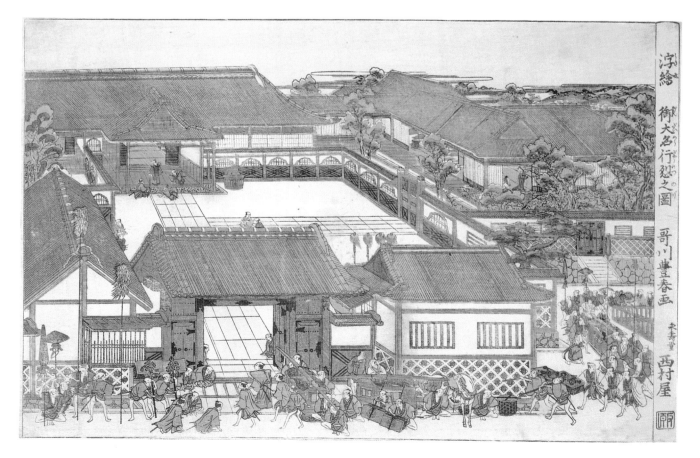

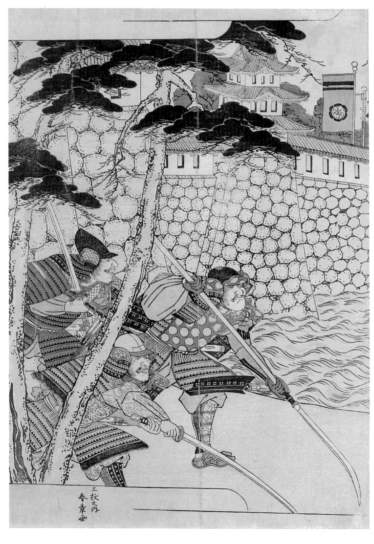

14 (far left) Iron openwork *tsuba* in the form of two interlocking *mokkō* shapes from the mounting of a *katana* by Yokoyama Sukenaga (no. 50). Early Edo period, 17th century. 1958.07-30.204

15 (left) *Tsuba* from the mounting of a *katana* by Yokoyama Sukesada (no. 46). *Shakudō* sculpted in the form of a stylized chrysanthemum blossom, and pierced with a *tomoe* in negative and a Buddhist 'wheel of the law' in positive silhouette. Edo period, 19th century. 1958.07-30.143

17 Utagawa Kuniyoshi (1797–1861). 'Ushioda Masanojō Takanori', from the series 'Biographies of the True and Faithful Samurai Retainers' (*Seichū gishi den*). About 1847. Colour woodblock, published by Ebiya Rinnosuke, Edo, 37.8 x 25.8 cm. 1906.12-20.01150

16 Katsukawa Shunshō (d. 1792). 'Three-sheet Perspective Picture of Tōyama Saemon Munemochi and Makino Aratarō Munezumi Leading the Attack on Kurosaki Castle against Emoto Magoroku and Tanaka Yaheita' (*Tōyama Saemon Munemochi, Makino Aratarō Munezumi, Kurosaki no shiro ni nukekake shite, Emoto Magoroku, Tanaka Yaheita o utsu no zu, uki-e sammai-tsuzuki no uchi*). About early 1780s. Colour woodblock triptych, publisher unknown, each sheet about 36.2 x 24.5 cm. 1910.4-18.0180

18 Pair of *tsuba* for a *daishō* (nos 56, left, and 55, right), with dragons in gold high-relief inlay on a *shakudō* ground. 19th century. 1958.07-30.163 (left) and 1958.07-30.5 (right)

19 *Wakizashi* mounting for a blade by Etchū no kami Masatoshi (no. 19). Black-lacquered scabbard and metal fittings with autumn flowers in high-relief gold inlay on a *shakudō* ground. 17th- to 18th-century Mino school. 1958.07-30.46

20 Mounting for the above (col. pl. 19) disassembled into its components, and with the *kozuka* and *kōgai* drawn from their pockets in the scabbard. 1958.07-30.46

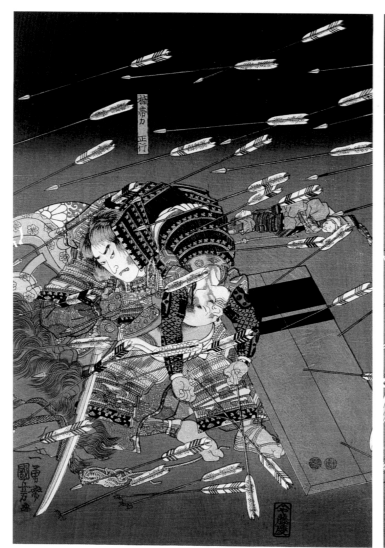

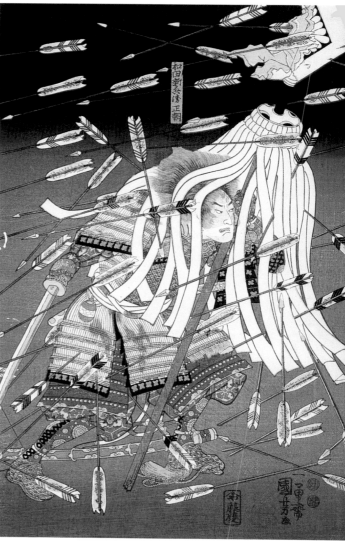

22 (right) Mounting for an unsigned *wakizashi* (no. 85). The scabbard is of brown lacquer with dragons in silver and gold *makie*. The hilt is bound with 'whale's beard'. The metal fittings include dragons among clouds in silver and iron with details in gold inlay. School of Tōryūsai, Meiji era, late 19th century. 1958.0730.129

21 (left) Utagawa Kuniyoshi (1797–1861).
'Fight to the Death of Heroic Samurai
of the Kusunoki Clan at Shijō Nawate'
(*Kusunoki-ke yūshi Shijō Nawate nite
uchijini*). About 1847–52.
Colour woodblock triptych, published
by Fujiokaya Keijirō, each sheet about
36.8 x 24.5 cm. 1907.5-31.0229

24 (below) Mounting for an *ito maki no tachi* with a gold *nashiji*-lacquered scabbard, which has the triple 'paving stone' *mon* of the Tsuchiya family of the Tsuchiura clan in both gold *makie* and gold foil, and the same *mon* repeated on all the metal fittings in gold inlay on a *shakudō nanako* ground. Edo period, 18th century. 1958.07-30.149

23 Hayakawa Shōzan (1850–92). 'The Killing at Namamugi' (*Namamugi no hassatsu*). 26 January 1877. Colour woodblock triptych, published by Kobayashi Tetsujirō, each sheet about 36.5 x 25.0 cm. 1949.5-14.011(1–3)

26 Iron *tsuba* from the mounting of the unsigned *wakizashi* no. 85 (col. pl. 22 on pp. 60–61), with dragons among clouds in high relief and gold inlay on a *tsuchime* (hammered finish) ground. Meiji era, 19th century. (1958.07-30.129)

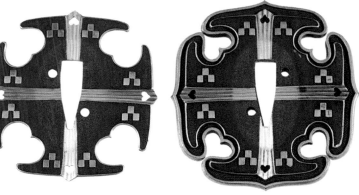

25 (left) *Shakudō tsuba* of the *ito maki no tachi* below (col. pl. 24). Of three-part construction typical on such *tachi*, it is shown separated from its two *ōseppa*, which fit either side of it, and with four standard *seppa* of gilt copper. Edo period, 18th century. (1958.07-30.149)

27 Ogata Gekkō
(1859–1920). 'The
Swordsmith of Mt Inari'
(*Inariyama kokaji*),
from the series
'Miscellaneous
Drawings by Gekkō'
(*Gekkō zuihitsu*). 1893.
Colour woodblock,
published by
Takekawa Risaburō,
36.7 x 24.8 cm.
1982.5-27.01,
given by Tim Clark

small *ashi*. On the *ura*, in particular, there are *gunome ashi*. The *bōshi* is *komaru* with a slightly pointed return.

The scabbard is richly lacquered with gold *nashiji* over which dark-lacquered ribbing has been applied. The *fuchi* and *kashira* are of plovers inlaid in high-relief coloured metal inlay, and there is a gold inlaid inscription 'Yasuchika' on the *fuchi*, which alludes spuriously to the eighteenth-century metalworker Nara Yasuchika. The *menuki* are in the form of immortals riding respectively on a crane and a turtle, in gold and *shakudō*. The *kozuka* is of copper, sculpted with a dragon. The *kurikata* is in the form of a turtle, and the chape of the scabbard is carved with a wave pattern. The *tsuba* is of *shibuichi* and has a stylized chrysanthemum profile, with paulownia, water plants and scrolling grasses in brass level inlay.

26 *Wakizashi* blade

Echizen Tsuguhiro (late 17th century)
Signed on the *omote* 'Echizen kuni Shimosaka Tsuguhiro' (Shimosaka Tsuguhiro of Echizen Province)
L 48.6 cm, C 1.1 cm
1958.07-30.118, bequeathed by R W Lloyd Esq.

This *wakizashi* blade is *shinogi zukuri* and has a medium *kissaki*. There are deep engravings of bamboo and plum blossoms on the *omote*, and of a *kurikara* on the *ura*. The tang has one hole and the file marks are *katte sagari*. The tang tip is *kengyō*. The grain is *itame* mixed with *komokume*. The *hamon* is *suguha* in *nie* with *ashi*, and deeply returning *komaru bōshi*.

There were two generations of smiths named 'Tsuguhiro', who worked from the 1660s through the 1690s. The family were originally from Mino Province. Both were recipients of the title 'Ōmi no kami', and sometimes signed 'Ōmi no kami Fujiwara Tsuguhiro'. The first generation worked in Echizen and Edo, and the second in Echizen.

27 *Katana* blade and *tachi* mounting

Echizen Masanori (17th century)
Signed on the *omote* 'Yamato daijō Fujiwara Masa[nori]'
L 70.6 cm, C 1.7 cm
1958.07-30.164, bequeathed by R W Lloyd Esq.

This blade is *shinogi zukuri* with a medium *kissaki*. It has been shortened so that the character 'nori' has been cut away from the inscription. The sword was originally at least 80 cm in cutting length, and *bōhi* on both sides of the blade were carved after the blade was shortened. The tang has two holes and the file markings are *sujigai* on the original part of the tang, and *kiri* on the portion of the tang that originally formed part of the cutting edge. The tang tip is *kiri*. The grain is an ordered, rather prominent *itame*. The *hamon* is *suguha* in *nie* with a hint of *notare* with *gunome* and *ashi*. The *bōshi* is a pointed *komaru* with *haki*.

Masanori I was originally from Tango Province, but worked in Kyoto and later moved to Echizen. Masanori II worked in Fukui in Echizen Province and also in Edo during the Kambun era (1661–73).

The blade has been mounted as a *tachi*. The gold *makie*-lacquered scabbard has longitudinal panels along the sides containing family *mon* of triple folding fans in *makie*. The metal fittings are polished and patinated iron with applied gold *mon*. The *tsuba* is a hollyhock *mokkō* type with a *nanako* surface, with the same family *mon* engraved on the ō-*seppa*. Although this is not a formal *tachi* style, it is of fine quality and was most probably made to the taste of a feudal lord or other high-ranking person.

28 *Wakizashi* blade and mounting

Fujiwara Shigenori (Jōkyō era, 1684–8)
Signed on the *omote* 'Hizen [no] kami Fujiwara Shigenori'
L 29.3 cm, C 0.3 cm
1958.07-30.115, bequeathed by R W Lloyd Esq.

This blade is of *naginata naoshi* shape (i.e. it was made in the form of a *naginata* that has been converted into a sword by reshaping the *mune*). On either side of the blade there are *naginata hi* and *soehi* which taper off on the tang. The unmodified tang has one hole and the file marks are *taka no ha*. The tang tip is *kurijiri*. The grain is a large, flowing *itame*. The *hamon* is standard narrow *suguha* with a tight *nioiguchi* culminating in a *komaru bōshi*. The smith was originally from Mino Province, but moved to Musashi Province and was active in Edo during the Jōkyō era (1684–8).

The scabbard (not illustrated) is decorated with plum flowers in black and vermilion merging outlines. The *fuchi* and *kashira* have stylized scrolling grasses, known as *karakusa* (literally 'Chinese grass'), in gold linear inlay. The gold *menuki* are in the form of pheasants. The *tsuba* are shaped as gourds and the *kozuka* and *kurikata* depict flowers and are of inlaid coloured enamels. The mounting and its fittings date from the nineteenth century.

Other *shintō* blades (nos 29–32)

29 *Katana* blade and mounting

Ōtsuki Kunishige (c.Manji era, 1658–61)
Signed on the *omote* 'Yamashiro daijō Minamoto Kunishige' and continued on the *ura* 'Bitchū kuni Mizuta jū' (resident of Mizuta, Bitchū Province)
L 64.8 cm, C 0.7 cm
OA+3781

This shallow curved blade is *shinogi zukuri* and has a medium *kissaki*. The upper half of the blade has a thin *kasane* probably due to the polishing away of the damaged surface some time in the past. The tang has one hole and the file marks are *sujigai*. The tang tip is *ha agari kurijiri*. There are carvings of a *sō no kurikara* on the *omote*, and a Sanskrit character and *gomabashi* with claws on the *ura*. The grain is closely packed *koitame* with *jinie*, and there is some *muneyaki*. The *hamon* is overall *suguha* with large *gunome* in places, rich in *nie*. The *bōshi* is deep *komaru*. The smith was Ōtsuki Ichizō Kunishige, younger brother of Ōyogo (act. *c*.Shōhō era, 1644–8), so this blade probably dates to about the Manji era (1658–61).

The scabbard (not illustrated) is black lacquer with a spiral probably formed using a piece of thread in the base layer. The small fittings are of *shakudō* with birds, cherry and chrysanthemum blossoms in high-relief coloured metal inlay. The *fuchi* is signed Yoshiteru, and the *tsuba* is of iron pierced and roundly carved with bamboo leaves.

30 *Katana* blade and mounting

Monju Shigekuni (mid-17th century)

Signed on the *omote* 'Nanki [ni] oite Monju Shigekuni kore [o] tsukuru' (Monju Shigekuni made this at Nanki, i.e. the southern part of Kii Province)

L 69.6 cm, C 1.6 cm

1958.07-30.194, bequeathed by R W Lloyd Esq.

This blade is *shinogi zukuri* with a medium *kissaki*. The high *shinogi* narrows slightly from the *monouchi* region upwards. The tang has one hole and the file markings are *sujigai*. The tang tip is *kengyō*. The grain is strongly flowing *itame* with much *jinie*, becoming pure *masame* on *shinogi ji*. The *hamon* is a broadly undulating *gunome* in *nie* with much variation and overall *sunagashi*. The *bōshi* is *komaru*.

The first-generation Shigekuni came from Yamato, and was originally retained by Tokugawa Ieyasu and then by the Tokugawa family of Kii Province (modern Wakayama Prefecture). He was particularly skilful in the Sōshū and Yamato traditions, and his tradition continued for several generations in Kii. This sword is by the second-generation Shigekuni, and reflects aspects of both Yamato and Sōshū traditions.

The black-lacquered scabbard has the Satsuma-family *mon* (a cross within a circle) and paulownia *mon* lightly incised in *yozakura* (literally 'evening cherry blossom') style. The metal fittings are of black-lacquered iron, with a single cherry-blossom *mon* on the *kashira*. The *menuki* are of gilt dragons and the *tsuba* is iron pierced with twelve stylized birds in twelve segments. The unusual *kashira* has limbs extending several centimetres along the hilt, possibly imitating a Western style.

31 *Katana* blade

Minamoto Yoshimasa (c.1680)

Signed on the *omote* 'Kōzuke [no] suke Minamoto Yoshimasa'

L 69.1 cm, C 1.4 cm

1958.07-30.76, bequeathed by R W Lloyd Esq.

The blade is *shinogi zukuri* with a shallow curve and has a medium *kissaki*. The unmodified tang has one hole and the file marks are *keshō* with *sujigai*. The tang tip is *kurijiri*. The grain is closely packed *itame*, with a flowing aspect in places. The *hamon* is *suguha* with some *komidare*, with a deep *nioiguchi* of close-packed *nie*. The *bōshi* is somewhat pointed *komaru*.

The sword is a majestic, well-made example of a Kambun-era (1661–73) *shintō*. Yoshimasa worked in Musashi Province and later moved to Tosa. In addition to the title 'Kōzuke no suke' his work is also sometimes inscribed with the title 'Kōzuke daijō'.

32 *Katana* blade and mounting

Fujiwara Kunimasa (c.Kyōhō era, 1716–36)

Signed on the *omote* 'Fujiwara Kunimasa' with a carved triple-hollyhock *mon*

L 61.4 cm, C 0.9 cm

1958.07-30.130, bequeathed by R W Lloyd Esq.

This blade is *shinogi zukuri* with a medium *kissaki* and round-ended *bōhi* either side of the blade. The tang has one hole and the file marks are *katte sagari*. The tang tip is shallow *kurijiri*. The grain is *itame* with *jinie*. The *hamon* is *gunome* with a deep *nioiguchi* in dense *nie*, and with *sunagashi* throughout. The *bōshi* is *komaru* with *haki*.

Either of two smiths Kunimasa III and Kunimasa IV, who both used the signature 'Fujiwara Kunimasa', could have produced this sword. Both smiths worked in Musashi Province at about the same time and both belonged to the Hōjōji school. Kunimasa III, who was active about the Kyōhō era (1716–36), was the first Kunimasa to be retained by the Edo *bakufu* working in Edo together with the Yasutsugu family and may well have been granted the hollyhock *mon*. Kunimasa IV, who was active about the Kampō era (1741–44), is recorded as having used the hollyhock *mon*. Permission for use of the hollyhock *mon* by the smith was probably approved by the shogun Tokugawa Yoshimune (r. 1716–45) himself, who was renowned for his patronship of swordsmiths.

The mounting (not illustrated) has a black-lacquered scabbard with metal fittings of *shishi* and peonies in high-relief coloured metal inlay on *shakudō*. The *tsuba* is of brass sculpted in high relief with flowers and insects.

Shintō blades in the Mino tradition (nos 33–7)

Mino Province had been a major centre of sword-making during the Muromachi period (1392–1573), but, as at Bizen, activity there declined during the Edo period. Many smiths moved to other provinces, however, and the Mino tradition was thereby enabled to continue and came to influence considerably the new *shintō* styles.

33 *Katana* blade and mounting

Jimyō (Kambun era, 1661–73)
Signed on the *omote* 'Jimyō'
L 60.3 cm, C 1.0 cm
1958.07-30.134, bequeathed by R W Lloyd Esq.

This blade is *shinogi zukuri* narrowing evenly towards the point, with the shallow curve of a Kambun-era *shintō*, and has a medium *kissaki*. The unmodified tang has one hole and the file marks are *higaki*. The tang tip is *kurijiri*. The grain is a whitish *koitame*, with *masame* on the *shinogi ji*. The *hamon* is an ordered, pointed *gunome* with a tight *nioiguchi* in *nioi* and *sunagashi*. The *bōshi* is *komaru* with *midare komi* and *haki*.

Although the sword is not particularly elegant and there are a number of cracks and blisters in the surface steel, it is nevertheless well made and would be an effective weapon. This Kambun-era *shintō* smith worked in Ōgaki in Mino Province.

The scabbard is luridly decorated with blossoms, *hanabishi* lozenges and long-tailed birds, all in a thick gold *makie* lacquer that might have been added at a later period. The *fuchi* and *kashira* are made of *shibuichi* with coloured metal inlaid chrysanthemums, and the *menuki* have designs of bows and arrows. The *kozuka* has *shishi* and peonies in gold pinned onto the *shakudō nanako* ground. The iron *tsuba* is pierced and carved with *shōjō*, demons and *yamabushi* in a mountainous landscape, with details in coloured metal inlay, and is signed 'Sōheishi nyūdō Sōten sei' (made by monk Sōheishi Sōten).

34 *Katana* blade

Kanenobu (17th century)
Signed on the *omote* 'Mutsu no kami Fujiwara Kanenobu'
L 63.4 cm, C 1.5 cm
1958.07-30.188, bequeathed by R W Lloyd Esq.

This broad *shinogi zukuri* blade has a shallow curve, and a medium *kissaki*. The tang has one hole and the file marks are *taka no ha*. The tang tip is *kurijiri*. The grain is a flowing, closely packed *itame*, although the steel is somewhat coarse. The *hamon* is a regular pattern of pointed *gunome* with a tight *nioiguchi*, so forming *sambon sugi*, and has faint *sunagashi* throughout. The *bōshi* is *midare komi* and *komaru*.

The first-generation Kanenobu worked in about the Meireki era (1655–8) at Kambe in Mino Province. This blade appears to be the work of the third generation, who worked in the Genroku era (1688–1704) and specialized in the *sambon sugi* style of *hamon*.

35 *Katana* blade

Kanemoto (17th century)
Signed on the *omote* 'Kanemoto'
L 70.5 cm, C 1.2 cm
1958.07-30.74, bequeathed by R W Lloyd Esq.

This blade is *shinogi zukuri* with an elongated *kissaki*, and has been shortened by about 3 cm. The *shinogi* is high and the blade is of broad dimension, giving it the appearance of a Yamato-school blade. The tang has two holes and the file marks are *taka no ha*. The tang tip is *iriyamagata*.

The grain is a somewhat coarse prominent *itame*, and there is some blistering. The *hamon* is a *sambon sugi* pattern of repeating sets of three pointed *gunome* undulations with one higher than the surrounding. It is predominantly in *nioi* with a tight *nioiguchi*. The *bōshi* has *midare komi* with *hakikake*.

The Kanemoto smiths originally worked in Akasaka in Mino Province (modern-day Gifu Prefecture). The first generation was active from around 1500, and a number of his swords bear dates and inscriptions including the name of his village, Akasaka. There were several subsequent generations who signed just with the two characters of the name. The work of the second generation, known as 'Magoroku', excels that of the others, but after him it is difficult to distinguish between the later generations of smiths. The characteristic *hamon* is particularly regular and contrived on swords of the later generations into the Edo period.

36 *Wakizashi* blade and mounting

Kaneuji (17th century)
Signed on the *omote* 'Nōshū Seki jū Kaneuji' (Kaneuji, resident of Seki, Mino Province)
L 32.4 cm, C 0.3 cm
OA+3807

This blade is *hira zukuri* and is very slightly curved. The tang has two holes and the file marks are *ōsujigai*. The tang tip is *kurijiri*. The grain is an unruly, flowing *itame* mixed with *masame* and with some *shirake*, the faint white form of *utsuri* found on many Seki-school swords, along the *mune*. The *hamon* is an ordered *gunome* with *togariba*, and the *bōshi* has a pointed return.

The lacquered scabbard has roundels of dragons in gold *makie*. The metal fittings are all of *shibuichi* carved and lightly gilded with clouds and dragons, and are all signed 'Narinobu'. The metalworker is probably Umetada Narinobu, who worked in Edo in the late Edo period and specialized in the technique of rubbing gold onto other metals.

37 *Wakizashi* blade and mounting

Fujiwara Hidetoshi (c.Hōei era, 1704–11)

Signed on the *omote* 'Kawachi [no] kami Hidetoshi'

L 32.6 cm, C 0.4 cm

1958.07-30.54, bequeathed by R W Lloyd Esq.

This curved blade is *hira zukuri* with a *mitsumune* and has been slightly shortened. There are *koshihi* and *soehi* on both sides. The tang has two holes and the file marks are *katte sagari*. The tang tip is *kiri*. The grain is *itame* with *jinie*. The *hamon* is *notare* with *gunome* in *nie*, breaking into *tobiyaki* at the *monouchi* on the *ura*. The *bōshi* is *komaru* with a long return on the *omote*, and *midare komi* with *hakikake* and a long return on the *ura*. This smith worked around the Hōei era (1704–11) in Mino and Kai Provinces.

The scabbard is lacquered with stylized clouds on an *ishime* ground. The fittings are of black-lacquered horn, with gold and *shakudō menuki* in the form of *shishi*.

Shintō blades of the Kansai region (nos 38–41)

38 *Yari* blade

Heianjō Shimosaka (early 17th century)

Signed on the *shinogi* side of the tang 'Heianjō jū Shimosaka' (Shimosaka, resident of Heianjō [i.e. Kyoto])

L 38.7 cm

OA+7081

This large-bodied *yari* blade is of shallow and symmetrical triangular cross-section with a broad *bōhi* on the wide side. The *kerakubi* section defining the boundary between the blade and the tang is octagonal. The unmodified tang has two holes and the file marks are *sujigai* in the upper part changing to *sensuki* at the lower part of the tang. The grain is flowing *itame* tending towards *masame*. The *hamon* is *suguha* overall, with *midareba* and *gunome* in *nie*, and with a *komaru bōshi*. This blade dates to the late Momoyama or early Edo period (early seventeenth century).

39 *Katana* blade (1682)

Echizen no kami Minamoto Rai Nobuyoshi

Signed on the *omote* 'Echizen [no] kami Minamoto Rai Nobuyoshi' with a carved chrysanthemum *mon*, and dated on the *ura* 'Tenna ni nen hachi gatsu jitsu' (a day in the eighth month in the second year of the Tenna era) in accordance with 1682

L 69.6 cm, C 1.6 cm

1958.07-30.75, bequeathed by R W Lloyd Esq.

This broad blade is *shinogi zukuri* with a medium *kissaki*. The grain is well-forged *itame* with *jinie*, and is predominantly *masame* on the *shinogi ji*. The *hamon* has an inclined, straight, Osaka-style *yakidashi* and continues with large, deeply undulating *gunome* dense in *nie*, with some spherical *tobiyaki*. The *bōshi* is a standard *komaru*.

The inscription on this sword dates its manufacture to 1682, the second year of the Tenna era (1681–4). The signature 'Echizen no kami Nobuyoshi' is that of the third-generation Nobuyoshi. The first-generation Nobuyoshi was known as 'Shinano no kami' and worked from the Shōhō era (1644–8) through the Meireki era (1655–8). The second-generation Nobuyoshi, also known as 'Shinano no kami' worked during the Empō era (1673–81) and through the Genroku era (1688–1704). The third-generation Nobuyoshi worked at about the same time, from the Meireki era (1655–8) to the Genroku era (1688–1704). He may have been the younger brother of the second-generation Nobuyoshi and was the most skilful of the three Osaka smiths. This sword is a well-forged and dignified, classic Kambun-era (1661–73) *shintō*.

40 *Tantō* blade and mounting

Fujiwara Hisakuni (early 18th century)

Signed on the *omote* 'Kōzuke daijō Fujiwara Hisakuni'

L 23.8 cm, C (*uchi zori*)

1958.07-30.41, bequeathed by R W Lloyd Esq.

This blade is *hira zukuri* and has a thick *kasane*. The tang has one hole and *ōsujigai* file marks and has been slightly cut down and re-shaped into *kiri* style. The grain is closely packed *koitame*. The

hamon is medium-width *suguha* in *nie*, with a *komaru bōshi*, which returns into a long section of *muneyaki*.

The smith Hisakuni (d. 1741) worked in Tosa Province. He used the title 'Kōzuke no kami' and subsequently received the title 'Kōzuke daijō' sometime during the Hōei era (1704–11). He studied under Ōmi no kami Kinshirō Hisamichi (d. 1711, aged eighty-five), who had been a pupil of Kimmichi of the Sampin school in Yamashiro Province (modern-day Kyoto) (cf. no. 19 by Etchū no kami Masatoshi, also of the Sampin school).

The scabbard is lacquered black and lightly sprinkled with gold *makie*, depicting sparrows in gold *takamakie*. The hilt is bound with 'whale's beard'. The main silver fittings are all sculpted roundly with wisteria, including the *kozuka* and *wari-kōgai*, and the *menuki* are peonies on stylized tweezers. The *fuchi* and the *kozuka* are both signed 'Kōsai Yoshinobu', a pupil of Tōryūsai Kiyotoshi who was active from the 1860s through the Meiji era, when this mounting was probably made in Tokyo.

41 *Tantō* blade and mounting

Umetada Yoshinobu (possibly Genroku era, 1688–1704)

Signed on the *omote* 'Yamashiro kuni jūnin Umetada Yoshinobu' (Umetada Yoshinobu, resident of Yamashiro Province)

L 24.2 cm, C (*uchi zori*)

1958.07-30.56, bequeathed by R W Lloyd Esq.

This blade is *hira zukuri* and has *uchi zori* and a *mitsumune*. There is a carving of a dragon on the *omote* and of a *suken* on the *ura*. The tang has three holes and the file marks are *kiri*. The tang tip is *kurijiri*. The grain is bright, closely packed *itame*. The *hamon* is *gunome* in *nie*, with *ashi* and *sunagashi*. The *bōshi* is pointed slightly upwards and returns abruptly.

The smith of this sword, Yoshinobu, belonged to the lineage of Umetada Myōju of Kyoto, who was a skilful sculptor of dragons. Although this is a good sculpture, its position on the blade is somewhat unharmonious, indicating that it might have been carved by someone other than the swordsmith Yoshinobu.

The scabbard is lacquered in simulation of tree bark, with depictions of a scrolling vine and a seedpod inlaid with enamel, shell, coral and agate. The *kashira* is of copper in the form of a cicada larva, and the *fuchi* is *shakudō* with gold-inlaid dragons among waves. The *menuki* are of rats sculpted in the round in *shibuichi*. The *kozuka* pocket contains a *kōgai* decorated with horse equipment in high-relief coloured metal inlay on a *shakudō* ground, signed 'Rakusei jū' (resident of western Kyoto). The *kuidashi tsuba* is sculpted with pinks and is signed 'Jūkōsai Yoshinari' with a *kaō*. This ensemble dates from the Meiji era.

Shintō and *shinshintō* blades of the Ishidō and related schools (nos 42–5)

The Ishidō school originated in the village of Ishidō in Ōmi Province during the *kotō* era. Their *shintō*-era blades frequently reveal the grandiose *chōji hamon* of the Kamakura-period Ichimonji style, and they are often said to have descended from the Kamakura-period smith Ichimonji Sukemune, or from the Yoshioka Ichimonji group also of Bizen Province. In the Edo period groups of smiths using the name 'Ishidō' flourished in a number of regions. Notable among these were: Korekazu, Mitsuhira and Tsunemitsu in Edo; the school of Tosa Shōkan Tameyasu in Kii Province; and Fukuoka Koretsugu and Moritsugu in Chikuzen Province.

The first of three generations of smiths signing 'Tachibana Yasuhiro' and with the honorific title 'Bitchū no kami' moved from Kii Province to Settsu Province (Osaka) in the mid-seventeenth century. The school is associated with other Osaka smiths working in Ichimonji-style *chōji*, and their work is sometimes loosely named 'Ōsaka Ishidō'.

42 *Katana* blade and mounting

Sasaki Ippō (Genroku era, 1688–1704)

Signed on the *omote* 'Gōshū jūnin Sasaki Zenshirō Minamoto Ichi[hō]' (Sasaki Zenjirō Minamoto Ippō, resident of Ōmi Province)

L 65.0 cm, C 1.2 cm

1878.12-30.838, bequeathed by John Henderson Esq.

This blade is *shinogi zukuri* of shallow curve, and has a small *kissaki*. The tang has three holes and the file marks are *katte sagari*. The tang tip is *kiri*. The grain is *itame* with *jinie*, becoming *masame* on the *shinogi ji*. The *hamon* is *suguha* with a slight shallow *notare* in *nie* with a deep *nioiguchi*. The *bōshi* is *komaru* with a deep and long return. The blade is accompanied by a silver-clad, single-piece *habaki*.

This sword is by Ippō II, descended from Ippō I of the Ishidō school of Ōmi Province, from which branches of the school spread to Kii, Chikuzen, Edo and elsewhere. The maker of this sword, Zenjirō Ippō, worked at Akasaka in Edo during the Genroku era (1688–1704).

The scabbard of this fine quality *efudachi* mounting is of gold *ikakeji* lacquer with phoenixes in gold *takamakie*. The metal fittings are silver with engraved scrolling foliage. The *menuki* are in the form of stylized tweezers with family *mon*.

43 *Katana* blade and mounting

Tachibana Yasuhiro (17th century)

Signed on the *omote* 'Bitchū [no] kami Tachibana Yasuhiro', with a carved chrysanthemum *mon* on the *ura*

L 70.1 cm, C 2.4 cm

1958.07-30.141, bequeathed by R W Lloyd Esq.

This blade is *shinogi zukuri* of standard proportions and of deep curvature. The unmodified tang has one hole and the file marks are *sujigai*. The tang tip is *kengyō*. The grain is closely packed *itame* with *masame* on the *shinogi ji* and with some *muneyaki*. The *hamon* is deep and luxuriant *chōji* in *nioi* with many *ashi* and *yō*. The *bōshi* is *komaru* with a deep return.

The mounting forms a *daishō* with that for the *wakizashi* by Ikkanshi Tadatsuna (no. 44). The scabbard is of gold *mura nashiji* patches in black lacquer, and the hilt is bound with 'whale's beard'. The silver fittings have scenes of a farmer tilling the soil, and his wife at home in their hut, sculpted in high-relief coloured metal inlay. The *fuchi* is signed 'Gyokusai', a Meiji-era art-name, which is here spuriously inscribed as dating to the second year of the Ansei era (1854–60), in accordance with 1855. The mounting lacks a *tsuba*.

44 *Wakizashi* blade and mounting

Ikkanshi Tadatsuna (late 17th century)

Signed on the *omote* 'Awataguchi Ōmi (no) kami Tadatsuna'

L 54.8 cm, C 1.2 cm

1958.07-30.158, bequeathed by R W Lloyd Esq.

This blade is *shinogi zukuri*. The tang has two holes and the file marks are *sujigai*. The tang tip is *ha agari kurijiri*. The grain is a serene closely packed *itame*. The *hamon* has a sloping *yakidashi* leading to extravagant *chōji* with many *ashi*. The *bōshi* is *komaru* with a straight approach.

The smith known as 'Ikkanshi Tadatsuna' was the son of the first Awataguchi Ōmi no kami Tadatsuna, who worked first in Yamashiro (Kyoto), then Himeji in Harima Province, and finally in Osaka around the middle of the seventeenth century. The family was said to be descendants of the Kamakura-period smith Awataguchi Kunitsuna of the Yamashiro school. This is the work of the second-generation Ikkanshi Tadatsuna, known in the Edo period as 'Mandao', who was noted both for the fine quality of his steel and his skill in decorative carving on his blades. He made many *wakizashi* blades with fine sculptures of rather un-military motifs, and it has been said this indicates that many of his clients were merchants rather than samurai.

Tadatsuna II's early work often has a *chōji hamon*, like this blade, but later he made a form of *tōranba* (literally 'billowing hamon'), as did his contemporary Sukehiro (also of Osaka). His *jigane* is always very bright, tight *koitame*, as seen on this sword. The deep *chōji hamon* in clusters derives from the Kamakura-period Ichimonji school of Bizen, which was revived by the Ishidō school in the middle Muromachi period. Many smiths in Osaka during the seventeenth century worked in versions of this vivid and contrived large *chōji*. Although Tadatsuna is not formally recognized as belonging to the Ishidō school, it is interesting to compare this sword with the *katana* by Yasuhiro (no. 43) with which it forms a *daishō*.

The scabbard is similar to that for the *katana* (no. 43) with gold *mura nashiji* patches, and the silver fittings portray a fisherman and children also in high-relief coloured metal inlay. The fittings are signed 'Katsukei Gyokusai', the same maker as those for the long sword (see the comments to no. 43 and cf. nos 64, 86).

45 *Wakizashi* blade (1661)

Tachibana Yasuhiro

Signed on the *omote* 'Bitchū no kami Tachibana Yasuhiro' and dated on the *ura* 'Kambun gannen ni gatsu jitsu' (a day in the second month in the first year of the Kambun era), in accordance with 1661

L 45.0 cm, C 1.0 cm

1958.07-30.144, bequeathed by R W Lloyd Esq.

This small *wakizashi* blade is *shinogi zukuri* with a shallow curve and a medium *kissaki*. The unmodified tang has one hole and the file marks are *sujigai*. The tang tip is *iriyamagata*. The grain is *itame*, and there is faint *utsuri*. A sloping *yakidashi* rises to form a tight *hamon* of *chōji* with many *ashi* in *nioi*. The *bōshi* is slightly pointed *komaru*.

Shintō and shinshintō blades of the Yokoyama school of Osafune in Bizen (nos 46–52)

Sword-making declined in Bizen Province after the end of the civil wars of the sixteenth century. During the early Edo period Yamato Kōzuke no suke Sukesada (no. 46), the son of Shichibei Sukesada in Osafune village, established a line of smiths signing 'Yokoyama' who continued into the *shinshintō* era. Their work is a conscious revival of old Bizen styles, with extravagant *hamon* of *chōji* and *gunome* somewhat like the work of the Ishidō smiths.

46 *Katana* blade and mounting

Yokoyama Sukesada (17th century)

Signed on the *omote* 'Yokoyama Kōzuke daijō Fujiwara Sukesada' and on the *ura* 'Bishū Osafune jūnin' (resident of Osafune village, Bizen Province)

L 68.6 cm, C 1.5 cm

1958.07-30.143, bequeathed by R W Lloyd Esq.

This blade is *shinogi zukuri* and of Kambun-era (1661–73) *shintō* shape. The unmodified tang has one hole and the file markings are *kiri*. The tang tip is *kurijiri*. The grain is a well-ordered and prominent *itame*. The *hamon* is open *gunome* mixed with *togariba*, with a tight *nioiguchi* predominantly in *nioi*. The *bōshi* is a straight *komaru*.

Yokoyama was the family name of several generations of smiths working in the village of Osafune in Bizen Province during the Edo period from around the third decade of the seventeenth century. They signed with a number of titles including the 'Kōzuke daijō' of this sword and 'Kawachi no kami' (no. 47). This sword has a large *chōji hamon* in *nioi* in traditional Bizen style and a clear fine-grained body, although sometimes a form of *utsuri* is found on the work of the group.

The classic *uchigatana* mounting has a plain black-polished scabbard as required for formal wear in Edo. The *fuchi* and *kashira* bear scenes from the adventures of Minamoto no Yoshitsune, and the *menuki* represent helmets, *naginata*, and bows and arrows indicating the Gempei wars of the twelfth century. The *tsuba* (col. pl. 15) is of deep black *shakudō* in the form of a stylized chrysanthemum blossom, pierced with a gold-inlaid Buddhist *hōrin* (wheel of the law) and with a *tomoe* motif.

47 *Katana* blade and mounting

Kawachi no kami Sukesada (early 18th century)

Signed on the *omote* 'Kawachi [no] kami Sukesada' with carved chrysanthemum *mon* and *ichimonji*, and on the *ura* 'Bizen kuni Osafune jū' (resident of Osafune village, Bizen Province)

L 70.0 cm, C 1.8 cm

1958.07-30.184, bequeathed by R W Lloyd Esq.

This blade is *shinogi zukuri* with a shallow curve and has a medium *kissaki*. The unmodified tang has one hole and the file marks are shallow *katte sagari*. The tang tip is *kurijiri*. The grain is an attractive, closely packed *koitame*. The *hamon* is a standard *suguha* with a fluffy *nioiguchi*. The *bōshi* is a slightly pointed *komaru*. This healthy blade looks like Rai or Enju work of the Kamakura period and may be in conscious imitation of such. It is fitted with a silver *habaki* in the form of a *kuwagata* (helmet crest).

The black lacquer scabbard (not illustrated) has inlaid stylized cloud designs. The *fuchi* and *kashira* are iron with dragons in high relief in Mito-school style, but inscribed with the spurious signature 'Yanagawa Naomasa'. The *tsuba* is iron, decorated with a dragon passing over Mount Fuji in high-relief sculpture and with gold inlay, and signed 'Ōmi kuni Gessensai Minamoto Shigetsuyo' (Gessensai Shigetsuyo of the Minamoto clan in Ōmi Province). This mounting was assembled in the late Edo period.

48 *Katana* blade (*c.*1830) and mounting

Yokoyama Sukenaga

Signed on the *omote* 'Bishū Osafune jū Sukenaga' (Sukenaga, resident of Osafune village, Bizen Province) and continued on the *ura* 'Tomonari gojūroku-dai mago' (the fifty-sixth generation descendant of Tomonari)

L 64.6 cm, C 1.6 cm

1958.07-30.197, bequeathed by R W Lloyd Esq.

This blade is *shinogi zukuri* and has a medium *kissaki*. The unmodified tang has one hole and the file marks are *kiri*. The tang tip is *kurijiri*. The grain is closely packed, almost indiscernible *koitame*. There is a straight *yakidashi* to the *hamon*, leading to a rather luxuriant *gunome chōji* with *ashi* in *nioi* with a tight *nioiguchi*. The *bōshi* is standard *komaru* type.

The scabbard (not illustrated) is lacquered with powdered shell *nashiji*. The *fuchi* and *kashira* are of *shibuichi* illustrated with Chinese figures. The *menuki* and *tsuba* are also of *shibuichi* decorated with chrysanthemums sculpted and inlaid in coloured metals.

49 *Katana* blade (1824) and mounting

Yokoyama Sukenaga

Signed on the *omote* 'Bizen kuni Osafune jū Sukenaga' (Sukenaga, resident of Osafune, Bizen Province) and dated on the *ura* 'Bunsei nana nen hachigatsu jitsu' (a day in the eighth month in the seventh year of the Bunsei era), in accordance with 1824

L 63.1 cm, C 1.6 cm

1958.07-30.155, bequeathed by R W Lloyd Esq.

This is a *shinogi zukuri* blade with *saki zori* and a medium *kissaki*. The long unmodified tang has one hole and the file marks are *kiri*. The tang tip is *ha agari kurijiri*. The grain is an almost indiscernible, closely packed *koitame*.

There is a gently sloping *yakidashi* and the *hamon* is luxuriant *chōji* mixed with *kobushi gata chōji*, with *ashi*. The *bōshi* is straightforward *komaru*. The sword resembles the work of Kawachi no kami Kunisuke and may be a conscious imitation. It has a gilded, single-piece *habaki*.

The scabbard is lacquered black with alternating bands of polished and matt lacquer. The *fuchi* and *kashira* are of drums in gold inlay on *shakudō*, and the *menuki* are in the form of bows and arrows in gold and *shakudō*. The *tsuba* is of *shibuichi* with linked *cloisonné* patterns.

50 *Katana* blade (1842) and mounting

Yokoyama Sukenaga

Signed and dated on the *omote* 'Yokoyama Kaga no suke Fujiwara Minamoto Sukenaga kore [o] tsukuru Tempō jūsan nen ni gatsu kichijitsu' (Yokoyama Kaga no suke Fujiwara Minamoto Sukenaga made this on an auspicious day in the second month in the thirteenth year of the Tempō era), in accordance with 1842; continued on the *ura* 'Bizen Osafune jūnin' (resident of Osafune village, Bizen Province), with carved chrysanthemum *mon* and *ichimonji*

L 70.8 cm, C 1.6 cm

1958.07-30.204, bequeathed by R W Lloyd Esq.

This broad-bodied blade is *shinogi zukuri*, and has a shallow curve and medium *kissaki*. The unmodified tang has one hole and the file marks are *kiri*. The tang tip is *ha agari kurijiri*. The grain is closely packed *koitame*. The *hamon* is widely spaced *gunome* mixed with *chōji*, with many small *ashi* in *nioi*. The *bōshi* is *komaru* of *Jizō bōshi* form.

The scabbard is lacquered black with an *ishime* finish, and has an iron chape carved with dragonflies. The *fuchi* and *kashira* are of *shakudō nanako* with chrysanthemums in high-relief coloured metal inlay. The *menuki* are of peonies. The patinated iron *tsuba* (col. pl. 14) is pierced and carved in the form of interlocking *mokkō* forms, and dates to the early Edo period, considerably earlier than the rest of the mounting.

51 *Wakizashi* blade (1850) and mounting

Yokoyama Sukenaga

Signed and dated on the *omote* 'Yokoyama Kaga [no] suke Fujiwara Sukenaga Ka'ei san nen ni gatsu jitsu' (Yokoyama Kaga no suke Fujiwara Sukenaga; a day in the second month in the third year of the Ka'ei era), in accordance with 1850; continued on the *ura* 'Biyō Osafune jū' (resident of Osafune village, Bizen Province) with carved chrysanthemum *mon* and *ichimonji* character

L 45.6 cm, C 1.6 cm

1981.08-08.72, given by Captain Collingwood Ingram

This blade is *shinogi zukuri* and has a medium *kissaki*. The unmodified tang has one hole and the file marks are *kiri*. The tang tip is *kurijiri*. The grain is an indiscernible, closely packed *koitame*. The extravagant *hamon* is *chōji* with *ashi* in bright and even *nioi*. The *bōshi* has *midare komi*, *haki* and a deep *komaru*.

The scabbard is of brown lacquers with scattered pieces of straw beneath a top transparent layer forming an effect similar to gold *nashiji*. The *fuchi* and *kashira* are of *shibuichi* with birds inlaid in *shakudō* and coloured metals. The *tsuba* is of *shakudō* pierced and roundly sculpted with a flowering plum bough, and is inscribed 'Nara saku' (Nara make). The *kozuka* (col. pl. 9) and *kōgai* by Masamori of Kyoto (b.1656) have nestlings in high-relief coloured metal inlay on *shibuichi*.

52 *Katana* blade (1866) and mounting

Yokoyama Sukekane

Signed on the *omote* 'Bizen Osafune jū Yokoyama Sukekane tsukuru' (Yokoyama Sukekane, resident of Osafune village, Bizen Province, made this) and dated on the *ura* 'Keiō ni nen ni gatsu jitsu' (a day in the second month in the second year of the Keiō era), in accordance with 1866

L 71.0 cm, C 1.3 cm

OA+3791

This blade is *shinogi zukuri*, and has a shallow curve with *fumbari* and a small *kissaki*. The unmodified tang has one hole and the file marks are *kiri*. The tang

tip is *ha agari kurijiri*. The grain is closely packed *koitame*. The *hamon* is *suguha* with a somewhat tight *nioiguchi* and with *konie*. The *bōshi* is *komaru* form, and loses definition slightly on the *omote*. This blade is accompanied by a silvered single-piece *habaki*.

The scabbard (not illustrated) is lacquered in simulation of wood grain. The *fuchi* and *kashira* are of iron with dragons in gold *nunome zōgan* on iron. The *menuki* are of military equipment. The *tsuba* is patinated iron carved with a willow beneath the moon, and signed 'Nara Masanori'.

Shintō blades of the Hizen school (nos 53–6)

The family of Hashimoto Shinzaemon Tadayoshi was retained throughout the Edo period by the ruling Nabeshima family of Hizen Province. The first-generation Tadayoshi was sent by Nabeshima Katsushige to study in Kyoto under Umetada Myōju in the early Keichō era (1596–1615), and the Hizen school consequently owes something to Myōju's Shizu style, with its broad *hamon* of *konie* and *jinie*. The Nabeshima clan closely controlled technology and commerce within their domain, and industry flourished there during the Edo period. Just as the porcelain traditions continued little changed until the Meiji Restoration, so the swords retained their individual character. The blades are all well shaped and of elegant curve, have the finest *koitame hada* with even fine *jinie*, and *suguha*, *chōji* or *gunome hamon* in *nie*. The characteristic steel has been described as *konuka hada* (i.e. '*hada* like *konuka*', meaning facial skin made beautiful by washing with the use of a small silk bag of rice bran), since it is invariably fine and even. Smiths signing 'Tadakuni', 'Masahiro' (no. 53) and other signatures continued for some generations under the aegis of the Tadayoshi forge.

53 *Wakizashi* blade

Hizen Masahiro II (17th century)

Signed on the *omote* 'Hishū Kawachi [no] kami Fujiwara Masahiro' (Kawachi no kami Fujiwara Masahiro of Hizen Province)

L 48.9 cm, C 1.0 cm

1958.07-30.159, bequeathed by R W Lloyd Esq.

This blade is *shinogi zukuri* and has a medium *kissaki*. The unmodified tang has one hole and the file marks are *sujigai*. The very end of the tang tip has been cut off squarely, as *kiri*. The grain is closely packed *itame*, tending towards *nashiji*, with *jinie*. The *hamon* is a shallow *notare*, interspersed with *gunome*, in *nie*. The *bōshi* is a pointed *komaru*. This is the work of the second of six generations who signed 'Masahiro'. (See no. 99 for the mounting.)

54 *Wakizashi* blade and mounting

Hizen Tadayoshi VIII (early 19th century)

Signed on the *omote* 'Hizen kuni Tadayoshi' (Tadayoshi of Hizen Province)

L 45.2 cm, C 0.8 cm

1958.07-30.156, bequeathed by R W Lloyd Esq.

This small *wakizashi* blade is *shinogi zukuri* and has a medium *kissaki*. The tang has one hole and the file marks are *kiri*. The tang tip is *kurijiri*. The grain is closely packed *koitame*. The *hamon* is standard *suguha* in *konie*. The *bōshi* is *komaru* on the *omote*, and *ōmaru* with a return on the *ura*. Although the work of this smith is often classified as *shinshintō*, it is in traditional Hizen style.

The *wakizashi* mounting (not illustrated) has a black-lacquered scabbard. The *menuki* are in the form of frogs, and the *fuchi* and *kashira* are plain patinated *shakudō*. The *tsuba* is of *shakudō* with peonies and butterflies in gold level inlay in the *Kaga zōgan* style. The *kozuka* and *kōgai* are of *shakudō* with flying cranes in high relief on a *nanako* ground.

55 *Wakizashi* blade and mounting

Ōmi daijō Tadayoshi (early 18th century)

Signed on the *omote* 'Ōmi daijō Fujiwara Tadayoshi'

L 53.4 cm, C 1.2 cm

1958.07-30.5, bequeathed by R W Lloyd Esq.

This blade is *shinogi zukuri* and has a medium *kissaki*. The tang has one hole and the file marks are *kiri*. The tang tip is *kurijiri*. The grain is bright *koitame* tending to *nashiji*, with even *jinie*. The *hamon* is medium-width *suguha* with much *konie* and small *ashi*. The *bōshi* is standard *komaru*. The accompanying two-piece *habaki* is made of copper covered with *shakudō*. This blade is a typical example of a Hizen sword by Tadayoshi IV.

The *wakizashi* mounting is part of a *daishō*, the *uchigatana* also by Ōmi daijō Tadayoshi (no. 56). The scabbards (not illustrated) are black lacquered with powdered shell inlay under the top transparent layer forming scattered haphazard *chirakashi makie* (literally 'scattered *makie*'). The hilt fittings (col. pl. 18) are of *shakudō* with dragons in high-relief gold inlay.

56 *Katana* blade and mounting

Ōmi daijō Tadayoshi (early 18th century)

Signed on the *omote* 'Hizen kuni Ōmi daijō Fujiwara Tadayoshi' (Ōmi daijō Fujiwara Tadayoshi of Hizen Province)

L 75.9 cm, C 2.3 cm

1958.07-30.163, bequeathed by R W Lloyd Esq.

This blade is *shinogi zukuri* and has a medium *kissaki*. The unmodified tang has one hole and the file marks are *kiri*. The tang tip is *kurijiri*. The grain is closely packed *koitame* with *jinie*, and tending to *nashiji*. The *hamon* is a broad *suguha* with much *konie* and includes small *ashi* and *yō*. The *bōshi* is standard *komaru*. This blade shows a particularly clear example of the characteristic Hizen-school *suguha*.

The *uchigatana* mounting (not illustrated) forms a *daishō* with no. 55 and is identical except that it is larger and has a *kōgai*, whereas the *wakizashi* has a *kozuka*, both with dragons among waves.

Blades of the *shinshintō* era and later (nos 57–89)

Sword-making declined generally during the peaceful period around the middle of the eighteenth century, apart from the continuing traditions of the retained smiths in some of the castle towns. One smith, Suishinshi Masahide (d. 1826), became instrumental in the revival of ancient styles with the publication of his researches such as *Tōken jitsuyō ron* (Practical Sword Dissertation). He produced swords in a number of old traditions, including both *kotō* and the styles of certain of the Kambun-era (1661–73) smiths. Masahide is said to have directly taught many smiths, notably Taikei Naotane (see nos 62 and 63).

57   *Tantō* blade and mounting

Bitchū Kunishige (18th or 19th century)

Signed on the *omote* 'Bitchū jū Kunishige' (Kunishige, resident of Bitchū Province)

L 22.9 cm, C 0.3 cm

1958.07-30.93, bequeathed by R W Lloyd Esq.

This blade is *shōbu zukuri*. The tang has two holes and the file marks are *katte sagari*. The tang tip is a deep *kurijiri*. The grain is *itame* with *mokume* and develops into a flowing grain with *masame* towards the cutting edge. The *hamon* is well-ordered *gunome* in *nie*. The *bōshi* is a slightly pointed *komaru*.

The scabbard of the mounting is lacquered black with a design of slightly embossed snowflakes. The *fuchi* and *kashira* are of *shakudō* and portray geese crossing beneath the moon in coloured metal inlay. The *menuki* are gold *shishi*. The *kuidashi tsuba* is of *shakudō* with cherry blossoms and snowflakes in coloured metal inlay. The *kozuka* also depicts snowflakes in high-relief inlay, and the *umabari* shows a rush-cabined boat in coloured metal inlay. All the fittings are signed 'Gotō Mitsumasa'. This metalworker was the second son of Gotō Benjō and succeeded as head of the Gotō school on the death of his father in 1851. He was the cousin of Gotō Ichijō, the last great master of the school, and was active until around 1900.

58   *Katana* blade and *handachi* mounting

Tōshirō Kuniyoshi (c.1770–80)

Signed on the *omote* 'Bingo Fukuyama jū Tōshirō Kuniyoshi tsukuru' (Tōshirō Kuniyoshi, resident of Fukuyama, Bingo Province, made this)

L 71.6 cm, C 1.0 cm

1958.07-30.154, bequeathed by R W Lloyd Esq.

This blade is *shinogi zukuri*, and has a very shallow curve with slight *fumbari*, and a medium *kissaki*. The unmodified tang has two holes and the file marks are *katte sagari*. The tang tip is *iriyamagata* type. The grain is closely packed, almost indiscernible *koitame*. The *hamon* is *suguha* in *nie* with *gunome ashi*, and some *hotsure* on the *ura*. The *bōshi* is standard *komaru* on the *omote* and slightly pointed *komaru* on the *ura*.

Two smiths used a signature with this wording. One is recorded to have been active during the Keian era (1648–52), and the other during the An'ei era (1772–81). The smith of this *shinshintō* blade is the latter.

The *handachi* style mounting has a black-lacquered scabbard with designs of peacock's feathers in powdered shell *makie*. The fittings are all of *shakudō ishime* ground depicting chrysanthemums and scrolling in gold line inlay. The *wakizashi* mounting (1958.07-30.133) that forms a *daishō* with this *handachi* contains a poor quality blade that was not conserved in this project and has therefore not been included.

59   *Katana* blade

Tōshirō Nagakuni (c.Bunka era 1804–18)

Signed on the *omote* 'Iyo Kuni Onsen Gōri Ishide jūnin Tōshirō Nagakuni kore [o] tsukuru' (Tōshirō Nagakuni, resident of Ishide in Onsen Gōri of Iyo Province, made this)

L 84.0 cm, C 1.9 cm

1958.07-30.154, bequeathed by R W Lloyd esq.

This long blade has a relatively, even longer tang, like many *shinshintō*. It has a deep curve, and the blade narrows towards the point with a medium *kissaki*. The tang has one hole with *katte sagari* file marks and ends in a *kurijiri* tip. The grain is a prominent *itame* with much *mokume*. The *hamon* is *gunome* in *nie* with *ashi* and *sunagashi* overall, culminating in a *midare komaru bōshi*.

Nagakuni sometimes inscribed 'Matsuyama jū' (resident at Matsuyama) on his blades, as did one or possibly two smiths named Nagakuni working in Iyo Province during the middle seventeenth century. Although the family may have continued from that time, there are no other recorded smiths until the appearance of this Nagakuni around the Bunka era (1804–18).

60   *Wakizashi* blade and mounting

Namihira Yukimune (c.Bunka era, 1804–18)

Signed on the *omote* 'Namihira Yukimune'

L 40.8 cm, C 0.4 cm

1958.07-30.151, bequeathed by R W Lloyd Esq.

This *wakizashi* blade is *hira zukuri*. The tang has one hole and the file marks are *higaki*. The tang tip is *kurijiri*. The grain is somewhat prominent *itame* with *jinie*. The *hamon* is *suguha* with thick *nie*, with *notare* towards the base of the blade, and some large *kuichigai*. The *bōshi* is standard *komaru*.

This is a typical *shinshintō* of the Satsuma Namihira school. The smith Yukimune (Hashiguchi Jirōemon) was active during the Bunka era (1804–18). He was the son of the well-known smith Yukichika and the fourth recorded generation of the Hashiguchi family of swordsmiths.

The scabbard is lacquered black with clouds of gold *nashiji*, and has a chape of *shibuichi* in the form of a lobster. The silver hilt fittings are engraved with a wave motif. The iron *tsuba* has a skull carved in high relief and is pierced with a crescent moon. Scabbards with a lobster motif were particularly popular in the late seventeenth century; however, this piece dates from the later Edo period.

61 *Tantō* blade (1844) and mounting

Satsuma Masafusa

Signed on the *omote* 'Satsuma kuni Fujiwara Masafusa shingitae' (Fujiwara Masafusa of Satsuma Province [made this according to] the *shingitae* tradition) and dated on the *ura* 'Tempō jūgo nen shimotsuki' (the eleventh month in the fifteenth year of the Tempō era), in accordance with 1844

L 27.6 cm, C (*uchi zori*)

1958.07-30.52, bequeathed by R W Lloyd Esq.

This *tantō* blade is *hira zukuri* with a thick *kasane*, and with *uchi zori*. The unmodified tang has one hole and the file marks are *keshō* with *sujigai*. The grain is compact *koitame* with large rounded crystals of *jinie* (*kazu no ko nie*). The *hamon* is *gunome* with *nie*, and with large *kuichigai* and *kinsuji*. The *bōshi* has *hakikake* sweeping round the *komaru* return. The maker is the sixth-generation smith in Satsuma Province to have signed 'Masafusa'.

This *tantō* mounting forms a *daishō* together with the *katana* blade attributed to Tametsugu (no. 9). The scabbards are gold *nashiji* with *mon* in the form of fan papers within circles, in gold leaf and gold *makie*. The metal fittings are all of *shakudō* with a *nanako* surface and gold inlaid *mon*.

62 *Wakizashi* blade (1813)

Taikei Naotane

Signed and dated on the *omote* 'Bunka mizunoto tori [toshi] ni gatsu Kanzanshi [no] motome [ni] ōjite Taikei Naotane kore [o] tsukuru, Honjō Yoshitane horu' (Taikei Naotane made this in response to the order of Kanzanshi in the second month of the cock

year of the Bunka era, and Honjō Yoshitane did the carvings); continued on the *ura* 'fusatsu Sō shison eiden tame Tachibana Moritaka' (made for Tachibana Moritaka to forever avert slaughter of the Sō family and their descendants); the date corresponds to 1813

L 50.0 cm, C 0.8 cm

1958.07-30.12, bequeathed by R W Lloyd Esq.

This *wakizashi* blade is *shinogi zukuri*, of even breadth and curve. The tang has one hole and the file marks are *keshō* and *sujigai*. The tang tip is *kurijiri*. There are *hi* on both sides of the blade; the *hi* on the *omote* has an *ukibori* carving of *sōryū* (twin dragons), and the *hi* on the *ura* has an *ukibori* carving of a triple-pronged *vajra*-hilted sword. The grain is *itame* mixed with *mokume* with *nie*, and there is *chikei* all over the blade. Steels of differing quality have been mixed to contrive a vivid effect of light and dark layers within the grain. The *hamon* is *gunome chōji* with *ashi* and *yō*, and *sunagashi* and *kinsuji* throughout the blade. The *bōshi* is *midarekomi* and *komaru*.

63 *Wakizashi* blade (1833) and mounting

Taikei Naotane

Signed on the *omote* 'Taikei Naotane', with a carved kaō, and dated on the *ura* 'Tempō yon nen chūshun' (mid-spring in the fourth year of the Tempō era), in accordance with 1833.

L 45.0 cm, C 0.9 cm

1952.10-28.19, given by Mrs Margaret Plass

This broad blade is *hira zukuri* and has a *mitsumune*. The tang has one hole and the file marks are *keshō* with *sujigai*. The tang tip is *kurijiri*. On the *omote* there are *gomabashi* and a *bōhi* with an inset *ukibori* carving depicting Fudō Myō-ō under a waterfall; on the *ura* there are *gomabashi* and a *bōhi* with an inset *ukibori* carving of a *vajra*-hilted sword. The grain is well-ordered, serene *itame*. The *hamon* is *gunome* mixed with *chōji*, with many *ashi*. It has a somewhat pointed *bōshi*. The fine carving is probably the work of Honjō Yoshitane (compare the *wakizashi* by Naotane, no. 62).

  Taikei Naotane (1778–1857) studied directly under Suishinshi Masahide in

Edo and, like Masahide, fostered many pupils (such as Naokatsu, no. 78). He travelled widely around Japan and has left swords with inscriptions including place names such as Sagami, Kyoto and Ise. He specialized in the Sōshū and Bizen traditions, but his Bizen-style work is the superior.

The scabbard (also col. pl. 10) is ribbed and lacquered black. All the metal fittings have paulownia and chrysanthemums in gold inlay on a *shakudō nanako* ground. The *midokoro-mono* (matching set of *menuki*, *kozuka* and *kōgai*) are Gotō family work.

64 *Tantō* blade (1833) and mounting

Hatakeyama Masamitsu

Signed on the *omote* 'Kairakuen [ni] oite Hatakeyama Yamato no suke Minamoto Masamitsu tsutsushinde kore [o] tsukuru' (Hatakeyama Yamato no suke Minamoto Masamitsu respectfully made this at Kairakuen); dated on the *ura* 'Tempō yon [nen] mizunoto mi toshi hachi gatsu jitsu' (a day in the eighth month of the snake year, the fourth year of the Tempō era) in accordance with 1833, with a carved chrysanthemum *mon*

L 22.6 cm

1958.07-30.91, bequeathed by R W Lloyd Esq.

The *tantō* blade is *hira zukuri* with a shallow curve, and has a *mitsumune*. The tang has one hole and the file marks are *keshō* with *sujigai*. The tang tip is *kurijiri*. The grain is closely packed *koitame*. The *hamon* is shallow *notare* rich in *nie*, with a deep clear *nioiguchi*, and with evenly arranged spherical *tobiyaki* on both sides of the blade. The *bōshi* is a deep *komaru*.

  Masamitsu was a pupil of Yasutoshi of Harima Province, who is recorded to have moved at some time to Osaka. It is rare to find a blade by this smith inscribed with the chrysanthemum *mon*.

The scabbard is lacquered black with a wood-grain effect and has a persimmon depicted in coral inlay. All of the silver fittings have designs of monkeys and persimmons in high-relief coloured metal inlay. The *fuchi* and *kozuka* are signed 'Kiyotsugu'. The mounting dates from the Meiji era (cf. nos 43, 44, 86).

65 *Katana* blade (1861)
and mounting

Tsunatoshi and Koretoshi

Signed on the *omote* 'Kōfu [ni] oite Chōjusai Tsunatoshi' (Chōjusai Tsunatoshi, in Kōfu, i.e. Edo) and continued and dated on the *ura* 'Chōunsai Koretoshi Bunkyū gannen hachi gatsu kichi jitsu' (Chōunsai Koretoshi, an auspicious day in the eighth month in the first year of the Bunkyū era), in accordance with 1861

L 70.1 cm, C 1.4 cm

1878.12-30.840, bequeathed by John Henderson Esq.

This blade is *shinogi zukuri*, has a shallow curve and a small *kissaki*. The unmodified tang has one hole and the file markings are *keshō* with *ōsujigai*. The grain is almost indiscernible, closely packed *koitame*. The *hamon* is an even *suguha* in *nie* with a tight *nioiguchi*. The *bōshi* is *komaru* with a somewhat pointed return.

This blade was the joint endeavour of Tsunatoshi and Koretoshi, who were father and son. Chōjusai (originally Chōunsai) Tsunatoshi (d. 1863) was the son of Katō Kunihide who studied under Suishinshi Masahide. Together with his brother Tsunahide, he moved from his native Ushū (Dewa) Province to go to Edo. His pupils include Unju Korekazu (see no. 67). In 1856 he gave the name Chōunsai to his son Koretoshi, and assumed the name Chōjusai. The *habaki* is comprised of a single piece, and has gold cladding.

The scabbard has designs of plum blossoms formed from ray fish skin inlaid into black lacquer and polished flat. The *fuchi*, *kashira* and *menuki* have scenes from the Gempei wars in *shakudō* with high-relief coloured metal inlay. The iron *tsuba* has similar scenes pierced and roundly carved, with details in gold inlay.

66 *Tantō* blade (1854) and mounting

Chōunsai Tsunatoshi

Signed on the *omote* 'Chōunsai Tsunatoshi' and dated on the *ura* 'Ka'ei shichi nen hachi gatsu jitsu' (a day in the eighth month in the seventh year of the Ka'ei era), in accordance with 1854

L 29.5 cm

1958.07-30.47, bequeathed by R W Lloyd Esq.

This *tantō* blade is *hira zukuri*. The tang has one hole and the file marks are *keshō* with *sugikai*. The tang tip is *kurijiri*. The grain is closely packed *koitame* with *nie*. The *hamon* is *chōji* in *nie* with many *ashi* and gentle *sunagashi* on the *omote*, and more violent *sunagashi* on the *ura*. The *bōshi* is *komaru*.

The scabbard is vermilion lacquered with a regular pattern of raised black dots. The gilt copper alloy fittings are roundly sculpted with dragons and *shishi*. The *kozuka* is of *shibuichi* with a tiger carved in sunken relief. The *fuchi* is signed 'Umetada Narikazu'.

67 *Tachi* blade (1861) and mounting

Unju Korekazu

Signed on the *omote* 'Ishidō Fujiwara Korekazu kore [o] tsukuru' (Ishidō Fujiwara Korekazu made this) and dated on the *ura* 'Bunkyū gannen jūichi gatsu jitsu' (a day in the eleventh month in the first year of the Bunkyū era), in accordance with 1861

L 71.4 cm, C 1.6 cm

1958.07-30.174, bequeathed by R W Lloyd Esq.

This *tachi* blade is *shinogi zukuri* and has a medium *kissaki*. The unmodified tang has one hole and the file marks are *keshō* with *ōsujigai*. The tang tip is *ha agari kurijiri*. The grain is a bright, closely packed *koitame* with *jinie*. The *hamon* is an ordered regular *gunome* in *nie* with substantial *ashi*. The *bōshi* is *Jizō* type. The curve of the blade continues in an unbroken line through the length of the tang.

The smith Unju Korekazu was a pupil of Chōunsai Tsunatoshi (nos 65, 66) and styled himself the seventh-generation master of the Ishidō school. He was retained by the shogunate in Edo.

The *itomaki-no-tachi* mounting has a scabbard of gold *nashiji* lacquer with cherry blossom *mon* in applied gold. All the fittings are of *shakudō nanako* ground with gold cherry blossom *mon*. Although cherry blossom was not a formal family *mon*, the fact that it is found on such a fine quality mounting made shortly before the Meiji Restoration suggests that it had by that time come to be regarded as a national symbol of Japan. The coincidence of a similar *tachi* with a blade also by Ishidō Korekazu in the collection of the Victoria and Albert Museum might suggest that both swords were made as diplomatic gifts.

68 *Katana* blade (1859) and *handachi* mounting

Unju Nobukazu

Signed on the *omote* 'Tanshū jū Unju Nobukazu' (Unju Nobukazu, resident of Tamba Province) and dated on the *ura* 'Ansei roku nen hachi gatsu jitsu' (a day in the eighth month in the sixth year of the Ansei era), in accordance with 1859

L 70.0 cm, C 1.4 cm

1958.07-30.187, bequeathed by R W Lloyd Esq.

This broad blade is *shinogi zukuri*, and has a medium *kissaki*. The tang has one hole and the file marks are *keshō* with *ōsujigai*. The tang tip is severe *kurijiri*. The grain is a bright *koitame* with *jinie*. The *hamon* is a luxuriant *chōji* in *nioi*, with many *ashi*. The *bōshi* is standard *komaru*. This smith is recorded as living in Ayabe in Tamba Province, a pupil of Ishidō Korekazu. His work is similar in style and skill (compare no. 67).

The *handachi* mounting has a scabbard of silver or tin *nashiji* lacquer with paulownia *mon* in *makie*. There are four *mon* on the *omote* and three on the *ura*, as it was the traditional custom to place more on the side of the scabbard that could be seen when the sword was worn. The fittings are all of silver. The *menuki* are silver in the form of stylized tweezers with paulownia *mon* in gold inlay. The *tsuba* is *mokkō* shape, with a *nanako* ground, but otherwise undecorated.

69 *Katana* blade (1832) and *hosodachi* mounting

Koyama Munetsugu

Signed on the *omote* 'Seishū Kuwana jū Koyama Munetsugu Higuchi Yasukuni [no] tame kore [o] tsukuru' (Koyama Munetsugu, resident of Kuwana, Ise Province, made this for Higuchi Yasukuni) and dated on the *ura* 'Tempō san nen hachi gatsu jitsu' (a day in the eighth month in the third year of the Tempō era), in accordance with 1832

L 63.2 cm, C 1.9 cm

1958.07-30.138, bequeathed by R W Lloyd Esq.

This slender blade is *shinogi zukuri*, with a deep curve, and has a medium *kissaki*. *Bōhi* on both sides of the blade extend through to the end of the tang. The unmodified tang has two holes and the file marks are *keshō* with *sujigai*. The tang tip is *iriyamagata*. The grain is a fine, closely packed *koitame*. The *hamon* is *gunome chōji* with *ashi* in *nioi* and a tight *nioiguchi*. The *bōshi* is pointed *komaru* on the *omote* and *komaru* with *nijūba* on the *ura*.

Koyama Munetsugu was born in the castle town of Shirakawa in Mutsu Province and was retained by the lord Matsudaira Sadanobu (Rakuō). In 1830 he moved to Kuwana in Ise Province, and a year or two later to Edo, where he lived as a retainer of the ruling clan of Ise. It is believed that Katō Tsunahide schooled him during his time in Edo. Munetsugu is known to have been friendly with the sword tester Yamada Asaemon, and a number of his blades have *tameshi-giri* (test cut) results recorded on their tangs by Yamada. In 1845 he obtained the title 'Bizen no suke'. After the Meiji Restoration he worked in Tokyo as a gunsmith, and then at the age of seventy made a sword that was exhibited at the first National Exposition, held in Tokyo in 1872. Like other smiths of his time he sometimes worked in the Sōshū style, but he is best known for his Bizen-style *chōji hamon* in *nioi* and fine close *mokume* grain.

The *hosodachi*-type *tachi* was used on formal occasions in place of the earlier *kazari tachi*, or 'decorative long sword'. The scabbard is lacquered with *nashiji*,

but the ground preparation was insubstantial, presumably to save expense, and the lacquer is now breaking away. The metal fittings are of lightly gilded copper or copper alloy, decorated with engraved scrolling. The hilt has seven irregularly applied *tawara byō*, a formal requirement for such a mounting. Although the work is generally very poor, the *menuki* are solid gold, bearing *mon* of *omodaka* (a water plant with three-petalled flowers). It is thus probable that the mounting was hurriedly commissioned for a special event, and that the *menuki* were 'borrowed' from another mounting.

70 *Katana* blade (Tempo era, 1830–44) and mounting

Koyama Munetsugu (see no. 69)

Signed on the *omote* 'Munetsugu'

L 69.8 cm, C 2.2 cm

1958.07-30.195, bequeathed by R W Lloyd Esq.

The blade has a standard deep curve. The unmodified tang has one hole and the file marks are *keshō* and *sujigai*; the tang tip is *iriyamagata*. The grain is closely packed, bright *koitame*. The rather flamboyant *hamon* consists of *kawazu no ko chōji* and *fukuro chōji*, with considerable variation in depth and many *ashi*; it is predominantly of *nioi* but there is some *nie* at the crests of the *chōji*. The *bōshi* is *midare komi*.

The scabbard is contrived in the form of tree bark with black, brown and gold lacquer. The *fuchi* and *kashira* are silver, deeply carved with chrysanthemum blossoms. The gilt *menuki* are of ivy leaves. The *kogai* is of gilt copper, with a gilt *kurikara* on a *shakudō* insert. The mounting lacks a *tsuba*, *kozuka* and *kojiri*.

71 *Wakizashi* blade (1865) and mounting

Koyama Munetsugu (see no. 69)

Signed on the *omote* 'Bizen [no] suke Munetsugu' and dated on the *ura* 'Keiō gan nen hachi gatsu jitsu' (a day in the eighth month in the first year of the Keiō era), in accordance with 1865

L 36.7 cm, C 0.6 cm

OA+3794

This *wakizashi* blade is *shinogi zukuri* and has a medium *kissaki*. There are *bōhi* on both sides that taper off on the tang. The unmodified tang has two holes and the file marks are *kiri*. The tang tip is *iriyamagata*. The grain is closely packed, almost indiscernible *koitame*. The *hamon* is *gunome* with *ashi* in *nioi* and a tight *nioiguchi*. This is standard work of Munetsugu, although the tang is somewhat crudely finished.

The scabbard has an *ishime* surface formed with layers of vermilion and black lacquer, finely incised with lines to give the effect of a light shower of rain. The *fuchi*, *kashira* and chape are of *shibuichi* with inlaid depictions of Shōki, the Demon Queller, and demons in high-relief coloured metal inlay. The *fuchi* is signed 'Nambōtei Katsumasa'. The *menuki* are of skulls, in silver, *shakudō* and gold; the *kozuka* is decorated with fishermen in a boat in coloured metal inlay on *shibuichi*; the *tsuba* is of iron with Shōki portrayed in high-relief inlay.

72 *Katana* blade (1867) and *tachi* mounting

Koyama Munetsugu (see no. 69)

Signed on the *omote* 'Bizen [no] suke Fujiwara Munetsugu' and dated on the *ura* 'Keiō san nen ni gatsu jitsu' (a day in the second month in the third year of the Keiō era), in accordance with 1867

L 74.7 cm, C 1.2 cm

1958.07-30.27, bequeathed by R W Lloyd Esq.

This blade is *shinogi zukuri* and has a shallow curve with a medium *kissaki*. There are round-ended *bōhi* on both sides of the blade. The tang has two holes, one of which is a *shinobi ana*. The file marks are *kiri*. The grain is almost indiscernible, closely packed *koitame*. The *hamon* is extravagant *gunome chōji* in *nioi* and has many small *ashi*. The *bōshi* is *midare komi*.

The *tachi* mounting is of vermilion-lacquered wood carved in simulation of *tsuishu* lacquerwork. All metal fittings are of lightly gilded silver with paulownia carved in *katakiri bori* (oblique chisel work). The *menuki* are in the form of bats. The whole mounting has been artificially distressed to give an appearance of age, which was presumably done to make it more appealing for export.

73 *Wakizashi* blade (1856)

Minamoto Masao

Signed on the *omote* 'Minamoto Masao' and dated on the *ura* 'Ansei san nen roku gatsu jitsu' (a day in the sixth month in the third year of the Ansei era), in accordance with 1856

L 35.4 cm, C 0.3 cm

OA+3800

This blade is *shōbu zukuri* and of robust proportions. It has carvings of a *sō-no-kurikara* on the *omote* and a Sanskrit character with *gomabashi* on the *ura*. The tang has one hole and the file marks are *sujigai*. The tang tip is a deep version of *kurijiri*. The grain is *itame* with many dense patches of *jinie* that leap up to the *shinogi* in a form of *tobiyaki*. The *hamon* is wild *gunome* in *nie* with *ashi*, *kinsuji* and overall *sunagashi*. The *bōshi* is uncontrolled *midare komi*. This blade is accompanied by a gold-clad two-piece *habaki*.

Masao was the pupil of Minamoto Kiyomaru (1813–54), the greatest of all *shinshintō* smiths, whose standing was such that he became known as 'The Yotsuya Masamune' during his period of working in Edo. Kiyomaru worked in several ancient styles, but was particularly skilful at the Sōshū style established by the great fourteenth-century smith Masamune. His two pupils Kiyondo and Masao continued this tradition and both produced swords, like this dagger, in the Sōshū style. Masao was an ardent imperialist and it is said

that he always intended for his swords to be used by the imperial faction, who opposed the rule of the Tokugawa shoguns. He is believed to have made swords only from the 1850s up to 1866, just before the Meiji Restoration of 1868.

74 *Wakizashi* blade (1849) and mounting

Shimizu Hisayoshi

Signed on the *omote* 'Tōto [ni] oite Sakuragawabe Sagami Kuni [no] hito Shimizu Hisayoshi tsukuru' (Shimizu Hisayoshi, resident of Sagami Province, made this at Sakuragawabe in the eastern capital, i.e. Edo) and continued on the *ura* 'horimono Sessai Toshimasa tsukuru Ka'ei ni nen shōgatsu kichi jitsu' (Sessai Toshimasa made the carvings on an auspicious day of the first month in the second year of the Ka'ei era), dated in accordance with 1849

L 54.4 cm, C 0.9 cm

1958.07-30.132, bequeathed by R W Lloyd Esq.

This blade is *shinogi zukuri* with a *mitsumune* and a medium *kissaki*. There are *ukibori* carvings of Fudō Myō-ō in flames on the *omote* and lotus petals with Sanskrit characters on the *ura*. The unmodified tang is curved and has one hole; the file marks are *keshō* with *sujigai*. The tang tip is *kurijiri*. The grain is *itame* flowing strongly near the cutting edge, with *jinie*. The *hamon* is overall *suguha* with dense *nie* and *ashi* throughout, forming rounded *gunome* resembling *juzuba* with *sunagashi*. The *bōshi* is *komaru* with some *hakikake*. The carvings are particularly skilful examples of work by Sessai Toshimasa. The blade is in the style of the Masayoshi school.

The scabbard is of black lacquer with designs of clouds in gold *nashiji* and faintly embossed depictions of paulownia. The long chape, *fuchi*, *kashira*, *koiguchi*, *kozuka* and *wari-kōgai* are of *shibuichi* sculpted with paulownia blossoms, and the *menuki* are of pheasants and chrysanthemums sculpted in *shibuichi*. The *tsuba* is formed half of iron and half of *shibuichi*, with coloured metal inlay motifs of pheasants and chrysanthemums in high relief. The mounting dates from the Meiji era.

75 *Tantō* blade (1865) and mounting

Minamoto Yoshimune

Signed on the *omote* 'Fuji Sama [no] suke Minamoto Yoshimune' and dated on the *ura* 'Keiō gannen ushi-doshi hachi gatsu jitsu' (a day in the eighth month of the ox year, the first year of the Keiō era), in accordance with 1865

L 23.0 cm

1958.07-30.105, bequeathed by R W Lloyd Esq.

This blade is *kogarasumaru zukuri* with a *mitsumune*. The *shinogi* is high, and the upper portion of the blade is thus similar in shape to a *ken*-type sword. The tang has one hole and the file marks are *keshō* with *sujigai*. The tang tip is *kurijiri*. The grain is somewhat prominent *itame*, with a flowing aspect near the cutting edge, with *jinie* and *chikei*. The *hamon* is *suguha* in *nie* with *sunagashi*, *uchi noke*, some *hotsure* and some *nijūba*. The *bōshi* is *komaru* and has a long return, like the *bōshi* of the long sword named 'Kogarasu Maru' in the imperial collection. The finish of the tang is similar to the work of Yoshimune's teacher, Hosokawa Masayoshi, who had studied under Suishinshi Masahide.

The scabbard is lacquered red with black bands, with butterflies in gold and coloured *makie*. The *fuchi*, *kashira* and *menuki* are of *shibuichi* with *shakudō* and gold depicting leaves. The *kozuka* has Jurōjin, one of the Seven Lucky Gods, carved in sunken relief on dark *shibuichi*.

76 *Tantō* blade (1865) and mounting

Hisayuki

Signed on the *omote* 'Bakufu shi Hisayuki tsukuru' (Hisayuki, in the service of the Bakufu, made this) and dated on the *ura* 'Keiō gan [nen] ushi doshi hachi gatsu jitsu' (a day in the eighth month of the ox year, the first year of the Keiō era), in accordance with 1865

L 25.2 cm, C 0.1 cm

1958.07-30.30, bequeathed by R W Lloyd Esq.

This is a *hira zukuri* blade. The tang has three holes and the file marks are *keshō* with *sujigai*. The tang tip is *ha agari kurijiri*. The grain is *itame*, forming a tight *masame* towards the cutting edge. The *hamon* is *suguha* in small *nie* with some slight *hotsure*. The *bōshi* is *komaru* with a pointed return.

The smith Fujiwara Hisayuki (or Kawai Hisayuki) was a pupil of Hosokawa Masayoshi together with Minamoto Yoshimune (no. 75). He was active over a long period, as evidenced by dated swords as far apart as the Bunsei era (1818–30) and the second year of the Meiji era (1869).

The scabbard is lacquered black with designs of water-plants in gold *makie*. The *kashira* and the chape of the scabbard are silver in the form of lobsters. The silver *fuchi* depicts a carp in high-relief *shakudō* inlay, and the *menuki* are also carp. The *kurikara* is in the form of a frog on a lotus leaf in the same metals. The hilt is bound with 'whale's beard'. This mounting dates from the Meiji era.

77   *Katana* blade (1842)

Enju Nobukatsu (d. 1871)

Signed on the *omote* 'Enju Nobukatsu tsukuru' (Enju Nobukatsu made this) and dated on the *ura* 'Tempō jūsan nen hachi gatsu jitsu' (a day in the eighth month in the thirteenth year of the Tempō era), in accordance with 1842

L 80.2 cm, C 2.5 cm

1958.07-30.66, bequeathed by R W Lloyd Esq.

This blade is *shinogi zukuri* and has a medium *kissaki*. There are square-ended *bōhi* with *soehi* both sides of the blade. The tang has one hole and the file marks are *kiri*. The tang tip is *kurijiri*. The grain is *itame* mixed with a flowing grain, with large *jinie* (*kazu-no-ko nie* or *hada nie*). The *hamon* is *gunome chōji* with numerous *ashi*, and there are many hard, glinting areas of steel along the crest. The *bōshi* is *midare komi* with a *komaru* return.

78   *Tantō* blade (1869) and mounting

Naokatsu

Signed on the *omote* 'Naokatsu' and dated on the *ura* 'Meiji ni [nen] chūshun' (mid-spring in the second year of the Meiji era), in accordance with 1869

L 15.1 cm, C (*uchi zori*)

1958.07-30.107, bequeathed by R W Lloyd Esq.

This small blade is *hira zukuri*. The tang has one hole, and the file marks are *keshō* with *sujigai*. The tang tip is *kurijiri*. The grain is prominent *itame* with *jinie*. The *hamon* is *gunome* in *sakagakari* form, tending towards *kataochi gunome*, in *konie* with *ashi*. The *bōshi* is pointed, with *hakikake*. The smith is Shōji Yamon Naokatsu (d. 1884), the successor of Jirō Tarō Naokatsu (d. 1858), who was the adopted son of Taikei Naotane (nos 62 and 63).

The scabbard is lacquered black, depicting paulownia flowers in gold *makie*. The silver fittings, including the *kozuka* and the *wari-kōgai*, are carved with chrysanthemums. The hilt is bound with leather and lacquered. The assembled mounting dates from the Meiji era.

79   *Tantō* blade and mounting

Tenryūshi Masataka (19th century)

Signed on the *omote* 'Ozaki Nagato [no] kami mago Tenryūshi Masataka' (Tenryūshi Masataka, grandson of Ozaki Nagato no kami)

L 27.4 cm, C 0.4 cm

1958.07-30.101, bequeathed by R W Lloyd Esq.

This broad *tantō* blade is *hira zukuri*. There is a carving of a *sō kurikara* on the *omote* and there are square-ended *bōhi* with a *soehi* on the *ura*. The unmodified tang has two holes and the file marks are *keshō* and *sujigai*. The tang tip is *iriyamagata*. The grain is closely packed, almost indiscernible *koitame*. The luxuriant *hamon* is *chōji* in *nioi* with long *ashi*, many *yō* and a tight *nioiguchi*. On the *komaru bōshi* there is a *tobiyaki* formation known as *tsuki ni kumo* (literally 'clouds across a moon').

The shape of the blade is reminiscent of the fourteenth-century masterpiece known as 'Hōchō Masamune' (there are three *tantō* of identical shape named Hōchō Masamune, which are all designated as National Treasures) and may have been modelled on it. The grandfather of the smith referred to in the inscription was Ozaki Suketaka (d. 1805). He used the two titles 'Nagato no kami' and 'Nagato no suke'.

The scabbard is lacquered black with sparse gold *nashiji* and decorated with a damask of maple leaves in red lacquer, formed by using real leaves to make impressions in the lacquer, and then applying the coloured lacquer. All the fittings are of iron with inlaid depictions of maple leaves and cherry blossoms. The hilt is wrapped with silk and the *menuki* depict bamboo. The *fuchi* is signed 'Yoshiaki'. The assembled mounting dates from the Meiji era.

80   *Tantō* blade (1867)

Dokuseishi Masanaga

Signed on the *omote* 'Bingo Onomichi jū Dokuseishi Masanaga' (Dokuseishi Masanaga, resident of Onomichi in Bingo Province) and dated on the *ura* 'Keiō san nen hachi gatsu jitsu' (a day in the eighth month in the third year of the Keiō era), in accordance with 1867

L 29.9 cm, C 0.1 cm

1958.07-30.100, bequeathed by R W Lloyd Esq.

This blade is *hira zukuri*. On the *omote* there is a Sanskrit character engraved into the surface, and a *hi* groove with a carving of a *kurikara*; on the *ura* there is a carving of a triple-pronged *vajra*-hilted sword. The unmodified tang has one hole and the file marks are *keshō* with *sujigai*. The tang tip is *kurijiri*. The grain is almost indiscernible, closely packed *koitame*. The *hamon* is *suguha* with *nie* tending towards *hotsure*. The *bōshi* is *komaru* with a deep return. The smith is unrecorded. The name 'Dokuseishi' may be translated as 'one of solitary enlightenment'.

81 *Wakizashi* blade (1866) and mounting

Kaifu Ujiyoshi

Signed on the *omote* 'Ashū shin Kaifu Ujiyoshi' (Ujiyoshi of Kaifu, a retainer of Awa Province) and dated on the *ura* 'Keiō ni nen hachi gatsu jitsu' (a day in the eighth month in the second year of the Keiō era), in accordance with 1866

L 31.2 cm

1958.07-30.108, bequeathed by R W Lloyd Esq.

This straight *wakizashi* blade is *hira zukuri* and has a thick *kasane* like a *yoroi dōshi*. The tang has one hole and the file marks are *kiri*. The tang tip is *kurijiri*. The grain is closely packed *koitame*. The *hamon* is an even medium-width *suguha* with *konie*. The *bōshi* has a pointed return.

The family of Ujiyoshi in Kaifu is said to extend back to the Kōryaku era (1379–81), founded by Kaifu Tarō. This blade is by the fifteenth- or sixteenth-generation smith working in Awa Province either side of the Meiji Restoration (1868).

The *aikuchi*-style *wakizashi* mounting (not illustrated) is bound with rattan at intervals and lacquered black over both the hilt and the scabbard. The *kozuka* is brass and depicts in high-relief coloured metal inlay the Chinese hero Kan'u from the novel *Tale of Three Kingdoms*.

82 *Katana* blade (1860) and mounting

Katsuyama Yoshinori

Signed on the *omote* 'Mimasaka Katsuyama shin Yoshinori' (Yoshinori, a retainer in Katsuyama, Mimasaka Province) and dated on the *ura* 'Man'en gan[nen] saru [doshi] hachi gatsu jitsu' (a day in the eighth month of the monkey year, the first year of the Man'en era), in accordance with 1860

L 63.2 cm, C 2.0 cm

1958.07-30.148, bequeathed by R W Lloyd Esq.

The blade is *shinogi zukuri*. The tang has *kiri* file marks and one hole. The tang tip is *kurijiri*. The grain is closely packed *itame*. The *hamon* is *togariba* style *gunome* close to *sambon sugi*, with a tight *nioiguchi*. The crests of the *gunome* have a hard appearance. The *bōshi* is

komaru. The Katsuyama, Mimasaka Province, of the inscription refers to present-day Katsuyama town in Maniwa ward, Okayama Prefecture.

The scabbard is lacquered black with an *ishime* effect, and with iron metal fittings carved as chrysanthemums. The *fuchi* and *kashira* are of a copper alloy with a plain *nanako* surface. There is only one remaining *menuki* of gilt copper depicting wild boars. The *tsuba* is iron, representing a dragon among clouds in high relief with some gold *nunome zōgan* inlay in the style of the late Jingo school of Higo Province.

83 *Katana* blade

Suishinshi Nobutaka (19th century)

Signed on the *omote* 'Suishinshi Nobutaka kore [o] tsukuru' (Suishinshi Nobutaka made this)

L 75.4 cm, C 1.4 cm

1958.07-30.166, bequeathed by R W Lloyd Esq.

This long and broad-bodied blade is *shinogi zukuri* with a shallow curve, and has a large *kissaki*. The *bōhi* grooves taper away in *kakinagashi* style. The long tang has one hole and the file marks are *keshō* with *sujigai*. The tang tip is *kurijiri*. The *jigane* is *koitame* and has coarse patches. The *hamon* is *gunome* in *nie* with *ashi*, and overall *sunagashi*. The *bōshi* is *midare komi* and *komaru*. The finish of the tang is unsophisticated, and the maker of this sword is an unrecorded smith unlikely to be related to the famous Suishinshi Masahide.

84 *Tantō* blade (1869) and mounting

Minamoto Sadakazu

Signed on the *omote* 'Minamoto Sadakazu' with a carved *kaō* and dated on the *ura* 'Meiji ni [nen] mi [toshi] natsu' (summer in the snake year, the second year of the Meiji era), in accordance with 1869

L 19.1 cm, C (*uchi zori*)

1958.07-30.61, bequeathed by R W Lloyd Esq.

This *tantō* blade is *hira zukuri* with an *uchi zori* curve and *mitsumune*. The tang has *keshō* and *sugikai* file marks, two

holes and a *kurijiri* tip. The grain is *itame*, flowing into *masame* towards the cutting edge. The *hamon* is *notare* with dense *nie* that mingles into the grain to form *sunagashi*. The *bōshi* is pointed, has *hakikake* and a long return, which develops into *muneyaki* along the back of the blade.

Minamoto Sadakazu (1836–1918) was the successor of Gassan Sadayoshi (d. 1870). Sadayoshi continued the tradition of the Gassan school, which originated in Dewa Province; the school was for centuries associated with the religious cults of the famous Three Mountains of Dewa. Sadayoshi studied under Suishinshi Masahide, the founder of the *shinshintō* tradition, and his repertoire expanded to include traditions other than the classic Gassan style. Sadakazu is said to have imitated the work of famous earlier smiths and signed with their names after the Haitōrei (law instituted in 1876 prohibiting the wearing of swords in public), when demand for swords within Japan plummeted. He was appointed *teishitsu gigei-in* (imperial craftsman) in 1907.

The scabbard is ribbed and lacquered black. The *shibuichi* fittings are sculpted with waves. The hilt is lacquered in simulation of leather binding, with *menuki* of *shibuichi* roundels depicting a youth riding a turtle, from the story of Urashima Tarō. The mounting was assembled in the Meiji era.

85 *Wakizashi* blade and mounting

Unsigned (17th or 18th century)

L 46.2 cm, C 1.0 cm

1958.07-30.129, bequeathed by R W Lloyd Esq.

This blade is *hira zukuri*. The grain is *itame* mixed with a larger flowing grain. The unmodified tang has one hole and the tang tip is *iriyamagata*. The file marks are indistinct. The *hamon* is of small *gunome* in *nie* with *ashi*. On the *omote* there is a carving of Fudō Myō-ō surrounded by flames standing under a waterfall. The *bōshi* is *komaru*.

Close examination indicates that a

signature has been erased from the tang, and that the tang has been covered with a fine suspension of rust in lacquer to conceal this. This was probably done in the Meiji era to prepare the sword for export, as was the skilful but rather ostentatious carving of Fudō Myō-ō. This blade is probably earlier Echizen work, which might once have had a spurious signature so incredible (even for the overseas market) that it had to be removed.

The scabbard (also col. pl. 22) is lacquered brown, with large dragons among clouds in silver and gold *makie*. In place of the traditional pair of *menuki* there is a fine silver sculpture of a dragon, which winds around the hilt. All other fittings are iron and are carved with dragons among clouds, with the details in gold inlay (col. pl. 26) .

86 *Tantō* blade and mounting

Fujiwara Masachika (19th century)

Signed on the *omote* **'Fujiwara Masachika tsukuru' (Fujiwara Masachika made this)**

L 24.0 cm, C (*uchi zori*)

1981.08-08.71, given by Captain Collingwood Ingram

This blade is *hira zukuri* and has a thick *kasane*. There is a carving of a *kurikara* on the *omote* and *gomabashi* on the *ura*. The tang has *katte sagari* file marks, two holes and a *kuri*-type tip. The grain is closely packed *itame*. The *hamon* is predominantly *konie* with *gunome* at the base of the blade near the tang, but develops into *suguha* with variations from the middle of the blade upwards. The *bōshi* is *komaru* with a pointed return.

The scabbard is lacquered in simulation of bamboo with combed lines and groups of three encircling bands. The *shibuichi* fittings show boys at play with various toys and emblems carved and inlaid with coloured metals. The *fuchi* and *kozuka* are signed 'Tōgyokusai Katsukei Kiyotsugu' (compare nos 43 and 44 whose fittings are signed

'Katsukei Gyokusai', and no. 64 signed 'Kiyotsugu'). The assembly dates from the Meiji era.

87 *Katana* blade and *tachi* mounting

Zenjō Chikanori (Meiji era, 1868–1912)

Signed on the *omote* **'Seki Zenjō ke Chikanori tsukuru' (Chikanori of the Zenjō household in Seki made this)**

L 71.4 cm, C 1.7 cm

1912.10-12.22, given by Mrs H Seymour-Jones

This blade is *shinogi zukuri* with a medium *kissaki*. The tang has one hole and the file marks are *keshō* with *sujigai*. The tang tip is *kurijiri*. The grain is closely packed, almost indiscernible *koitame*, becoming *masame* on the *shinogi ji*. The *hamon* is essentially *suguha* with *gunome* and *ashi*, presenting a slight *juzuba* formation. The *bōshi* is a deep *komaru*.

The first Chikanori was active during the Keiō era (1865–8) in Hitachi Province and is distinguished by his use of *kiri* file marks. Zenjō Chikanori is Chikanori II, who was active during the Meiji era (1868–1912) in Mito, Hitachi Province.

The *tachi* scabbard is of black *ishime* lacquer with *mon* depicting sets of four *masu* (measuring boxes) in shell inlay and gold *makie*. Of the three sets of *mon* on the *omote* one is of shell and two of *makie*, and there are two *mon* of shell and two of *makie* on the *ura*. All the *shakudō* fittings have a *nanako* surface, with inlaid gold paulownia *mon*. The *menuki* are roundly carved depictions of paulownia flowers. The hilt is wrapped with blue silk brocade beneath the standard black silk binding. A *mokkō*-shaped iron *uchigatana tsuba* is fitted with *shakudō ōseppa* matching the rest of the metalwork, to adapt it for use on a *tachi*. The iron *tsuba* itself is carved in high relief, with depictions of phoenixes and paulownias on the *omote* and paulownia and flowing clouds on the *ura*, and details in gold *nunome zōgan* inlay.

It was customary during the Edo period to have more *mon* on the *omote*

than on the *ura* of the scabbard, but the reverse is the case with this mounting. The metal fittings are high quality, middle Edo-period workmanship, but they do not fit naturally to the mounting. Furthermore, the unconventional use of the iron *tsuba* also indicates that the *tachi* mounting was assembled for export in the Meiji era when the blade was made.

88 *Katana* blade (1910) and mounting

Miyamoto Kanenori (1831–1926)

Signed on the *omote* **'Teishitsu gigei-in Miyamoto Kanenori hachijū-issai tsukuru' (Imperial Craftsman Miyamoto Kanenori made this at the age of eighty-one) and dated on the** *ura* **'Meiji yonjūsan nen gogatsu kichijitsu' (an auspicious day in May in the forty-third year of the Meiji era), in accordance with 1910**

L 65.0 cm, C 1.5 cm

1998.12-17.02

This blade is *shinogi zukuri* and has a medium *kissaki*; its shape is similar to that of Kambun *shintō*. The tang has one hole and the file marks are *kiri*. The tang tip is *kurijiri*. The grain is prominent *itame*. The *hamon* is a deeply varying *saka gunome* and *chōji* in large *nie* and overall *sunagashi*. The *bōshi* is *komaru* with some *haki*.

Kanenori studied under Yokoyama Sukekane (no. 52) during the late Edo period. The blade is a valuable record of the 'imperial craftsman' system during the late Meiji era.

The *uchigatana* mounting was assembled long after the Haitōrei (law banning the public wearing of swords) of 1876, but it is in Edo-period style. The *menuki* are gold and *shakudō* chrysanthemum blossoms on flowing water. The *fuchi* and *kashira* have monkeys depicted in high-relief gold inlay on a *shakudō nanako* ground. The *tsuba* is *mokkō* shape in *shakudō* carved overall with a cluster of chrysanthemums. The later thick *seppa* might indicate that the *tsuba* has been changed since the mounting was assembled, although the sword is believed to have been a presentation piece and was in the possession of the same British family from 1911 until it was acquired by the museum in 1998.

89 *Katana* blade (1913) and sabre mounting

Minamoto Kaneharu

Signed on the *omote* 'Minamoto Kaneharu tsukuru' (Minamoto Kaneharu made this) and dated on the *ura* 'Taishō ni nen hachi gatsu jitsu' (a day in August in the second year of the Taishō era), in accordance with 1913

L 63.7 cm, C 1.8 cm

1998.12-17.03

The thin-bodied blade is *shinogi zukuri* with a deep curve. The cutting edge has *ubuha* (a few centimetres of original edge left unsharpened in the first polishing process). There are square-ended *bōhi* either side of the blade. The unmodified tang has one hole and the file marks are *kiri*. The tang tip is *kurijiri*. The grain is almost indiscernible closely packed *koitame*. The standard *hamon* is *suguha* in *nie* with a somewhat moist *nioiguchi*. The *bōshi* is *komaru*. The steel lacks lustre, and the blade might have been made using imported or industrial steel.

Kaneharu was a pupil of both Minamoto Kanenori (no. 88), and Kasama Shigetsugu (1885–1965), who was head teacher of the Akasaka Nippontō Denshūsho (an institute at Akasaka for studying the tradition of the Japanese sword).

The scabbard is of polished ray skin, all the fittings of gilt copper alloy with chrysanthemum blossoms in high relief. There is a silver triple-hollyhock leaf *mon* of the Tokugawa family applied to the back of the hilt strap. This is an interesting example of a Meiji- or Taisho-era sabre-like military sword and was likely to have been made for an important occasion.

Other mountings (nos 90–99)

90 *Wakizashi* mounting

19th century

1958.07-30.59

This *wakizashi* mounting is a lacquered black *ishime* ground with a design of wisteria in gold *togidashi makie*. There is a *kozuka* of *shakudō* and gold with a phoenix in high-relief coloured metal inlay, but the corresponding *kōgai* or *umabari* is missing. The *fuchi* and *kashira* are of polished *shibuichi* with scattered blossoms in coloured metals and shell level inlay. The *fuchi* is signed 'Kuwamura Moriyoshi'. The *menuki* are gold in the form of dancing cranes. The *tsuba* is *mokkō* shape of *shakudō nanako*, with feathers in high-relief coloured metal inlay.

The maker of the *fuchi*, Moriyoshi, was a samurai of Toyohara in Echizen Province. He went to Komatsu in Kaga Province where he studied metalwork under Gotō Kenjō, and was later retained by the ruling clan of Kaga. He died in 1711.

91 *Tantō* mounting

19th century

1958.07-30.59

This *tantō* mounting has a black-lacquered ribbed scabbard in *inrō kizami* style. The *fuchi*, *kashira* and *kozuka* are of gold and *shakudō* with line engravings of pine leaves. The *menuki* depict horses in gold or gilded copper. The *kuidashi tsuba* is of *shakudō* with insects in gold inlay; it is unsigned but probably Umetada school work.

92 *Tantō* mounting

19th century

1981.08-08.71, given by Captain Collingwood Ingram

The scabbard of this *tantō* mounting is lacquered black with waves depicted in powdered shell *makie*, with a dragon of silver and other *makie* winding around it. All the hilt and scabbard fittings are of *shibuichi* sculpted with waves, and the gold *menuki* are in the form of sea bream. The hilt is bound with 'whale's beard'.

93 *Tantō* mounting

19th century

1958.07-30.57

This *tantō* mounting is lacquered black with waves depicted in shell powder *makie*, and with shells depicted in gold leaf and gold *takamakie*. The *fuchi*, *kashira*, *menuki* and *origane* are decorated with shells in various coloured metal high-relief sculpture and inlay. The *kozuka* is brass, carved and inlaid with waves and shells, and is signed 'Hiryūsha', an art name used by Jōseki of Bizen Province (d. 1837). The *kuidashi tsuba* is of *shibuichi* sculpted with bellflowers and signed 'Tanaka Tadashige'. The mounting was assembled in the late Edo period.

94 *Tantō* mounting

19th century

1958.07-30.35

This is an *aikuchi tantō* mounting with the scabbard sculpted and lacquered in simulation of bamboo. The metal fittings, including the *menuki* and *kozuka* are all decorated with representations of Raiden, the god of thunder, in high-relief sculpture and coloured metal inlay. The hilt is bound with 'whale's beard'. The *fuchi* is inscribed 'Eiji kore (o) tsukuru' (Eiji made this), and the *kozuka* is signed 'Tōkōsai'. 'Tōkōsai' and 'Eiji' are both names used by the metalworker Okuda Setsuga (1854–1912). When this maker was thirteen, his father died and he became apprenticed to Takahashi Yoshitsugu, who gave him the adoptive name 'Eiji' (or 'Terutsugu'). From 1874 he was appointed to the imperial household as a maker of *tantō* mountings and everyday accessories. The mounting was assembled in the Meiji era.

95 *Tantō* mounting

19th century
1958.07-30.106

This is an *aikuchi tantō* mounting lacquered black with sparse immersed gold powder, depicting bamboo in *yozakura* style. The silver fittings carry depictions of dragons among clouds in silver with some coloured metal inlay. The *menuki* are in the form of tigers. The hilt is bound with 'whale's beard'. The mounting was assembled in the Meiji era.

96 *Wakizashi* mounting

19th century
1958.07-30.90

The scabbard is wrapped with leather and lacquered brownish red in the form of a stylized lobster. The *fuchi* and *kashira* are of plain *shakudō*, and the hilt and the scabbard are enveloped with silver sheaths engraved with flowers and *hanabishi* motifs. The *menuki* are dragons in roundels, and the *kozuka* has a dragonfly in high-relief *shakudō* inlay on copper. The *tsuba* is of *shibuichi* with the spurious signature 'Eishū'. The assembly dates from the late Edo period.

97 *Tantō* mounting

19th century
1958.07-30.55

This is an *aikuchi tantō* mounting with a scabbard of vermilion-lacquered polished ray skin. The *fuchi*, *kashira* and scabbard fittings are all of silver, sculpted with representations of chrysanthemums. The silver *kōgai* and *kozuka* are engraved with scrolling. The *menuki* are in the form of horses in gold and *shakudō*. The *kuidashi tsuba* is silver carved with a rope motif around the rim. The assembly dates from the Meiji era.

98 *Katana* mounting

19th century
1958.07-30.192

The scabbard is lacquered a cloudy vermilion. The *fuchi* and *kashira* have depictions of cranes and grasses in high-relief coloured metal inlay on *shakudō nanako*. The *menuki* are of chrysanthemums and praying mantises. The *tsuba* is of bright-polished iron pierced and carved with flowers and leaves. The mounting forms a *daishō* with the matching *wakizashi* mounting, no. 99, both probably assembled in the Meiji era. It carried a blade that was not conserved in this project.

99 *Wakizashi* mounting

19th century
1958.07-30.159

The scabbard and metal fittings are identical to those of the *katana* mounting, no. 98, which forms a *daishō* together with this *wakizashi* mounting, except that the birds are herons in this case. The *fuchi* is inscribed with the spurious signature 'Hiroyuki'. The scabbard of this sword carries a matching *kozuka* and *kōgai* with cranes in high-relief coloured metal inlay on inset *shakudō* panels. It carried the *wakizashi* blade by Kawachi no kami Masahiro (no. 53).

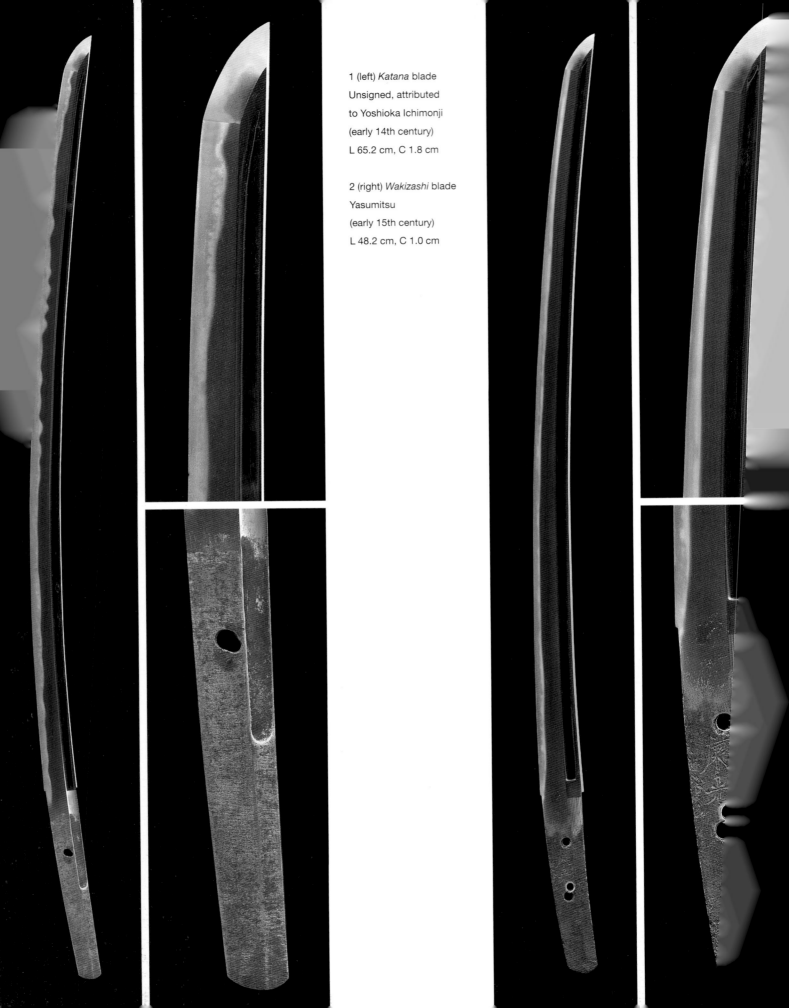

1 (left) *Katana* blade
Unsigned, attributed
to Yoshioka Ichimonji
(early 14th century)
L 65.2 cm, C 1.8 cm

2 (right) *Wakizashi* blade
Yasumitsu
(early 15th century)
L 48.2 cm, C 1.0 cm

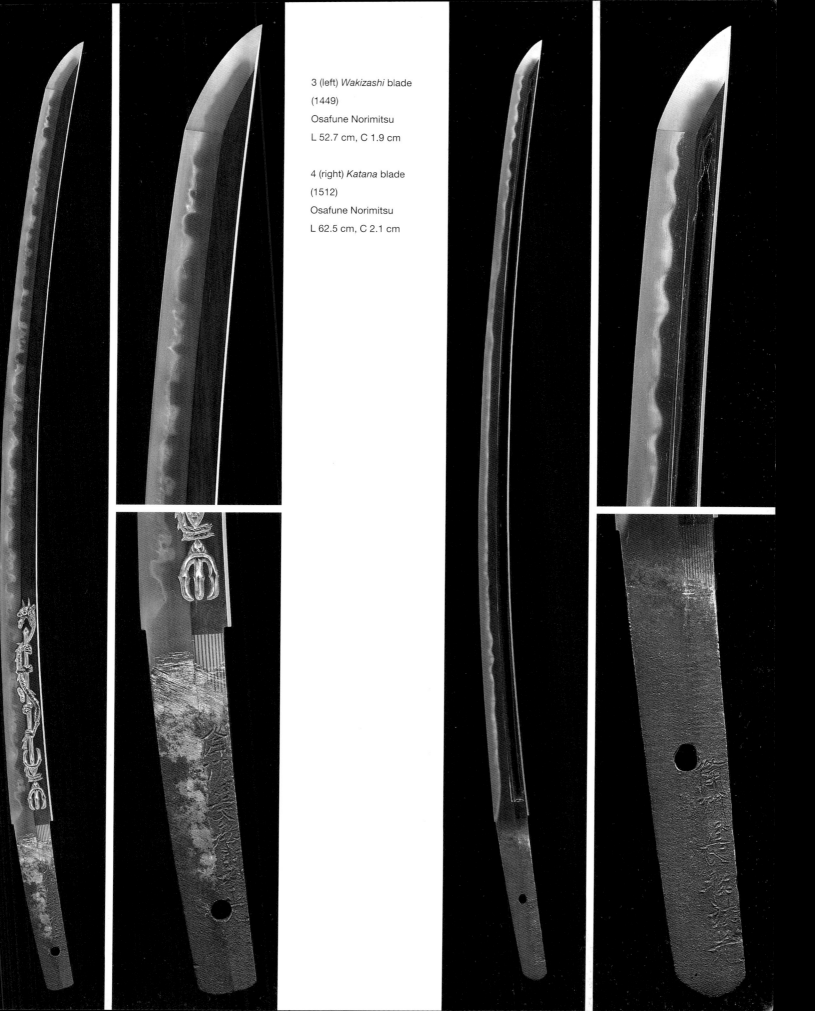

3 (left) *Wakizashi* blade
(1449)
Osafune Norimitsu
L 52.7 cm, C 1.9 cm

4 (right) *Katana* blade
(1512)
Osafune Norimitsu
L 62.5 cm, C 2.1 cm

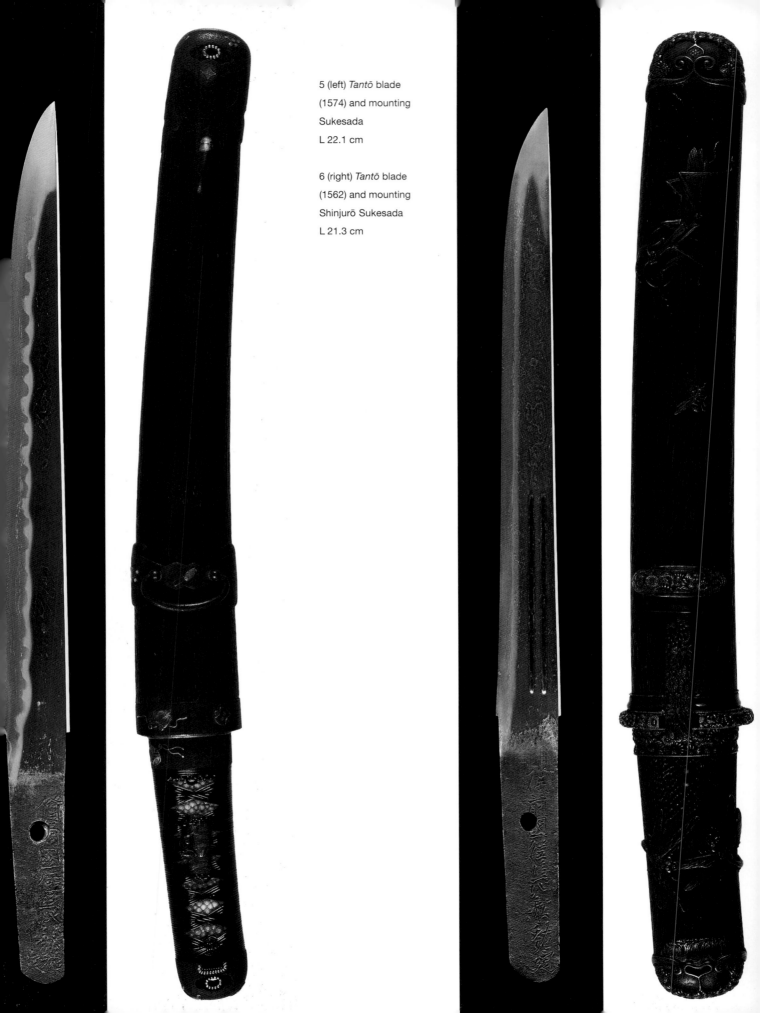

5 (left) *Tantō* blade
(1574) and mounting
Sukesada
L 22.1 cm

6 (right) *Tantō* blade
(1562) and mounting
Shinjurō Sukesada
L 21.3 cm

7 (left) *Tantō* blade
(1582) and mounting
Sukesada
L 22.2 cm, C (*uchi zori*)

8 (right) *Tantō* blade
and mounting
Sukesada (16th century)
L 20.5 cm, C (*uchi zori*)

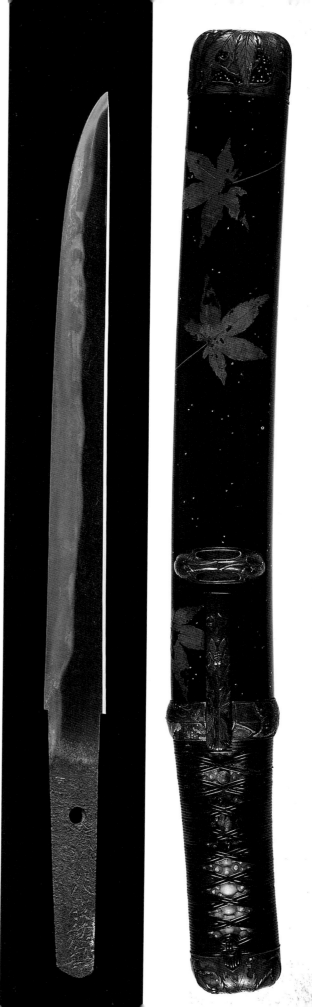

9 *Tachi* blade
and mounting
Unsigned,
attributed to Esshū
Tametsugu
(14th century)
L 71.7 cm,
C 1.7 cm

10 *Tantō* blade
and mounting
Unsigned, attributed
to Tsukushi Nobukuni
(Ōei era, 1394–1428)
L 32.5 cm, C (*uchi zori*)

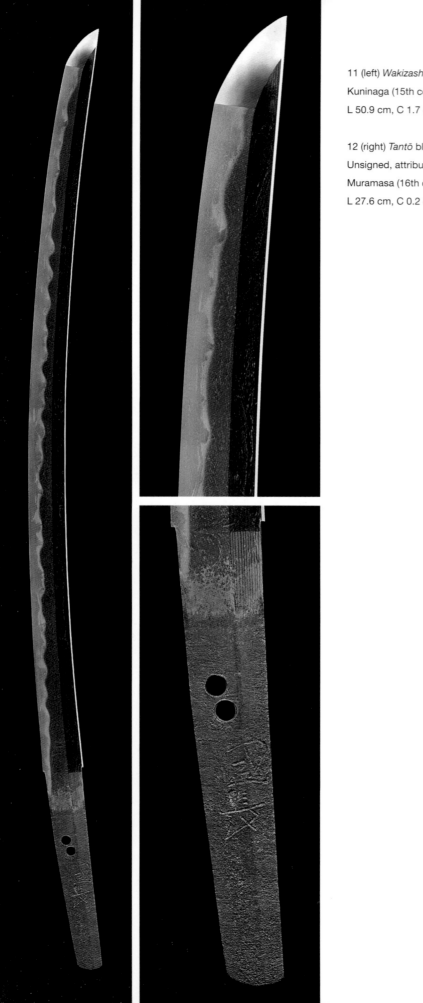

11 (left) *Wakizashi* blade
Kuninaga (15th century)
L 50.9 cm, C 1.7 cm

12 (right) *Tantō* blade
Unsigned, attributed to
Muramasa (16th century)
L 27.6 cm, C 0.2 cm

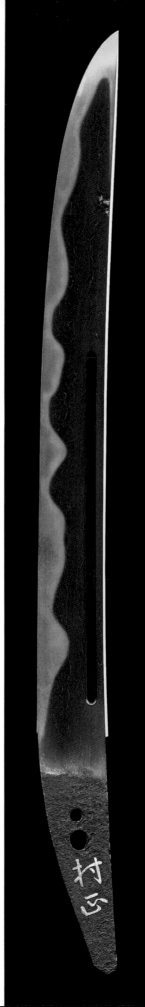

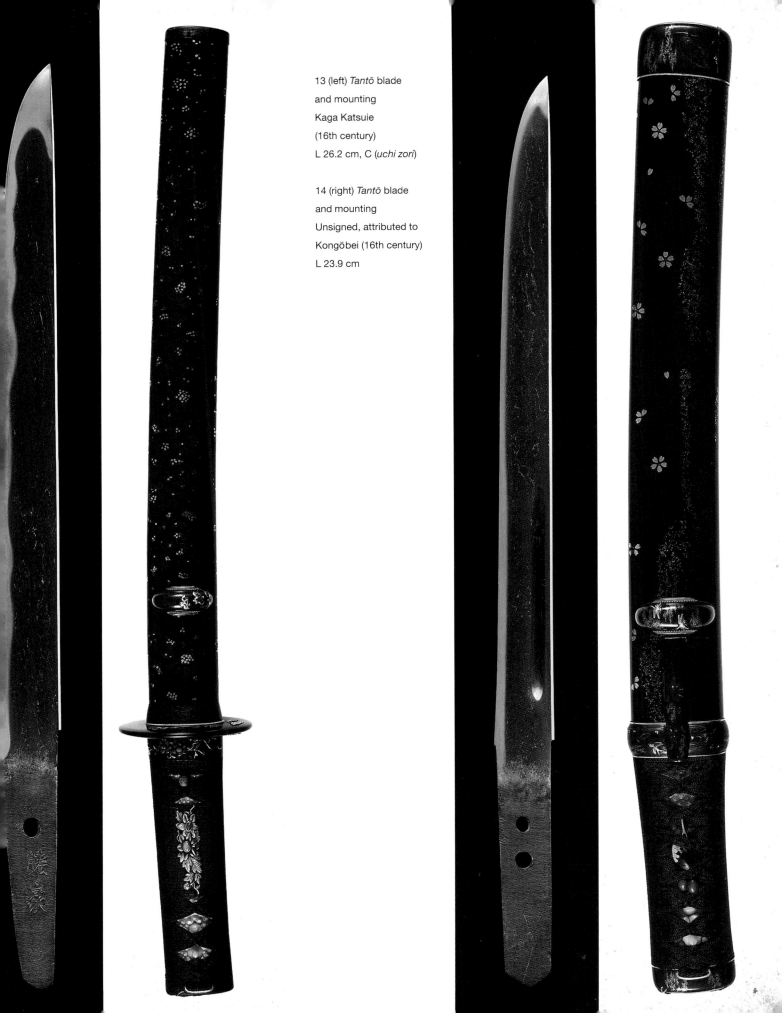

13 (left) *Tantō* blade
and mounting
Kaga Katsuie
(16th century)
L 26.2 cm, C (*uchi zori*)

14 (right) *Tantō* blade
and mounting
Unsigned, attributed to
Kongōbei (16th century)
L 23.9 cm

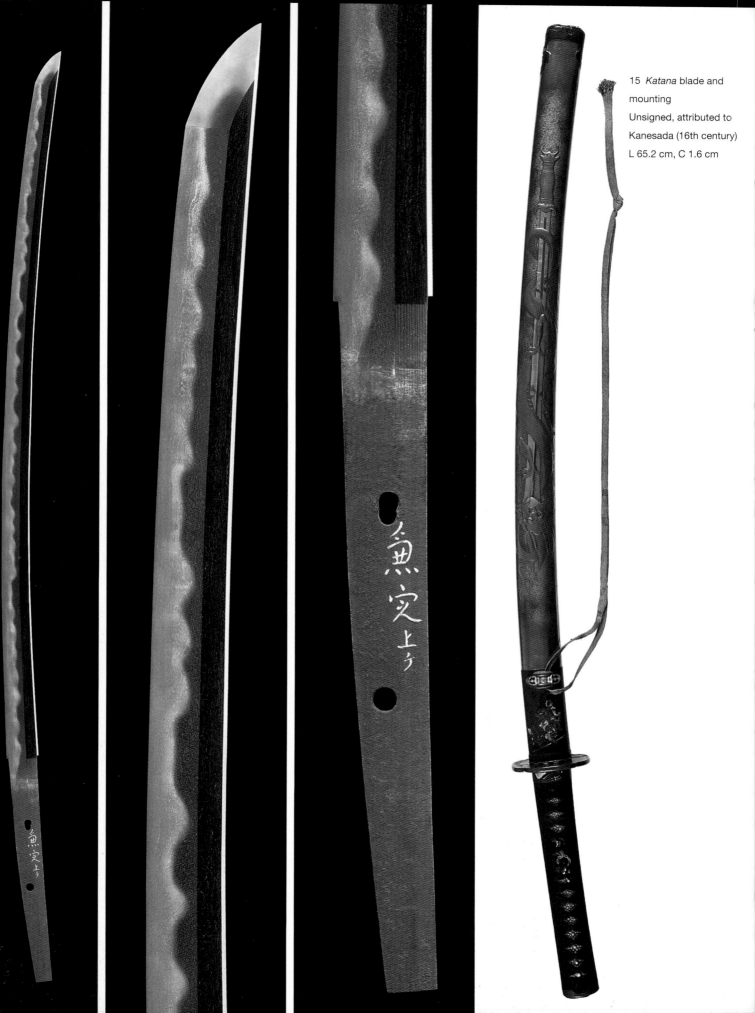

15 *Katana* blade and
mounting
Unsigned, attributed to
Kanesada (16th century)
L 65.2 cm, C 1.6 cm

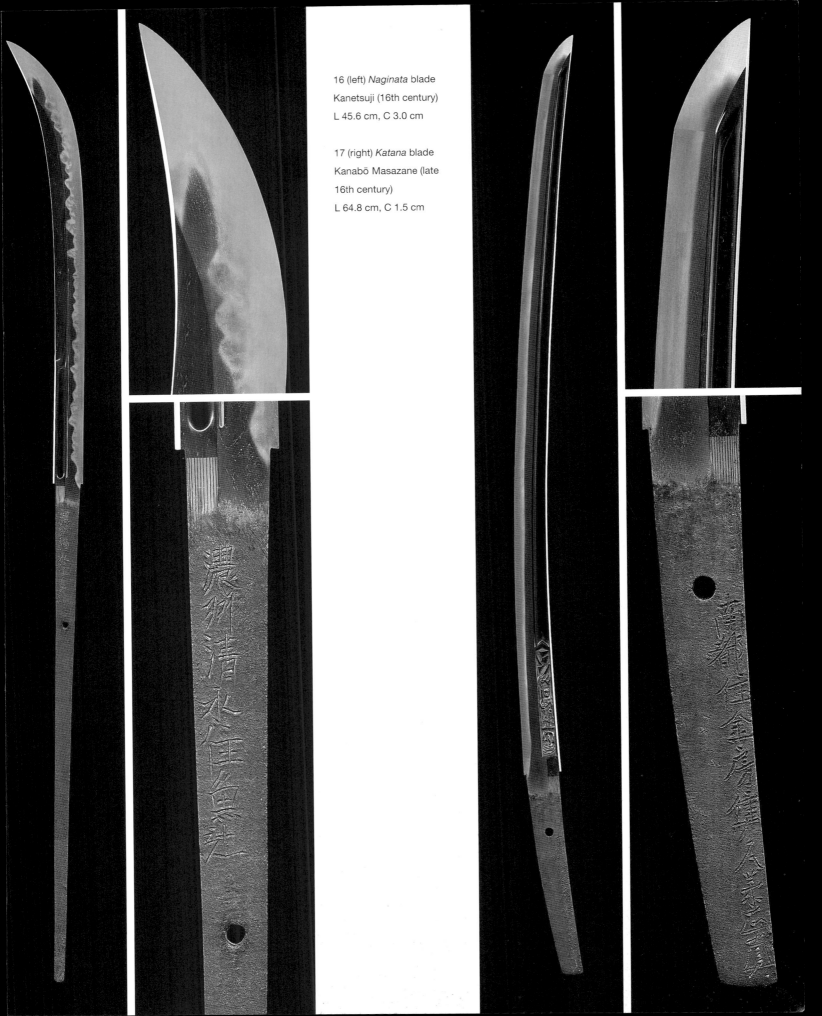

16 (left) *Naginata* blade
Kanetsuji (16th century)
L 45.6 cm, C 3.0 cm

17 (right) *Katana* blade
Kanabō Masazane (late
16th century)
L 64.8 cm, C 1.5 cm

18 *Wakizashi* blade
and mounting
Horikawa Kunihiro (early
Keichō era 1596–1615).
L 50.6 cm, C 1.0 cm

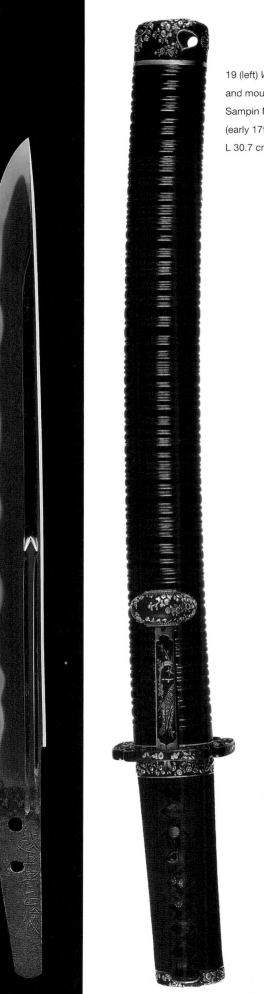

19 (left) *Wakizashi* blade
and mounting
Sampin Masatoshi
(early 17th century)
L 30.7 cm, C (*uchi zori*)

20 (left) *Tantō* blade
Shimosaka
(early 17th century)
L 29.9 cm, C (*uchi zori*)

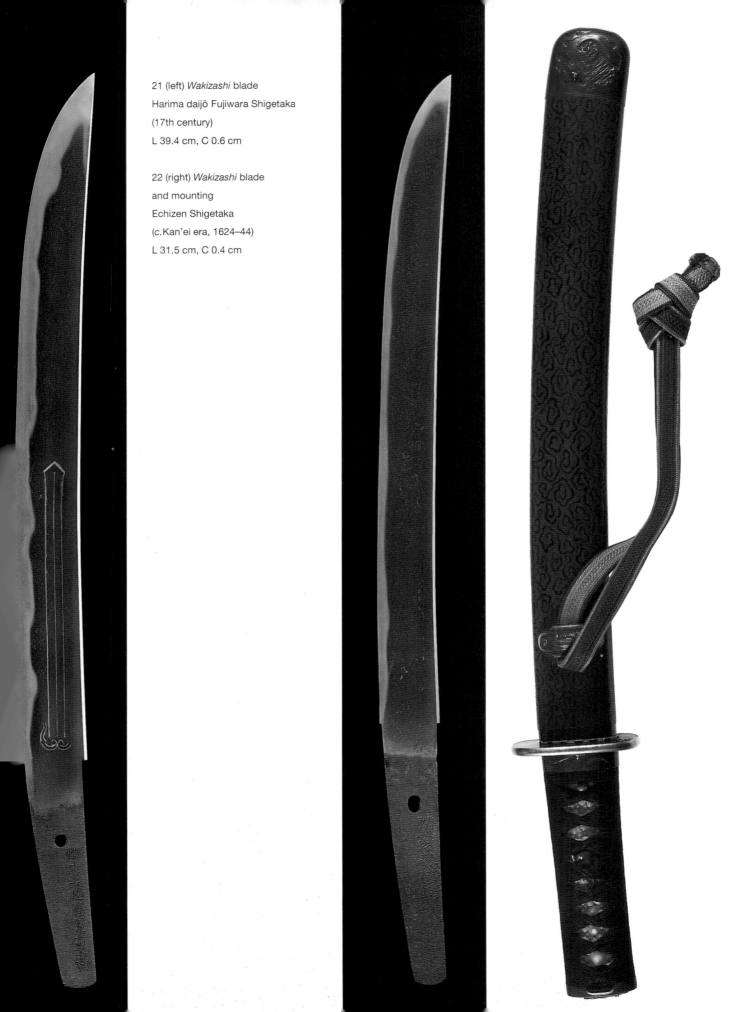

21 (left) *Wakizashi* blade
Harima daijō Fujiwara Shigetaka
(17th century)
L 39.4 cm, C 0.6 cm

22 (right) *Wakizashi* blade
and mounting
Echizen Shigetaka
(*c.*Kan'ei era, 1624–44)
L 31.5 cm, C 0.4 cm

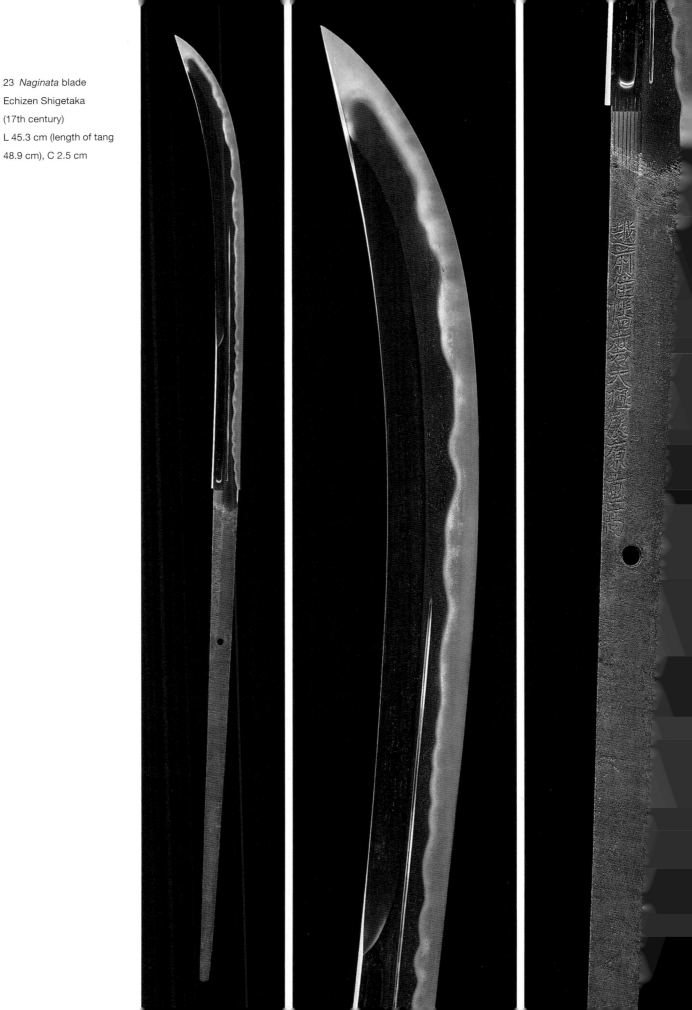

23 *Naginata* blade
Echizen Shigetaka
(17th century)
L 45.3 cm (length of tang
48.9 cm), C 2.5 cm

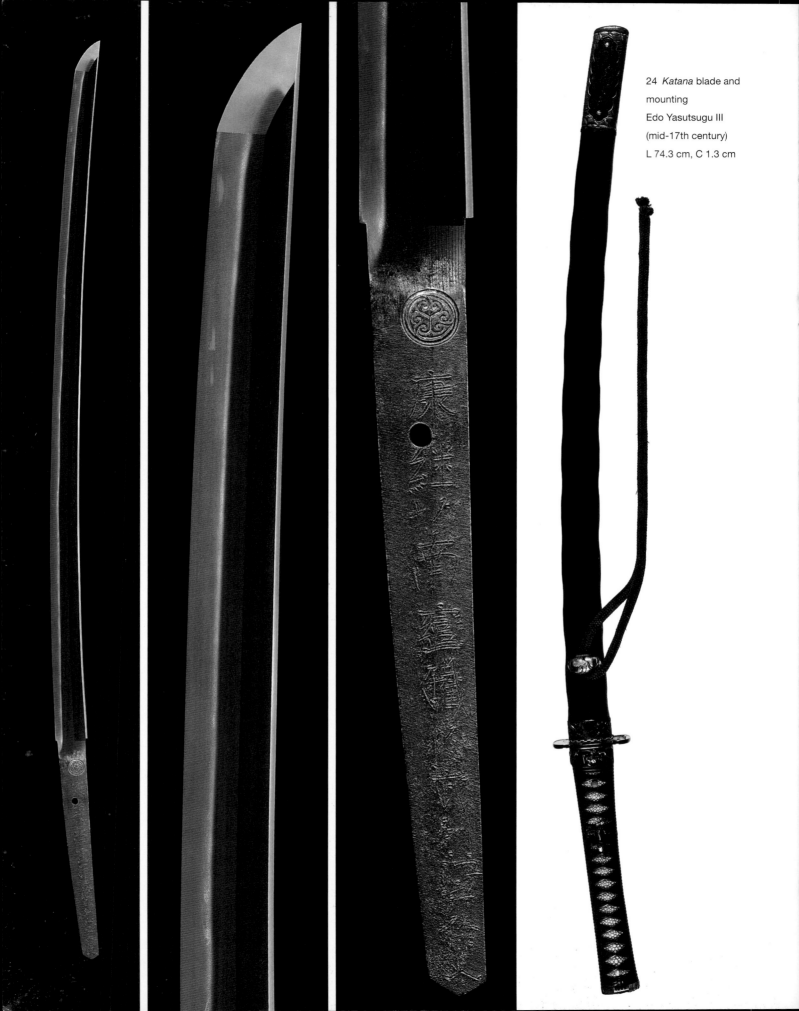

24 *Katana* blade and
mounting
Edo Yasutsugu III
(mid-17th century)
L 74.3 cm, C 1.3 cm

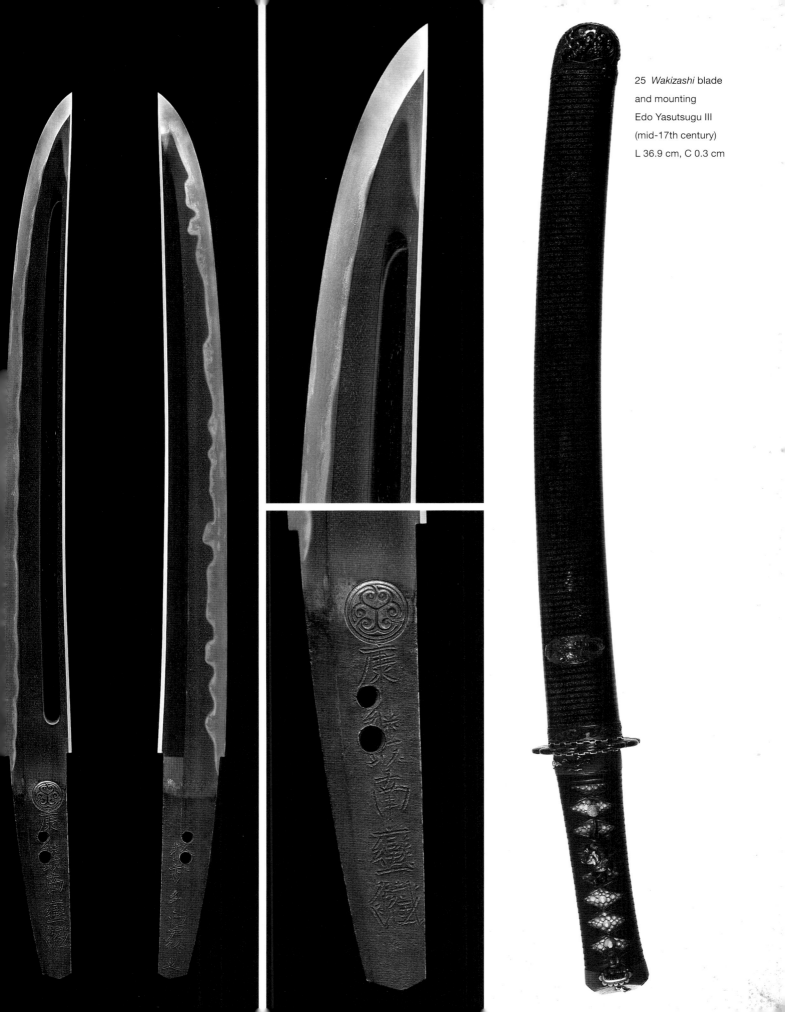

25 *Wakizashi* blade
and mounting
Edo Yasutsugu III
(mid-17th century)
L 36.9 cm, C 0.3 cm

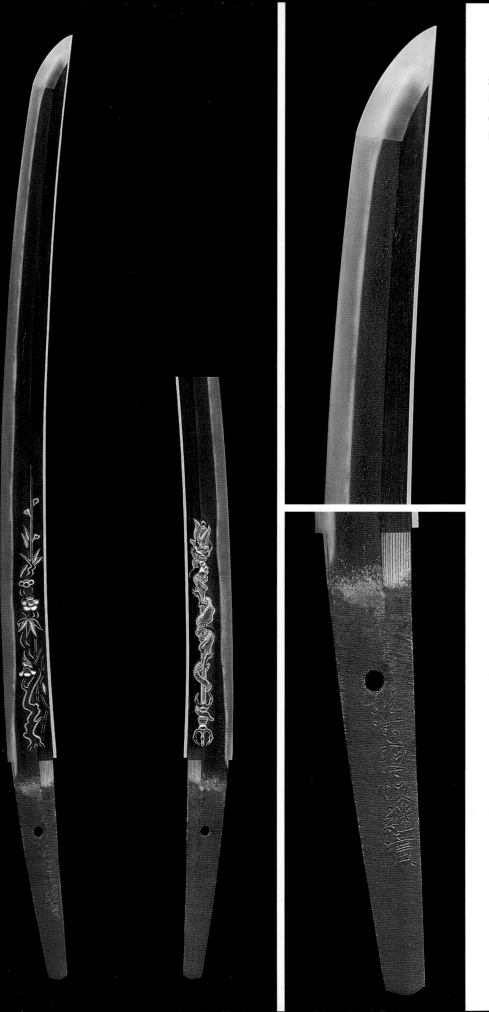

26 *Wakizashi* blade
Echizen Tsuguhiro
(late 17th century)
L 48.6 cm, C 1.1 cm

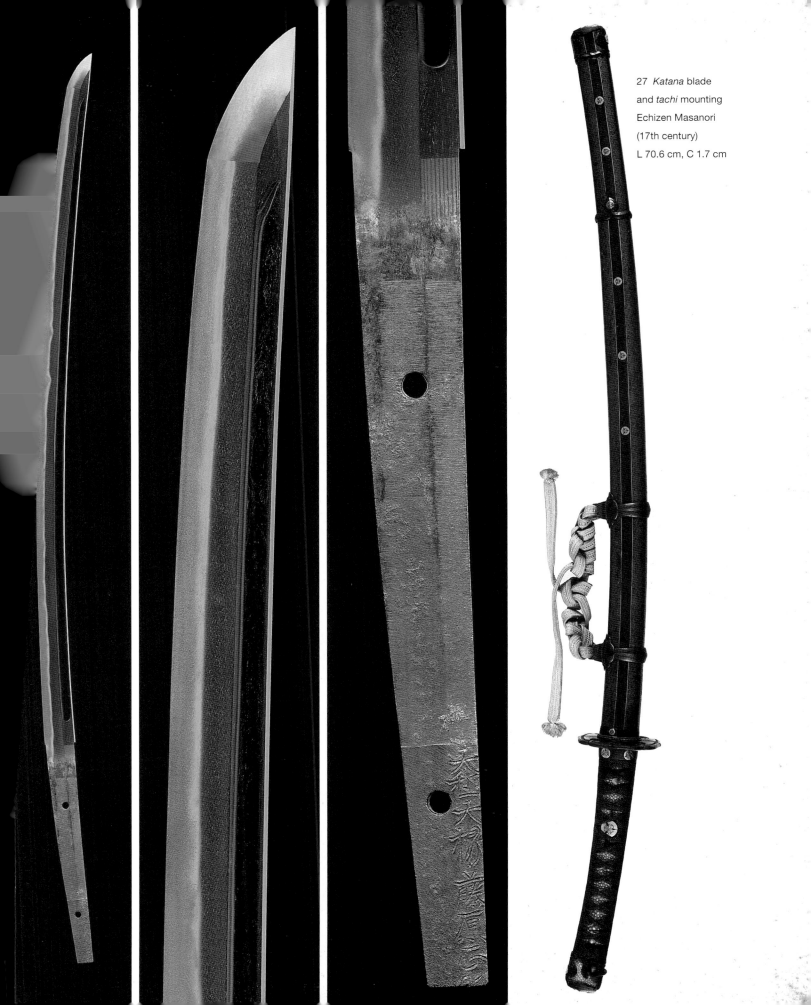

27 *Katana* blade
and *tachi* mounting
Echizen Masanori
(17th century)
L 70.6 cm, C 1.7 cm

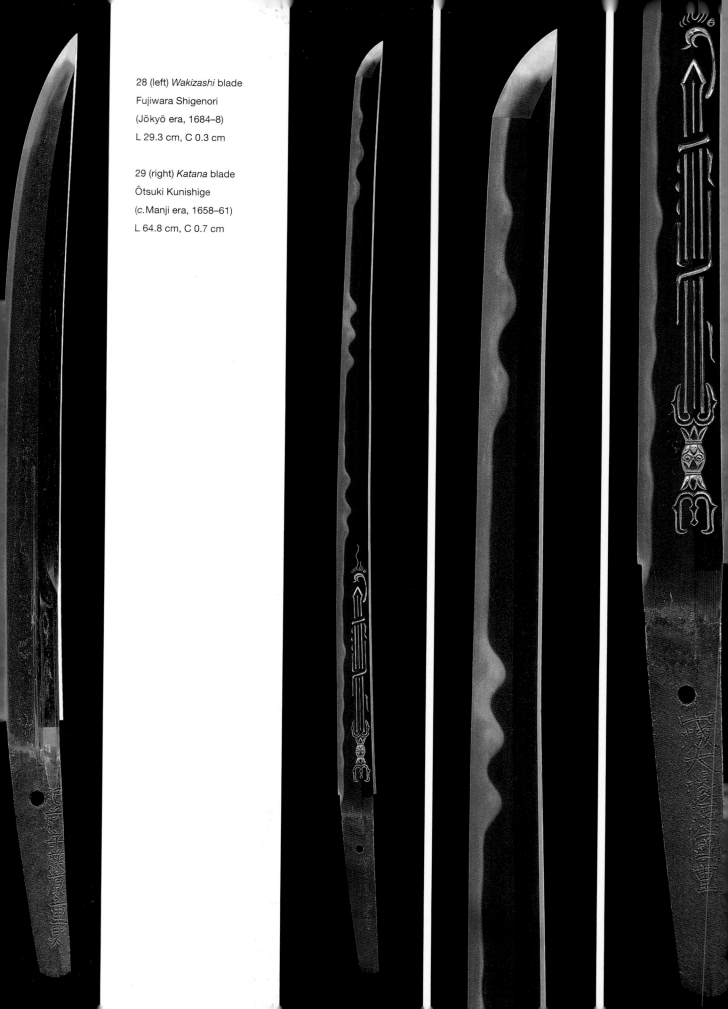

28 (left) *Wakizashi* blade
Fujiwara Shigenori
(Jōkyō era, 1684–8)
L 29.3 cm, C 0.3 cm

29 (right) *Katana* blade
Ōtsuki Kunishige
(*c.*Manji era, 1658–61)
L 64.8 cm, C 0.7 cm

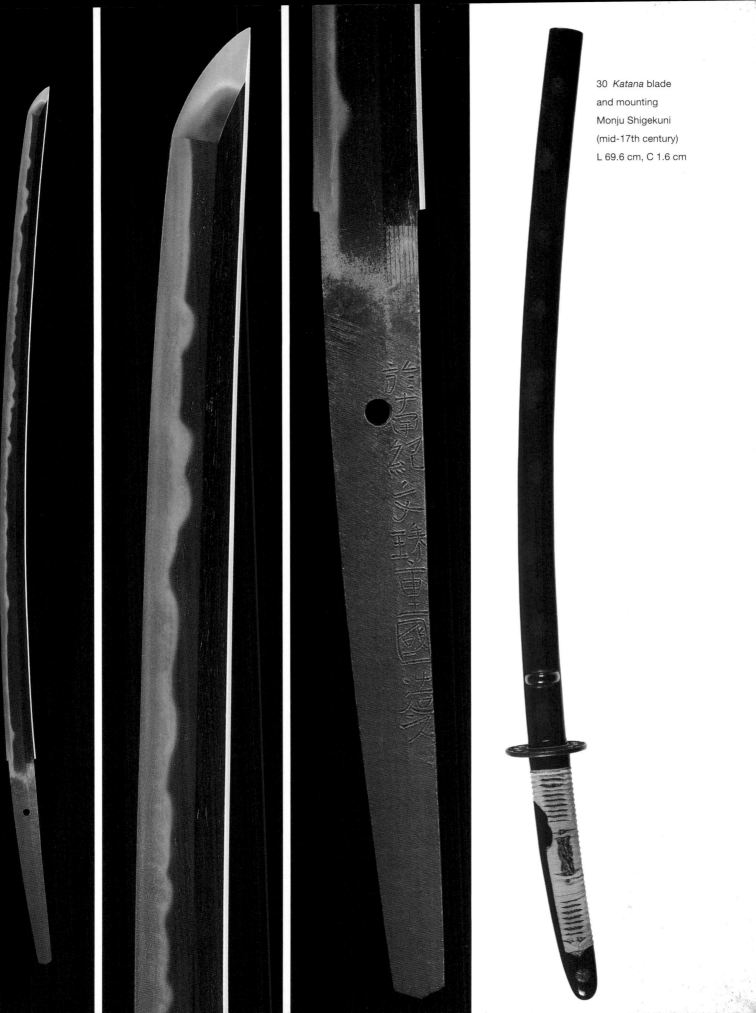

30 *Katana* blade
and mounting
Monju Shigekuni
(mid-17th century)
L 69.6 cm, C 1.6 cm

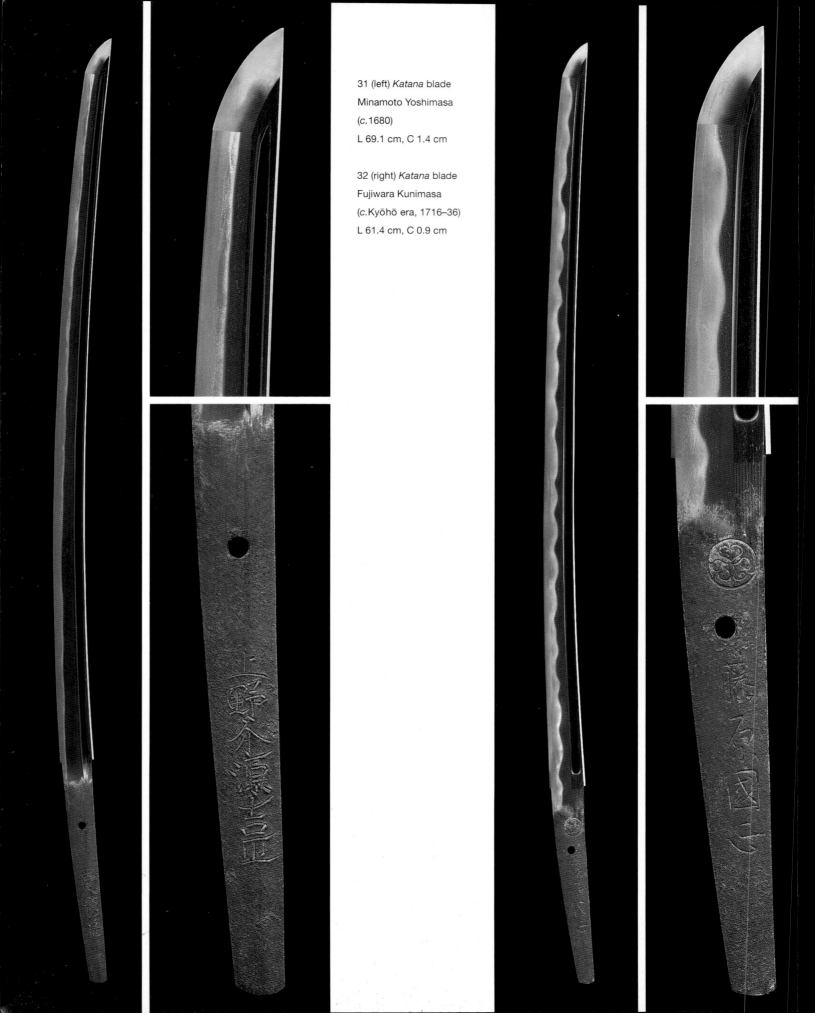

31 (left) *Katana* blade
Minamoto Yoshimasa
(*c*.1680)
L 69.1 cm, C 1.4 cm

32 (right) *Katana* blade
Fujiwara Kunimasa
(*c*.Kyōhō era, 1716–36)
L 61.4 cm, C 0.9 cm

33 *Katana* blade
and mounting
Jimyō (Kambun era,
1661–73)
L 60.3 cm, C 1.0 cm

34 (left) *Katana* blade
Kanenobu (17th century)
L 63.4 cm, C 1.5 cm

35 (right) *Katana* blade
Kanemoto (17th century)
L 70.5 cm, C 1.2 cm

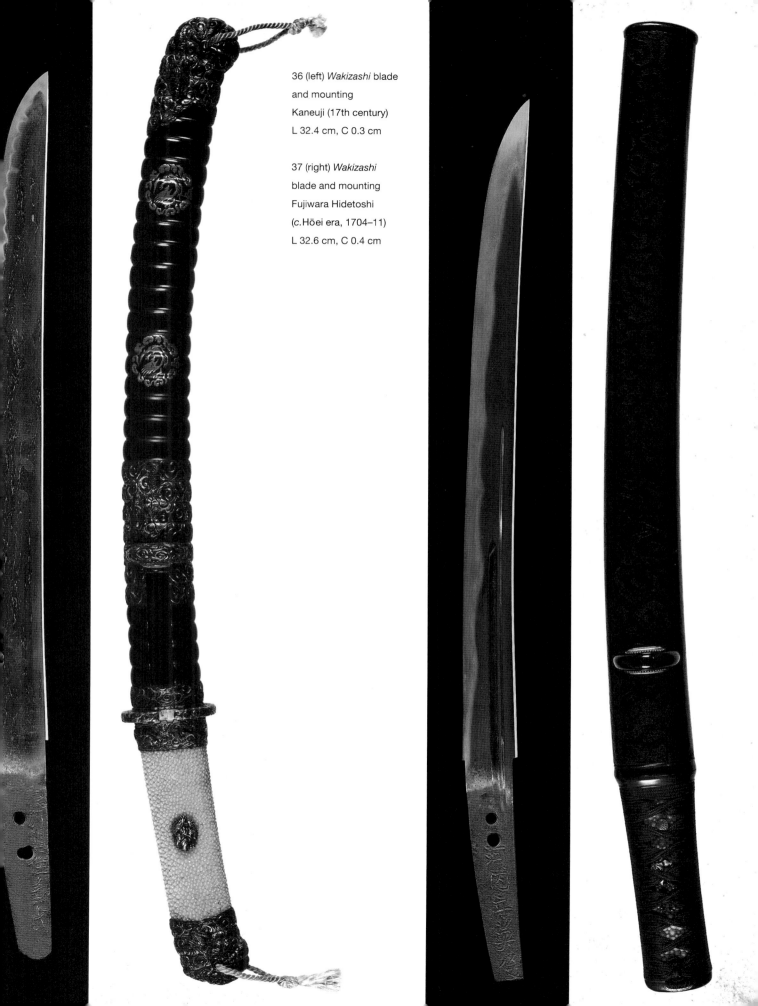

36 (left) *Wakizashi* blade
and mounting
Kaneuji (17th century)
L 32.4 cm, C 0.3 cm

37 (right) *Wakizashi*
blade and mounting
Fujiwara Hidetoshi
(*c.*Hōei era, 1704–11)
L 32.6 cm, C 0.4 cm

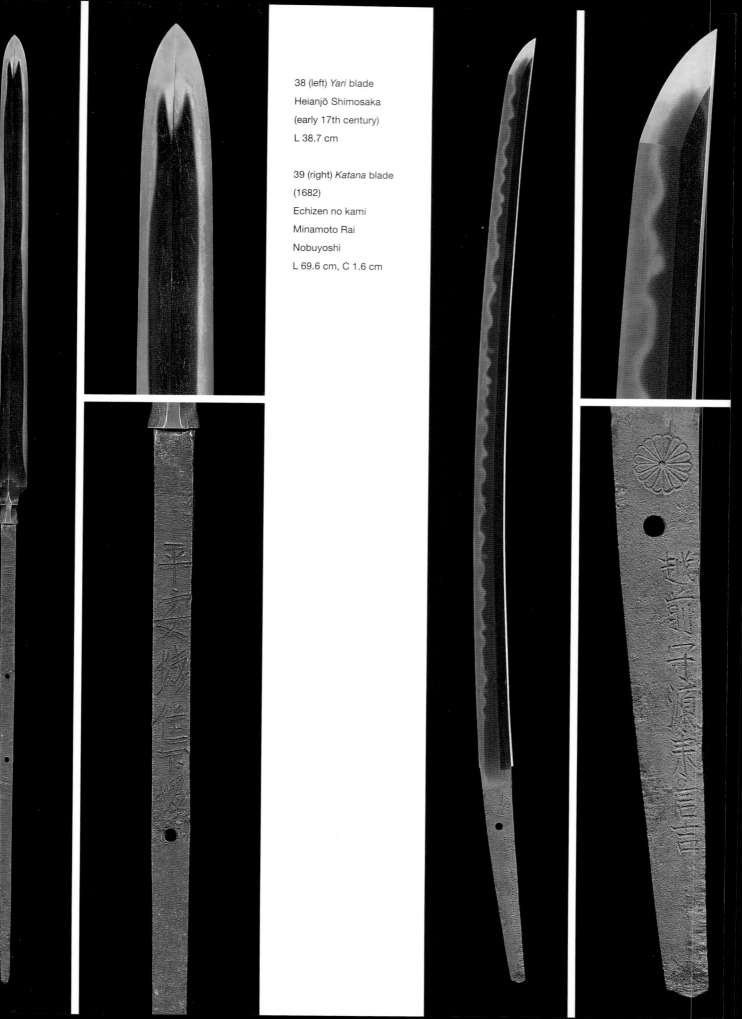

38 (left) *Yari* blade
Heianjō Shimosaka
(early 17th century)
L 38.7 cm

39 (right) *Katana* blade
(1682)
Echizen no kami
Minamoto Rai
Nobuyoshi
L 69.6 cm, C 1.6 cm

40 (left) *Tantō* blade
and mounting
Fujiwara Hisakuni
(early 18th century)
L 23.8 cm, C (*uchi zori*)

41 (right) *Tantō* blade
and mounting
Umetada Yoshinobu
(possibly Genroku era,
1688–1704)
L 24.2 cm, C (*uchi zori*)

42 *Katana* blade
and mounting
Sasaki Ippō (Genroku
era, 1688–1704)
L 65.0 cm, C 1.2 cm

43 *Katana* blade
and mounting
Tachibana Yasuhiro
(17th century)
L 70.1 cm, C 2.4 cm

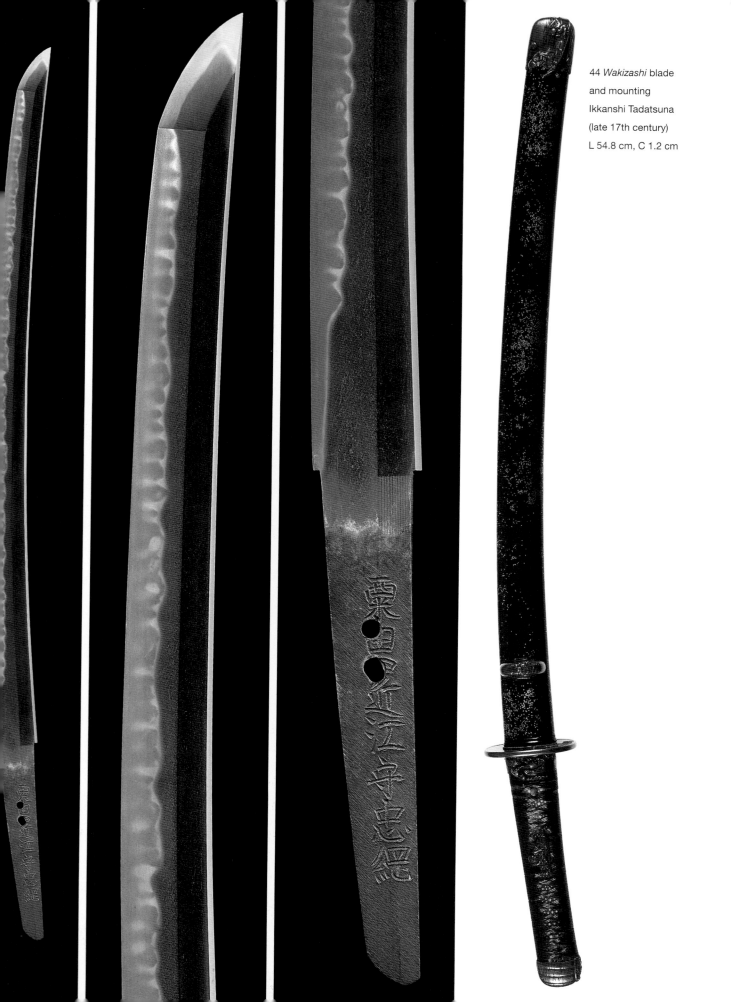

44 *Wakizashi* blade
and mounting
Ikkanshi Tadatsuna
(late 17th century)
L 54.8 cm, C 1.2 cm

45 *Wakizashi* blade (1661)
Tachibana Yasuhiro
L 45.0 cm, C 1.0cm

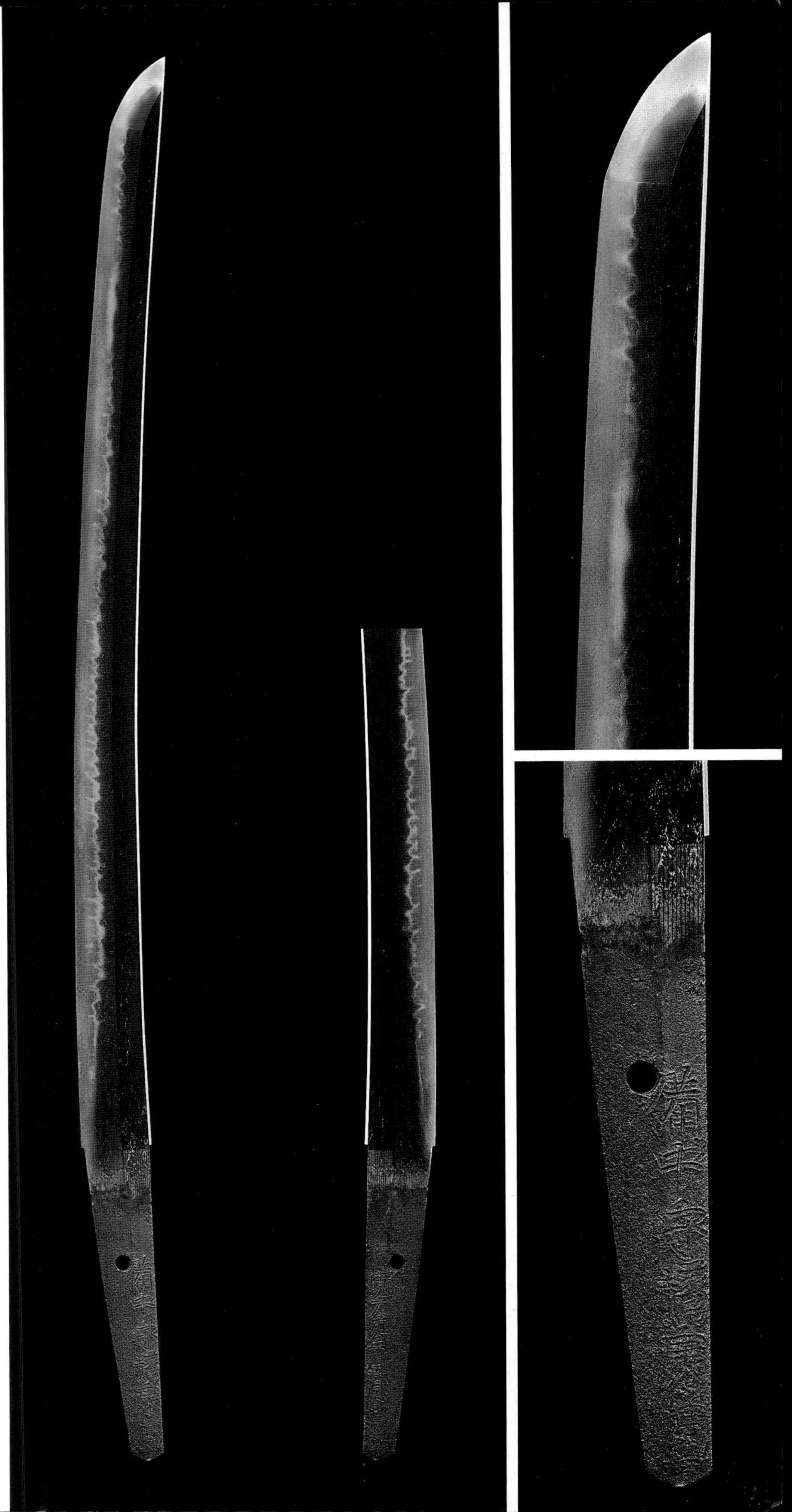

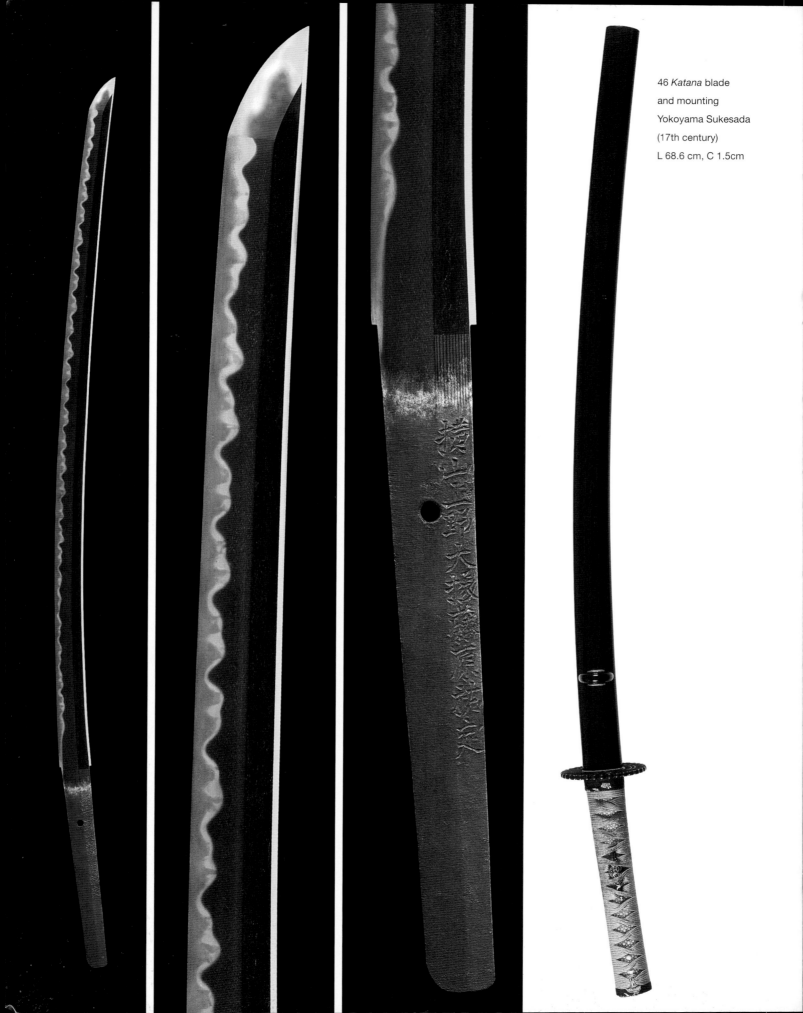

46 *Katana* blade
and mounting
Yokoyama Sukesada
(17th century)
L 68.6 cm, C 1.5cm

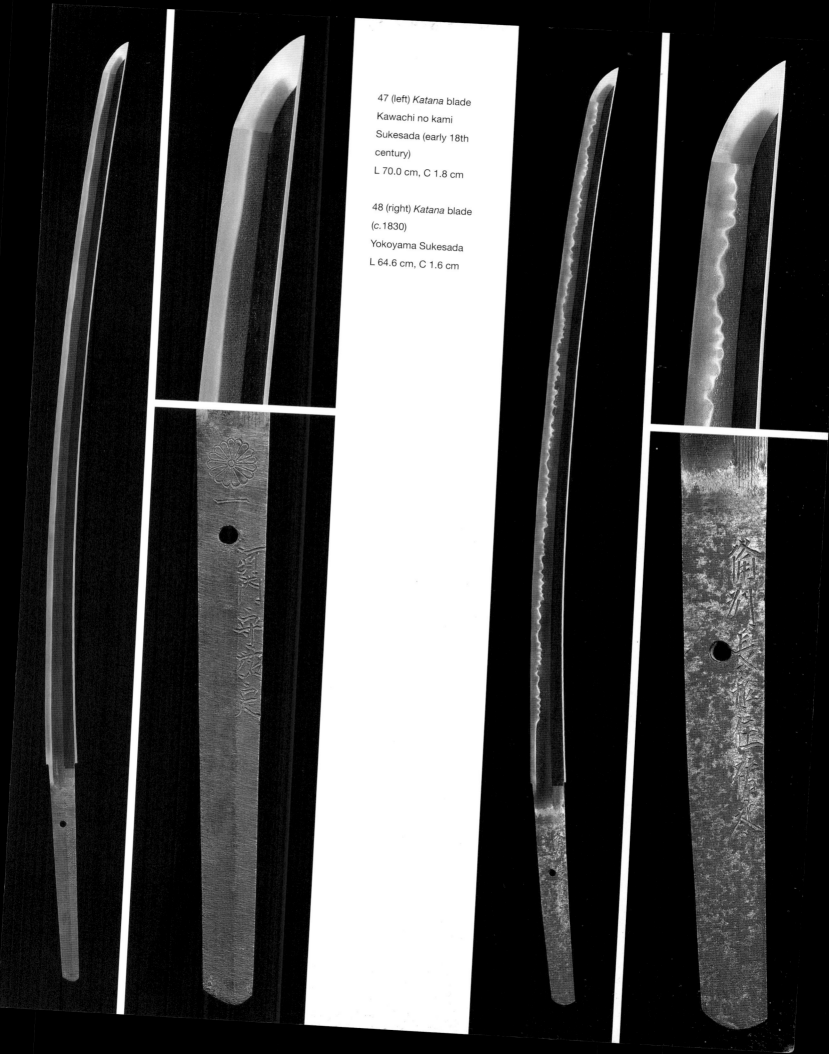

47 (left) *Katana* blade
Kawachi no kami
Sukesada (early 18th
century)
L 70.0 cm, C 1.8 cm

48 (right) *Katana* blade
(*c.*1830)
Yokoyama Sukesada
L 64.6 cm, C 1.6 cm

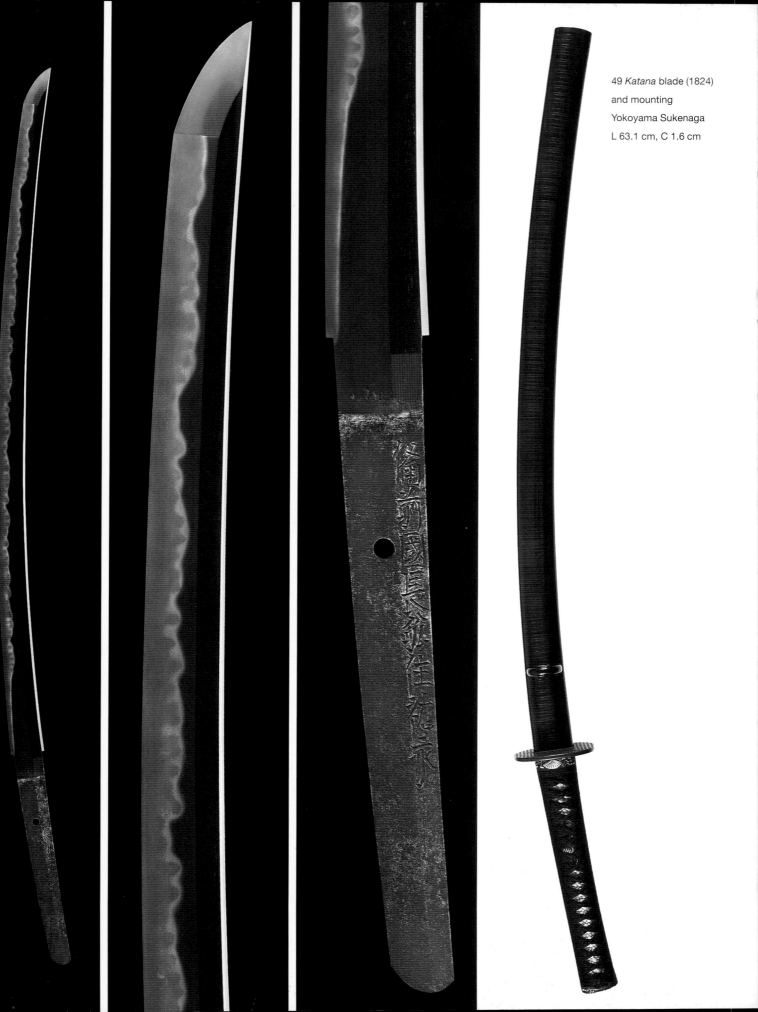

49 *Katana* blade (1824)
and mounting
Yokoyama Sukenaga
L 63.1 cm, C 1.6 cm

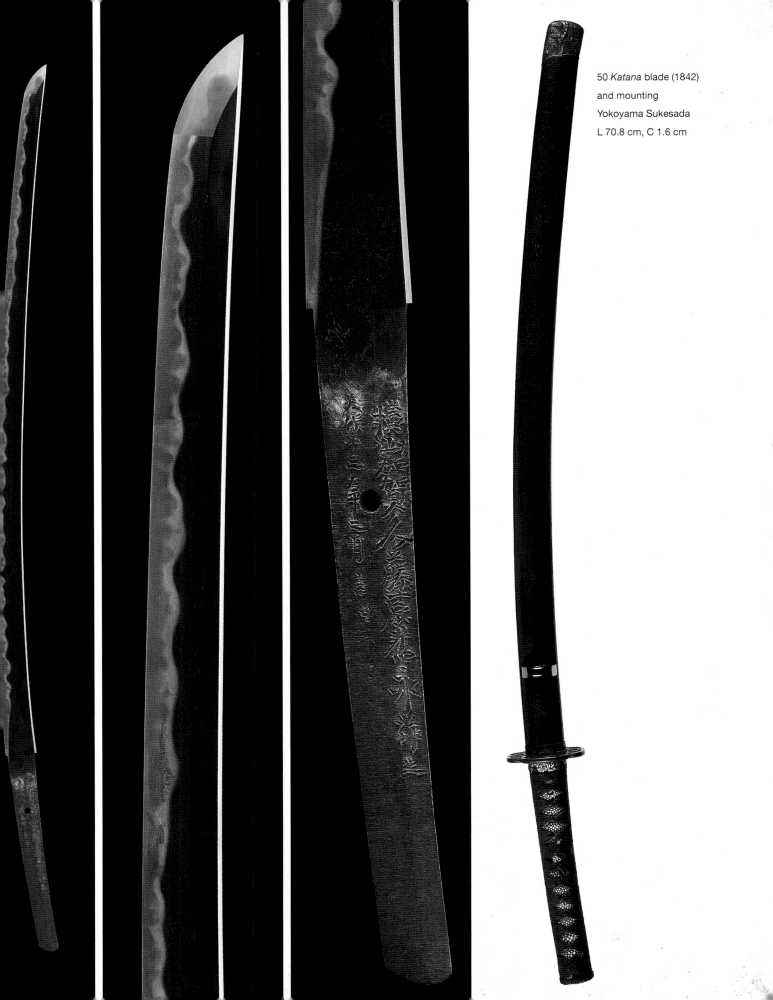

50 *Katana* blade (1842)
and mounting
Yokoyama Sukesada
L 70.8 cm, C 1.6 cm

51 *Wakizashi* blade
(1850) and mounting
Yokoyama Sukenaga
L 45.6 cm, C 1.6 cm

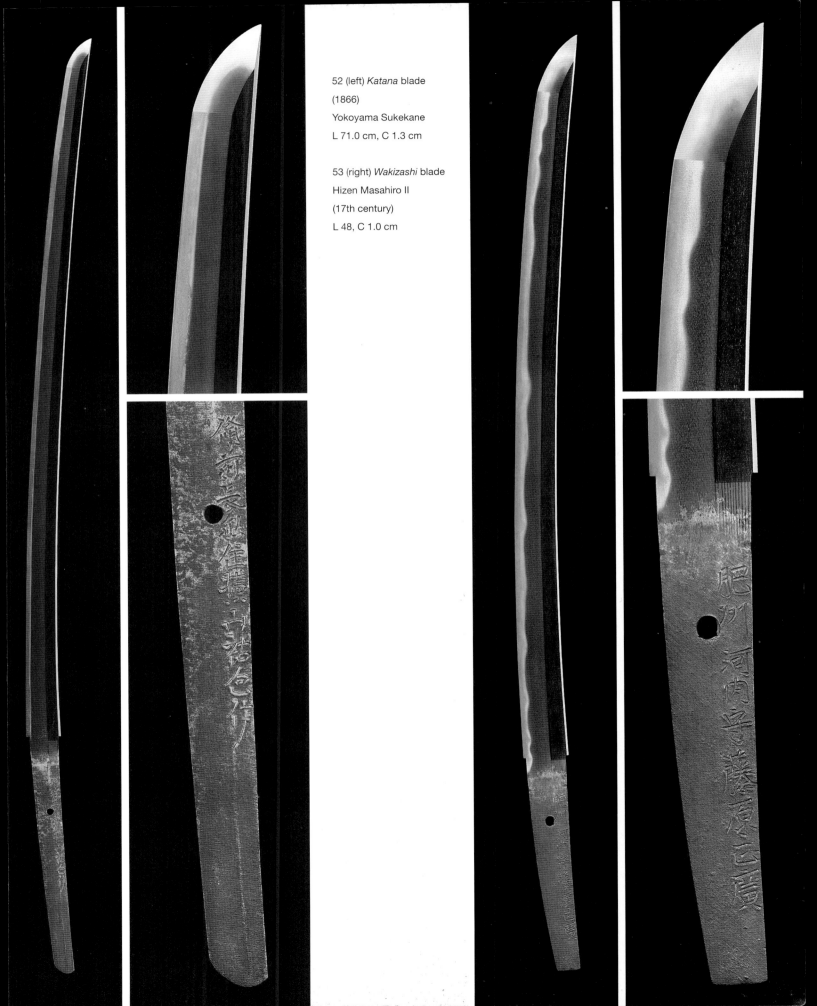

52 (left) *Katana* blade
(1866)
Yokoyama Sukekane
L 71.0 cm, C 1.3 cm

53 (right) *Wakizashi* blade
Hizen Masahiro II
(17th century)
L 48, C 1.0 cm

54 *Wakizashi* blade

Hizen Tadayoshi VIII

(early 19th century)

L 45.2 cm, C 0.8 cm

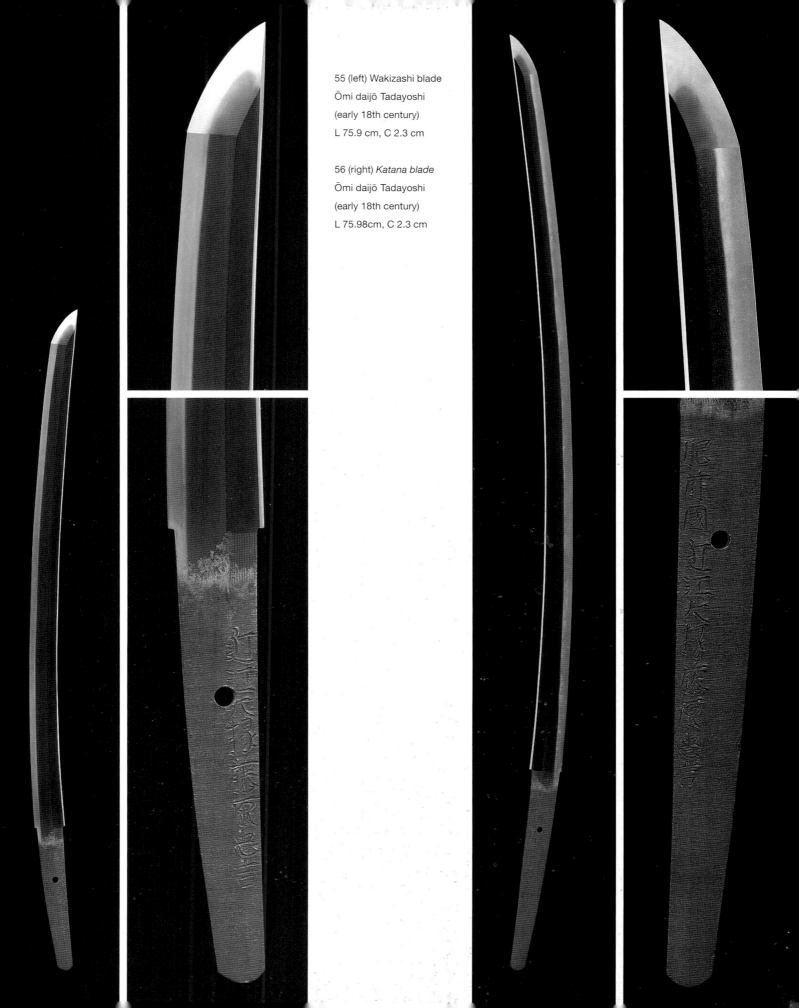

55 (left) Wakizashi blade
Ōmi daijō Tadayoshi
(early 18th century)
L 75.9 cm, C 2.3 cm

56 (right) *Katana blade*
Ōmi daijō Tadayoshi
(early 18th century)
L 75.98cm, C 2.3 cm

57 *Tantō* blade and mounting
Bitchū Kunishige
(18th or 19th century)
L 22.9 cm, C 0.3 cm

58 *Katana* blade and
handachi mounting
Tōshirō Kuniyoshi
(*c*.1770–80)
L 71.6 cm, C 1.0 cm

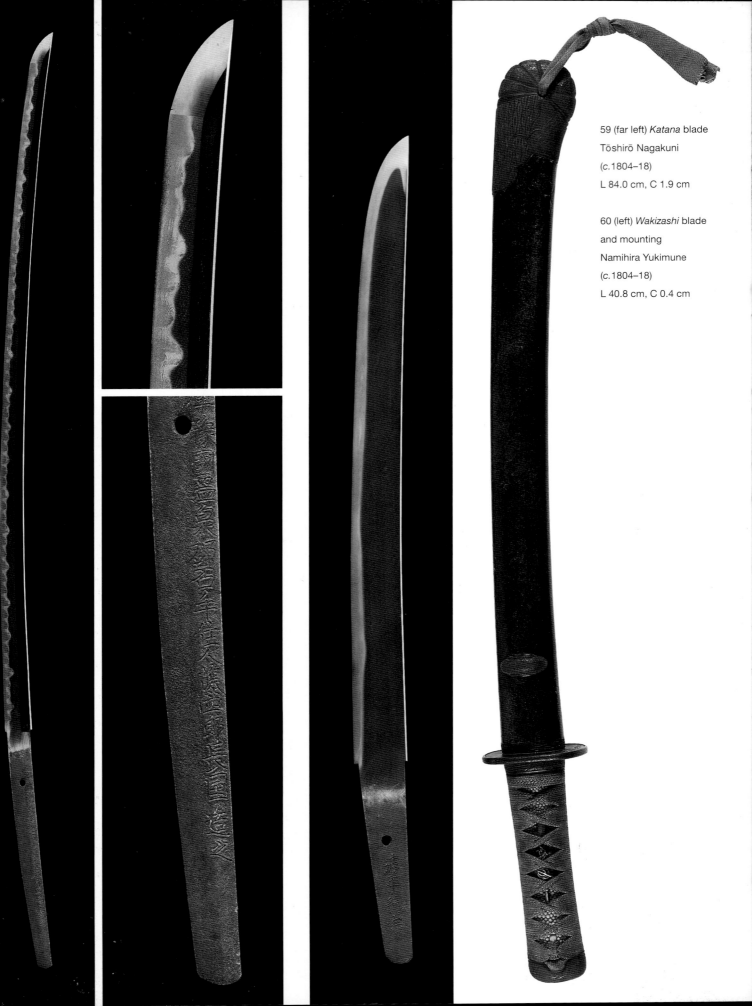

59 (far left) *Katana* blade
Tōshirō Nagakuni
(*c*.1804–18)
L 84.0 cm, C 1.9 cm

60 (left) *Wakizashi* blade
and mounting
Namihira Yukimune
(*c*.1804–18)
L 40.8 cm, C 0.4 cm

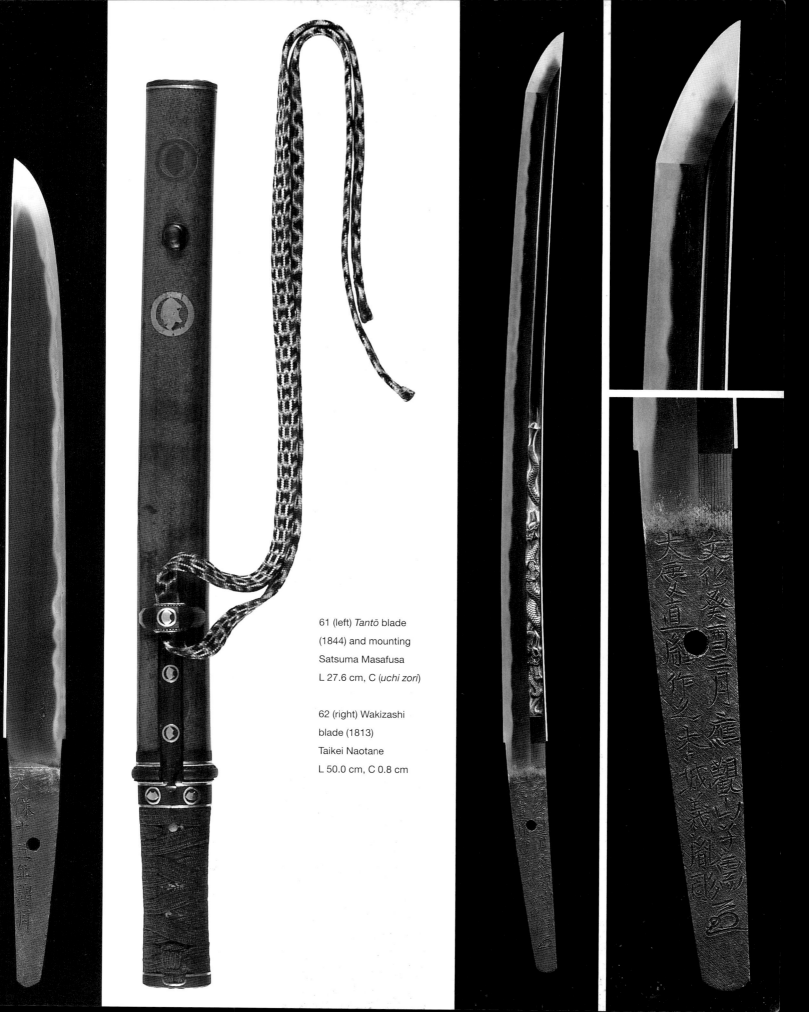

61 (left) *Tantō* blade
(1844) and mounting
Satsuma Masafusa
L 27.6 cm, C (*uchi zori*)

62 (right) Wakizashi
blade (1813)
Taikei Naotane
L 50.0 cm, C 0.8 cm

63 *Wakizashi* blade
(1833) and mounting
Taikei Naotane
L 45.0 cm, C 0.9 cm

64 *Tantō* blade (1833)
and mounting
Hatakeyama Masamitsu
L 22.6 cm

65 *Katana* blade (1861)
and mounting
Tsunatoshi and Koretoshi
L 70.1 cm, C 1.4 cm

66 *Tantō* blade (1854)
and mounting
Chōunsai Tsunatoshi
L 24.5 cm

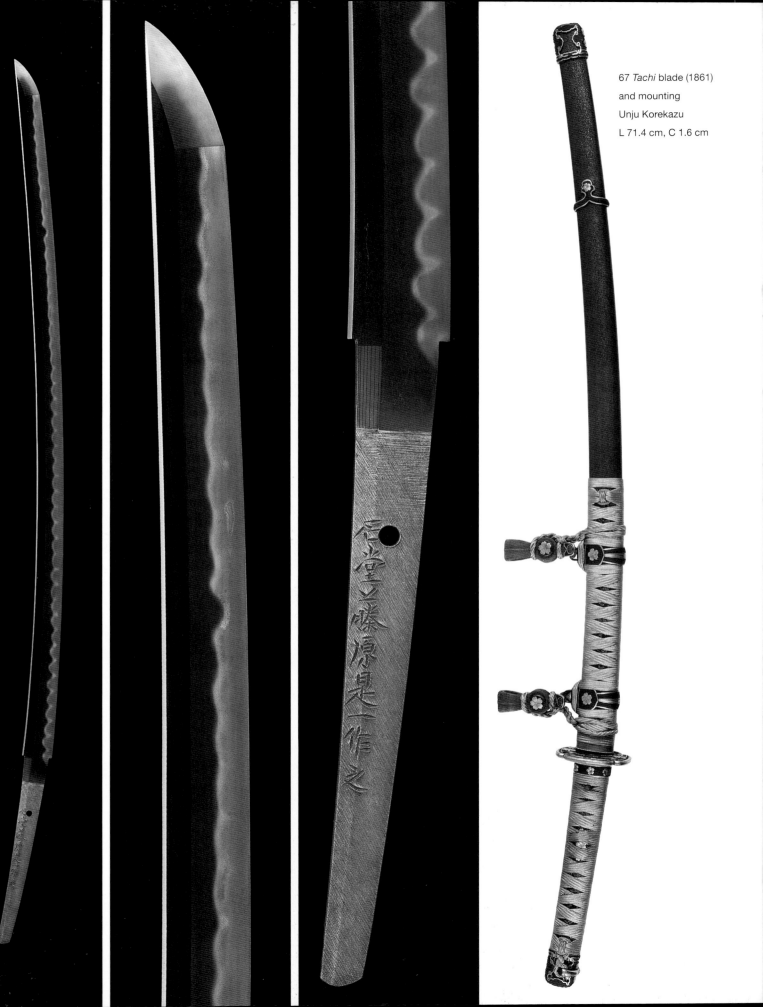

67 *Tachi* blade (1861)
and mounting
Unju Korekazu
L 71.4 cm, C 1.6 cm

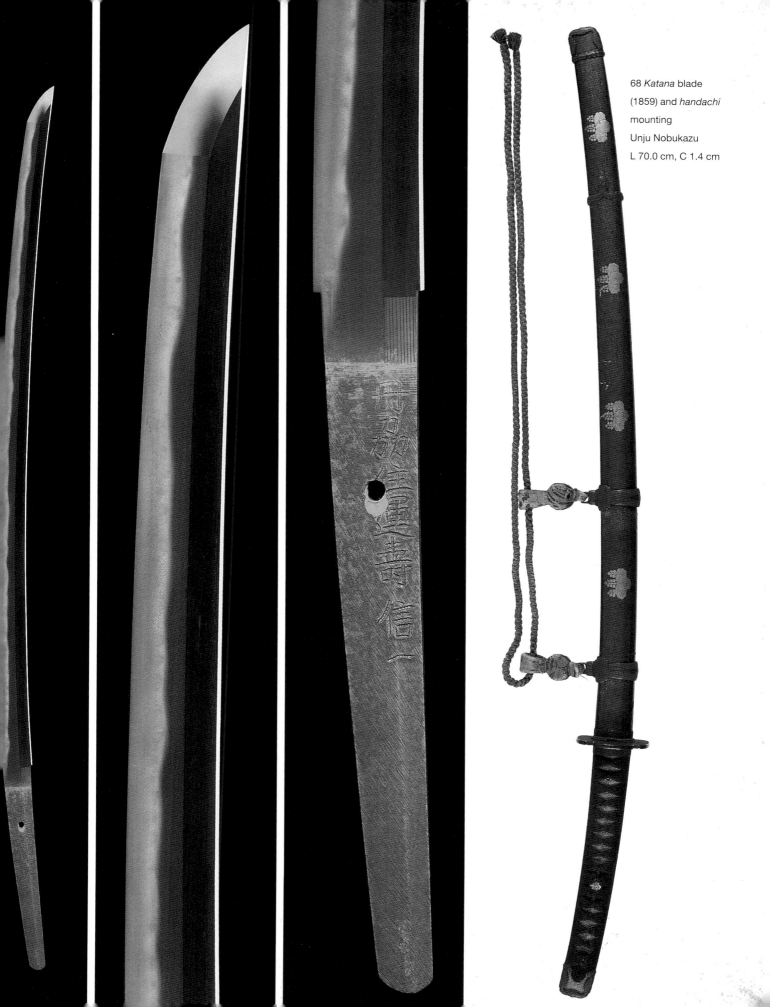

68 *Katana* blade
(1859) and *handachi*
mounting
Unju Nobukazu
L 70.0 cm, C 1.4 cm

備前介運壽信一

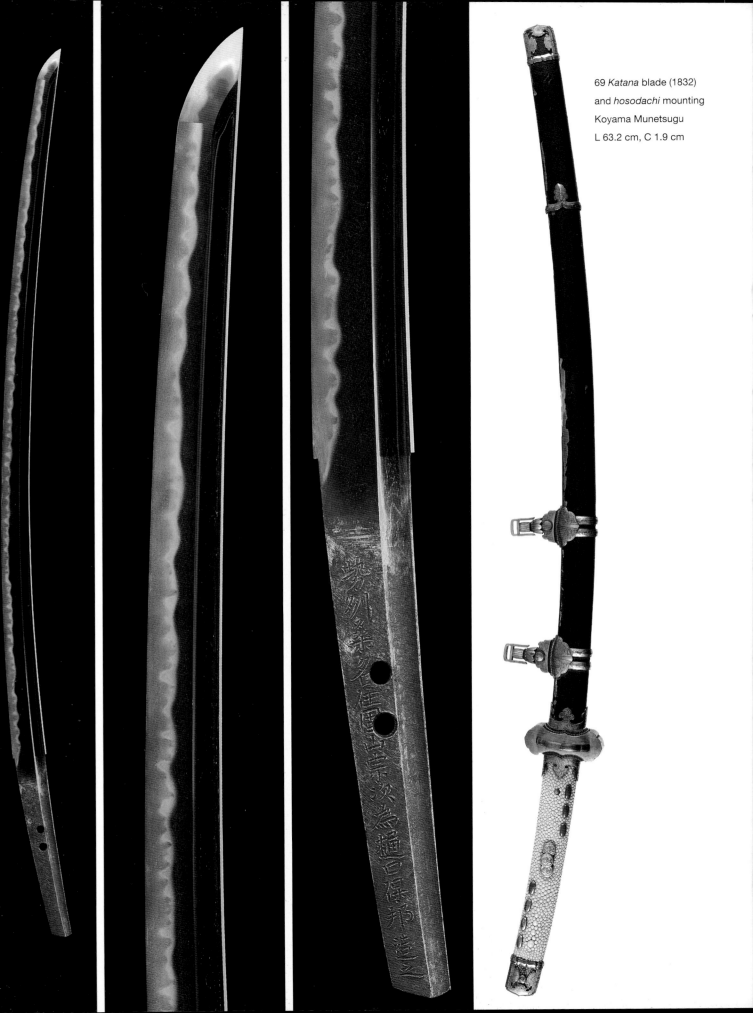

69 *Katana* blade (1832)
and *hosodachi* mounting
Koyama Munetsugu
L 63.2 cm, C 1.9 cm

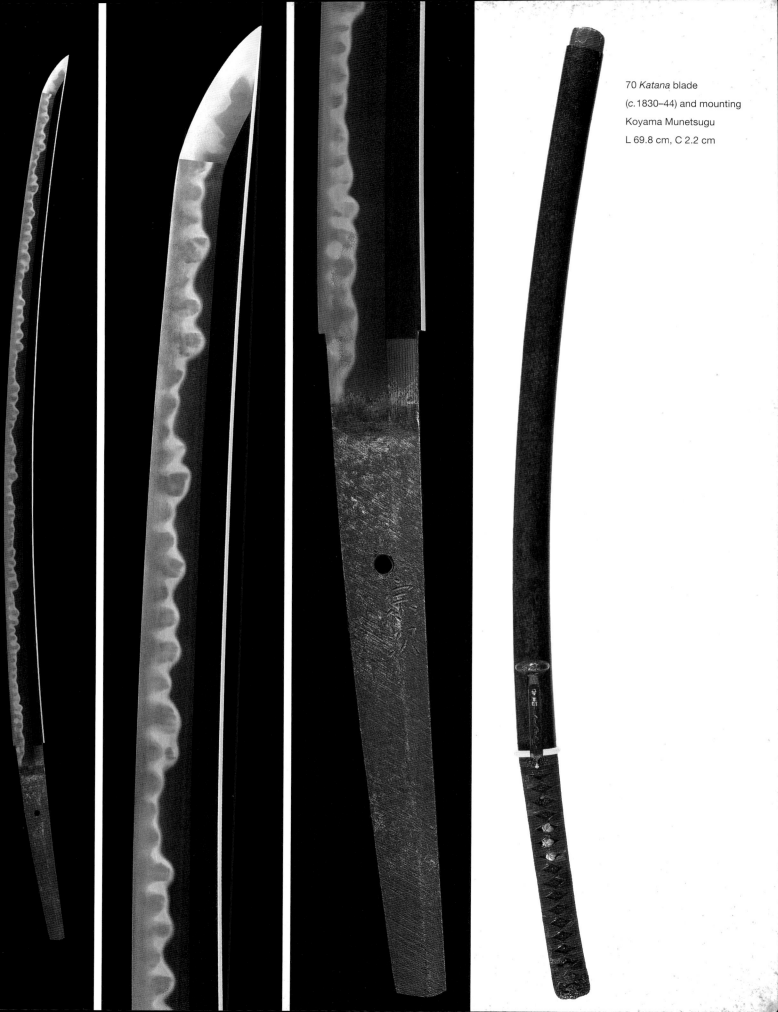

70 *Katana* blade
(*c.*1830–44) and mounting
Koyama Munetsugu
L 69.8 cm, C 2.2 cm

71 *Wakizashi* blade
(1865) and mounting
Koyama Munetsugu
L 36.7 cm, C 0.6cm

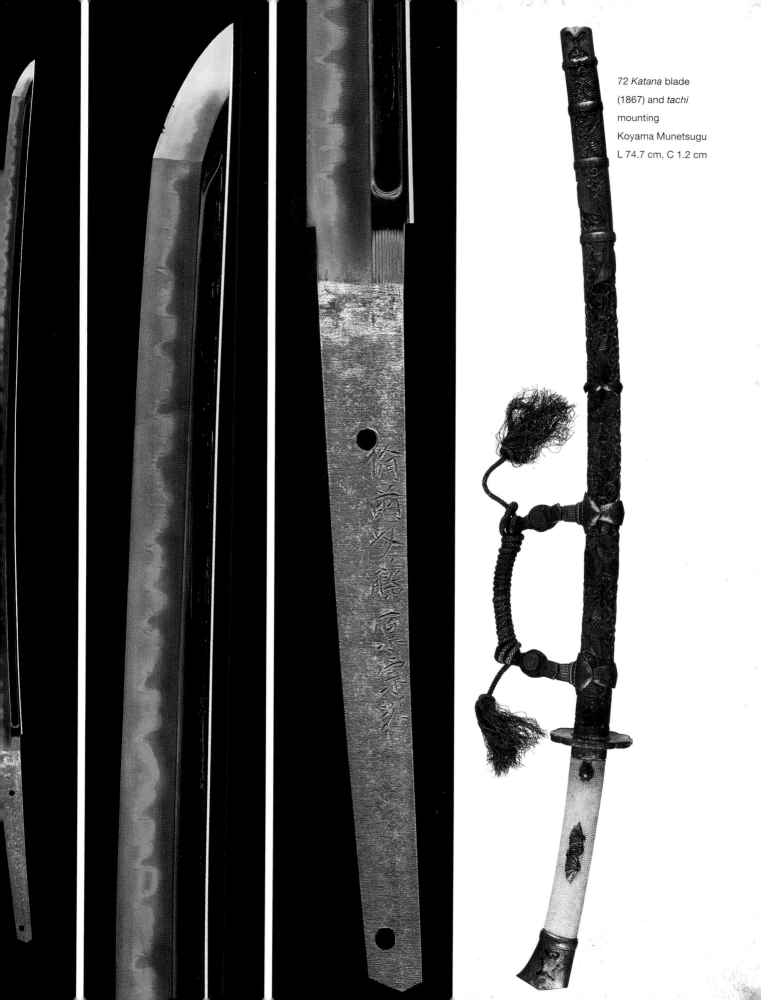

72 *Katana* blade
(1867) and *tachi*
mounting
Koyama Munetsugu
L 74.7 cm, C 1.2 cm

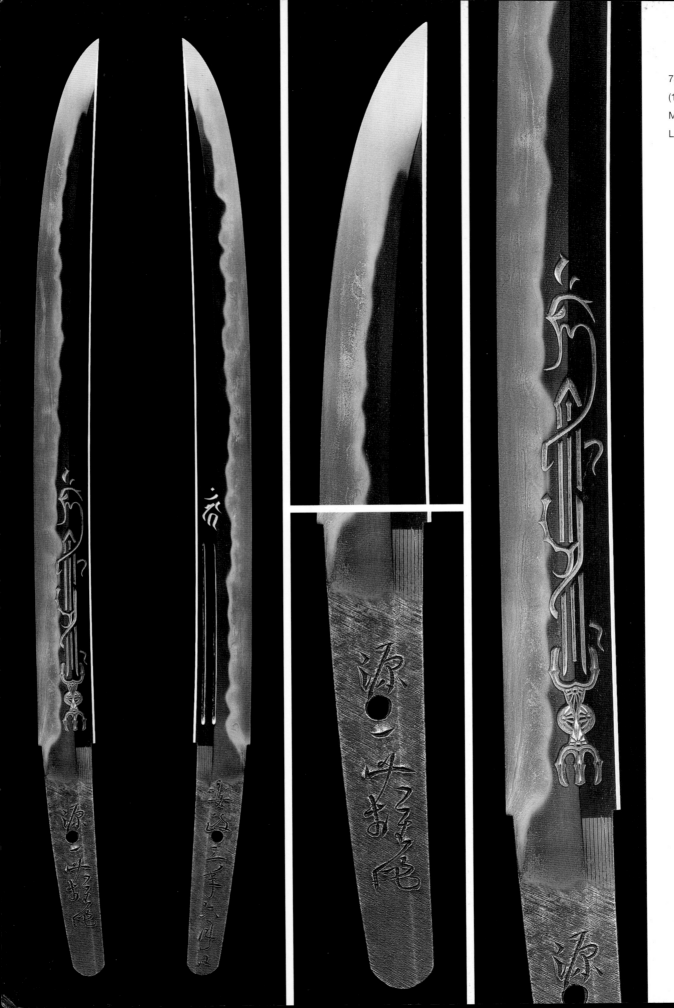

73 *Wakizashi* blade
(1856)
Minamoto Masao
L 35.4 cm, C 0.3 cm

74 *Wakizashi* blade (1849)
and mounting
Shimizu Hisayoshi
L 54.4 cm, C 0.9 cm

75 (left) *Tantō* blade
(1865) and mounting
Minamoto Yoshimune
L 23.0 cm

76 (right) *Tantō* blade
(1865) and mounting
Hisayuki
L 25.2 cm, C 0.1 cm

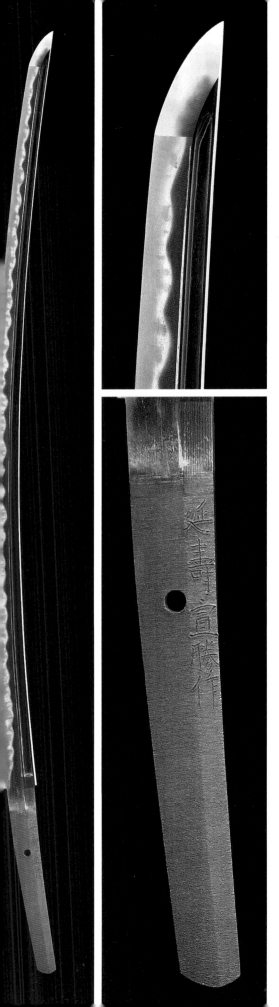

77 (left) *Katana* blade
(1842)
Enju Nobukatsu (d. 1871)
L 80.2 cm, C 2.5 cm

78 (right) *Tantō* blade
(1869) and mounting
Naokatsu
L 15.1 am, C (*uchi zori*)

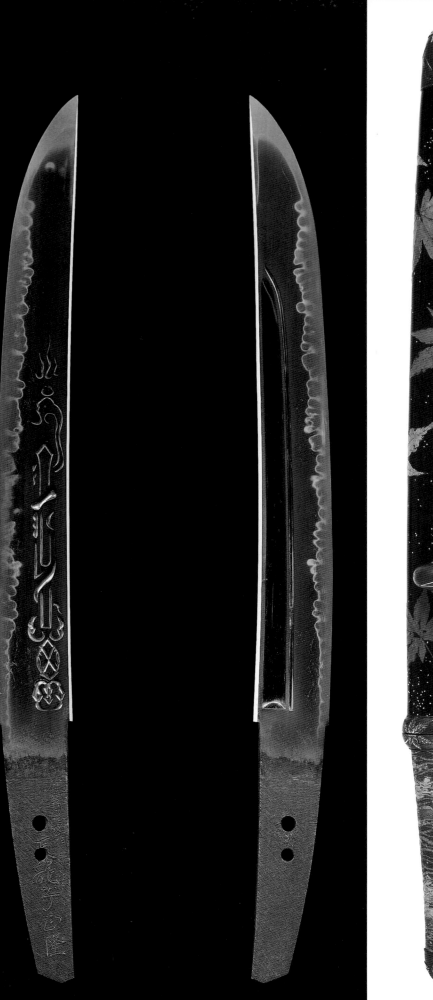

79 *Tantō* blade
and mounting
Tenryūshi Masataka
(19th century)
L 27.4 cm, C 0.4 cm

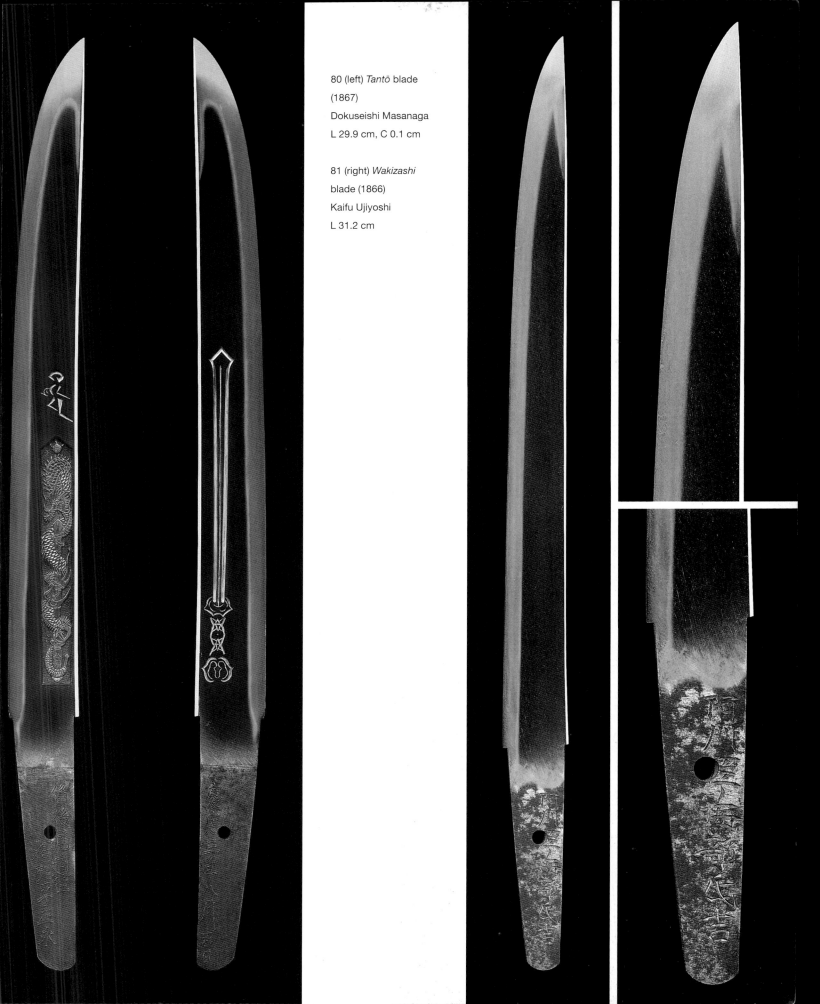

80 (left) *Tantō* blade
(1867)
Dokuseishi Masanaga
L 29.9 cm, C 0.1 cm

81 (right) *Wakizashi*
blade (1866)
Kaifu Ujiyoshi
L 31.2 cm

82 *Katana* blade (1860)
and mounting
Katsuyama Yoshinori
L 63.2 cm, C 2.0 cm

美濃住揚真武誠

83 *Katana* blade
Suishinshi Nobutaka
(19th century)
L 75.4 cm, C 1.4 cm

84 *Tantō* blade (1869)
and mounting
Minamoto Sadakazu
L 19.1 cm, C (*uchi zori*)

85 *Wakizashi* blade
and mounting
Unsigned
(17th or 18th century)
L 46.2 cm, C 1.0 cm

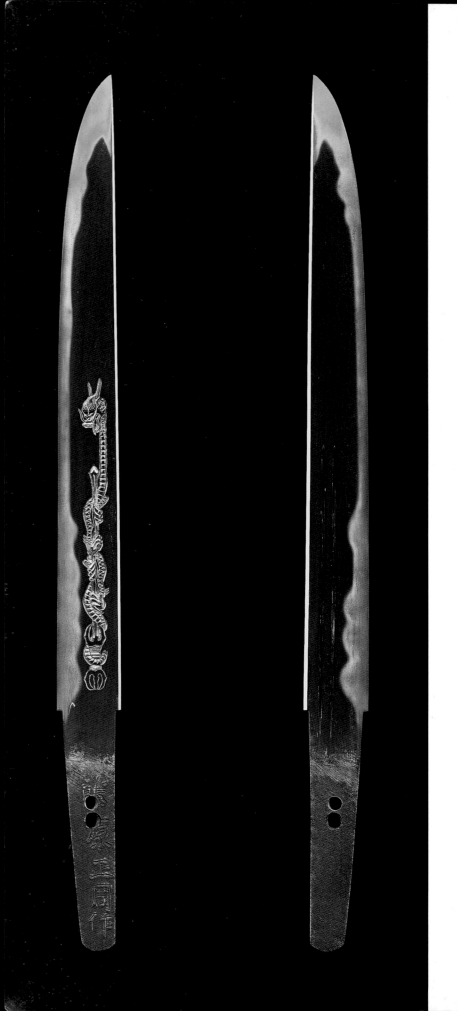

86 *Tantō* blade
and mounting
Fujiwara Masachika
(19th century)
L 24.0 cm, C (*uchi zori*)

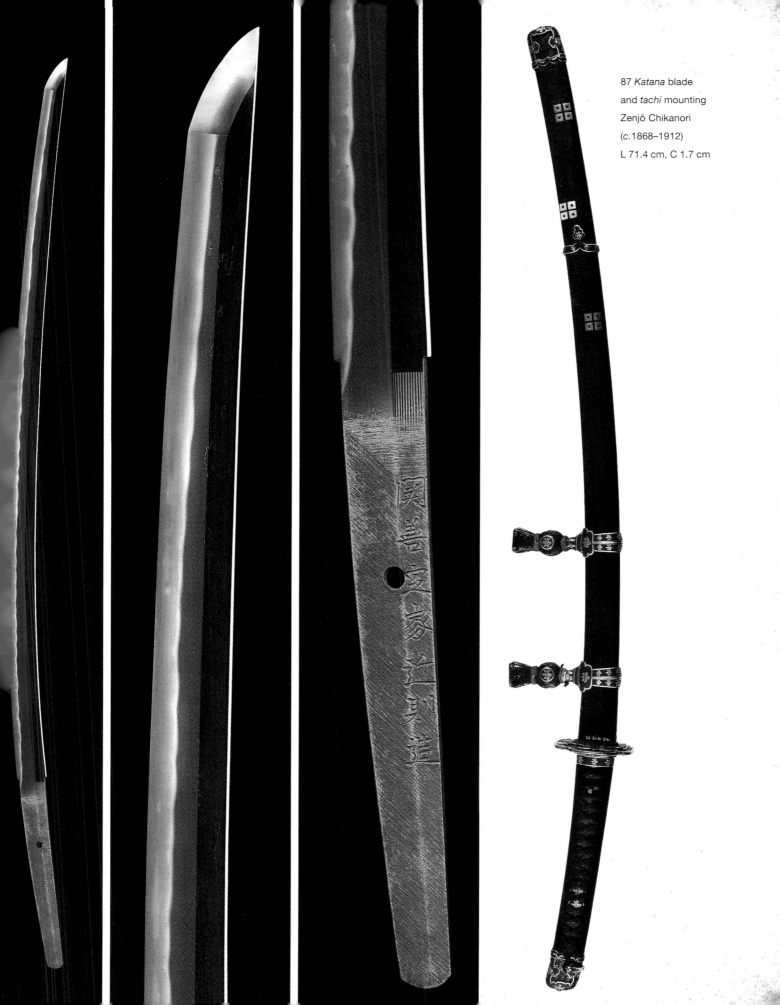

87 *Katana* blade
and *tachi* mounting
Zenjō Chikanori
(*c*.1868–1912)
L 71.4 cm, C 1.7 cm

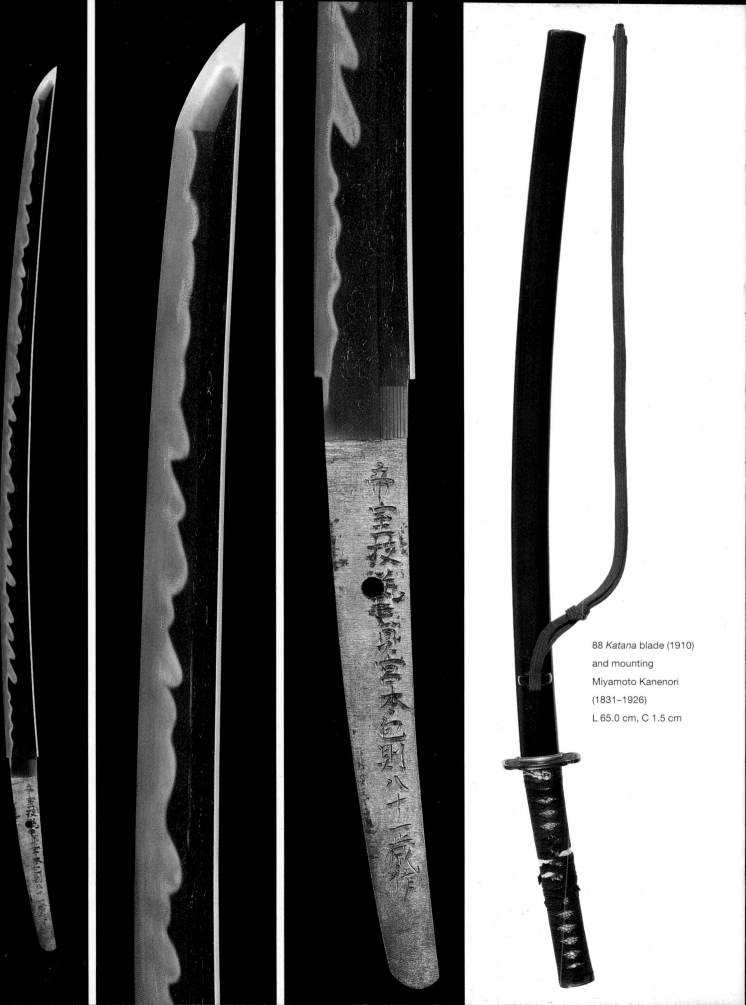

88 *Katana* blade (1910)
and mounting
Miyamoto Kanenori
(1831–1926)
L 65.0 cm, C 1.5 cm

89 *Katana* blade (1913)
and sabre mounting
Minamoto Kaneharu
L 63.7 cm, C 1.8 cm

90 *Wakizashi* mounting
19th century

91 (left) *Tantō* mounting
19th century

92 (right) *Tantō* mounting
19th century

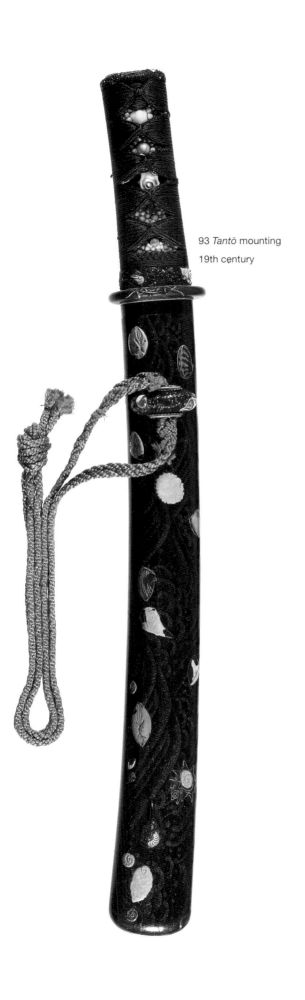

93 *Tantō* mounting
19th century

94 (right) *Tantō*
mounting (two views)
19th century

95 *Tantō* mounting
19th century

96 *Wakizashi* mounting
19th century

97 *Tantō* mounting
19th century

98 (right) *Katana* mounting
(matching pair with no. 99)
19th century

99 (far right) *Wakizashi*
mounting (matching pair
with no. 98)
19th century

Glossary

aikuchi (meeting mouths) A type of sword mounting without a *tsuba*.

aranie Coarse *nie*.

ashi (legs) Lines falling perpendicularly from the *hamon* towards the cutting edge.

ashigaru (light foot) An infantryman, not of samurai class, in the large armies of the Period of the Warring Provinces (*sengoku jidai*) in the 15th to 16th centuries.

ayasugi hada (cryptomeria twill skin) A sinusoidal grain pattern.

Bakufu Shogunal government by samurai.

banzashi (duty wear) A formal style of *daishō*, the matching pair of long and short swords, with black-lacquered scabbard and black metal fittings.

Bizen zori (Bizen curve) A description of the type of curve found particularly in early and middle Kamakura-period blades, whereby the bottom part of the blade exhibits a deep curve that straightens out towards the top. See also *koshi zori*.

bō utsuri (bar reflection) A straight form of *utsuri* found especially on Nambokuchō-period swords of the Aoe school and on Ōei-era (1394–1428) swords of the Bizen school.

bōhi (bar groove) A broad groove extending along the *shinogi ji* of the blade.

bōshi (cap) That portion of the *hamon* that turns back to meet the *mune* at the *kissaki* section.

bushi A member of the hereditary provincial military class, or samurai.

chikei (ground shadow) Bright lines of *nie* on the *ji* of the blade.

chirakashi makie (scattered *makie*) A style of *makie* application characterized by a contrived haphazard or sporadic appearance.

chirimen/chirimen hada (silk crêpe) A fine grain in a complex of round formations resembling silk crêpe.

chōji/chōji hamon (cloves) *Hamon* pattern resembling a row of packed clove buds.

chokutō A straight-bladed sword of the Kofun and Nara periods.

daimyō The lord of a province.

daishō (large and small) A matching pair of swords worn by samurai; see also *banzashi*.

efu-dachi Style of *tachi* mounting designated for palace guards.

fuchi An oval piece, usually metal, that fits round the blade over the end of the hilt next to the *tsuba*. It usually matches the *kashira* in material and decoration.

Fudō Myō-ō (the Unmoving) One of the five 'Kings of Light' deities of esoteric Buddhism.

fukuro chōji (bag *chōji*) An aspect of *chōji hamon* whereby the shape of the crests tends to flatten slightly, in the manner of upturned drawstring pouches.

fumbari (bottom or tenacity) A sudden widening of certain blades at the *koshi*.

fushi (thicket) Thickets in *hamon*, especially in the straight *hamon* of certain smiths of the Muromachi-period Mino school.

futasujibi Two narrow parallel grooves running the length of the blade.

Gempei wars Series of battles during a period of civil unrest in the 12th century, in which the Taira and Minamoto clans vied for precedence, culminating in a defeat for the imperial Taira faction at the battle of Dan-no-ura in 1185 and the subsequent establishment of the Minamoto shōgunate at Kamakura.

goban kaji Smiths who attended the sword-making Retired Emperor Gotoba-In in rotation.

gomabashi Carving in the form of two short parallel grooves representing Buddhist ritual tongs.

gunome An abruptly undulating form of *hamon*.

gunome chōji A type of *hamon* in which a basic *gunome* outline is traced with a small *chōji* pattern.

ha Hardened cutting edge of the blade.

ha agari A variety of *kurijiri* tang tip slanting more conspicuously on the side of the cutting edge.

habaki Collar that fits around the blade in front of the *tsuba*.

hada (skin) Surface steel of a blade; grain of a blade.

hadagane (skin steel) The outer layer of steel on a composite blade.

Haitōrei Governmental decree promulgated in 1876 prohibiting the wearing of swords in public without authorization.

haki (brushings) Wispy formations of *nie* sweeping along the *bōshi*.

hakikake (swept) A form of *bōshi* in which the *hamon* divides into fine lines that sweep up to meet the *mune*.

hako gunome *Hamon* with abrupt squarish undulations shaped like boxes.

hamachi Lower end of the sharp edge of a blade, where it abruptly narrows into the tang.

hamaguri ba (clam blade) A blade whose *hira ji* is of slightly convex cross-section, found on many blades up until the late Kamakura period.

hamon The crystalline pattern formed along the hardened edge of the blade.

hanabishi (floral lozenge) Tessellated design of rhomboids arranged as stylized petals of a flower, as found on *mon*.

handachi (half-*tachi*) A sword with metal fittings similar to a *tachi*, but worn through the belt like an *uchigatana*.

hi A groove carved along the length of a sword.

higaki Hatched file marks on a tang.

hijiki hada A *jihada* with thick bands of *jinie*, named after *hijiki*, a type of edible seaweed. See also *matsukawa*.

hira The 'flat' of a blade, i.e. the two opposing flat surfaces that meet to form the cutting edge.

hira ji (flat ground) The ground of the flat surfaces that meet to form the cutting edge of a blade.

hira zōgan Inlay work on sword-fittings that is level with the surface of the ground.

hira zukuri (flat make) Type of blade of triangular cross-section having no *shinogi*.

hitatsura A *hamon* that spreads into separate patches throughout the surface of the blade.

hitsuana The holes pierced through the *tsuba* to accommodate the blade and the passage of the *kozuka* and *kōgai*.

horimono Decorative, structural or religious carving on the blade of a sword.

hōrin (wheel of the law) Eight-spoked wheel signifying the Buddhist principle of Dharma.

hōshu (Buddhist 'treasure jewel') A Buddhist motif.

hosodachi (narrow *tachi*) Style of *tachi* mounting used by the court nobility.

hotsure (fraying) Lines of *nie* straying away from the *hamon* above and below, resembling frayed thread.

ichimai bōshi (single-sheet cap) A *bōshi* that fills the whole of the *kissaki* portion of the blade.

ichimonji (the character 'one') As found inscribed on work by the Ichimonji group of smiths, who flourished between the early Kamakura period and the Nambokuchō period. The appellation was first conferred on a selection of Bizen smiths by Retired Emperor Gotoba-In (1180–1239).

iebori (house carvers) Metal sword-fitting makers in the service of the Shogun during the Muromachi and Edo periods.

ikakeji An unburnished lacquer surface sprinkled overall, usually with gold particles.

ikubi kissaki (boar neck point) A stubby *kissaki* found on broad-bladed work of the middle Kamakura period.

inazuma (lightning) Lines of *nie* through and around the *hamon*.

inrō kizami Ribbed carving on scabbards and shafts resembling the shape of some *inrō* (medicine or seal containers).

iriyamagata Type of tang tip when the portion of the tang above the *shinogi* is perpendicular or nearly perpendicular to the *shinogi*, and that below the *shinogi* is at an obtuse angle to the lower edge of the tang.

ishime The stone-ground effect on metal sword fittings.

ishizuki The chape on a *tachi* scabbard.

itame (wood-plank grain) Type of grain on a blade resembling the cross-section of timber cut aslant.

ito maki no tachi A *tachi* mounting bound with braid on both the hilt and the upper part of the scabbard to prevent abrasion of the lacquer against armour.

ji (ground) The steel surface of a blade; *shinogi ji* refers to the surfaces of the region above the *shinogi*, and *hira ji* to the surfaces below, which meet at an angle forming the cutting edge.

jifu (ground spots) Patches of *nie* on the *ji*.

jigane (ground steel) See *ji*.

jihada (ground skin) See *hada*.

jinie *Nie* on the *ji* of the blade.

Jizō bōshi A *bōshi* rounded in a form resembling the shaven head of the Bodhisattva Jizō.

jūka chōji (banked *chōji*) A broad *hamon* with densely packed banks of *chōji*.

juzuba Type of *hamon* in the form of the row of beads of a rosary.

kabukimono Subcultural group of discontents, mainly *rōnin*, that emerged during the early Edo period.

kabuto gane (helmet metal) The *kashira* on a *tachi* mounting.

kaerizuno (return horn) Horn-shaped projection below the *kurikata* on an *uchigatana* mounting, preventing the scabbard from slipping upwards.

kage sukashi (shadow piercing) Pierced sculpture in negative silhouette.

kakinagashi Style of *hi* where the lower end tapers away.

kakitōshi Style of *hi* that continues through the end of the tang.

Kambun shintō Swords of shallow curve narrowing towards the point in a style established around the Kambun era (1661–73).

kami The gods of the Shintō religion.

kammuri otoshi (crown drop) Type of dagger blade shape with a partial double edge, and a distinctively shaped *shinogi ji*.

kani no tsume (crab's claws) Type of *hamon* in which the crests of the *gunome* break into pincer-like formations.

kaō An inscribed mark unique to a specific metalworker or swordsmith, often an illegible quasi-cursive character.

Kara [Chinese] **tsuba** A style of tsuba used on *hosodachi*.

kasane The thickness of a blade measured between the *shinogi* on the *ura* and *omote*.

kashira The pommel of a sword hilt, usually metal or horn.

katakiri bori Method of decorative carving with a chisel held at an oblique angle so as to vary the section and depth of the cut to simulate brush painting.

katakiri ha Blade shape perfectly flat on one side, and with a wide *shinogi ji* on the other, so that the *hira ji* slopes down abruptly from the *shinogi* to the cutting edge.

katana (sword) Any sword in general, but by convention those single-edged curved swords over 60 cm in length intended to be worn inserted through the belt with the cutting edge downwards.

kataochi gunome An aspect of *gunome* whereby the *hamon* slants downwards on one side to meet the valleys.

katte sagari File marks sloping slightly down towards the back of the tang.

kawarigata zukuri (of unusual shape) Any form of blade shape that does not fall into the categories *shinogi zukuri*, *hira zukuri*, *naginata zukuri*, *kogarasu maru zukuri*, etc.

kawazu no ko chōji (tadpole *chōji*) A *hamon* with high, round-ended *chōji* resembling the heads of tadpoles.

kazari byō Decorative pin or rivet head.

kazari tachi A decorative *tachi* mounting used at court from the Nara period until recent times.

kazu no ko nie (herring row *nie*) Large spherical form of *nie*.

kazu uchi mono (things made in numbers) Poor-quality swords made in large numbers during the Muromachi period.

ken A straight double-edged blade, primarily made for esoteric Buddhist ritual.

kendō (Way of the Sword) The spiritual study of swordplay.

kengyō (*ken* sword shape) Triangular tip of a tang.

kenuki gata tachi (tweezer-shaped sword) A form of *tachi* of the Heian period whose tang is shaped into the form of the hilt; the tang is pierced with a longitudinal hole that resembles opposed tweezers.

keshō (cosmetic) File marks forming narrow bands at different angles at the broad part of a tang.

kijimata (pheasant's thigh) A tang shape found on certain Heian- and Kamakura-period *tachi*.

kinsuji Usually applied to lines of *nie* similar to, yet shorter than, *inazuma* in the *hamon*.

kiri (cut) Horizontal file marks or a square-ended tang shape.

kissaki Point section of a blade.

kobushi gata chōji (fist-shaped *chōji*) A *hamon* devised by Kawachi no kami Kunisuke.

kōgai A kind of bodkin carried in a pocket at the side of the scabbard.

kogarasu maru zukuri Type of sword with a double edge extending partway along the blade, named after the sword called 'Kogarasu Maru' (Little Crow) in the collection of the imperial household.

koitame Small *itame* grain.

kojiri The chape of a scabbard.

komaru A small round return of the *bōshi*.

komidare Small *midare hamon*.

komokume Small *mokume hada*.

kongōtai The 'diamond', or ultimately real world, as opposed to the illusory world of human understanding.

konie Small or fine *nie*.

konuka hada (rice flour *hada*) A fine form of *itame* grain found on swords of Hizen Province during the Edo period, named after rice-based facial washing grains.

koshi (waist) Lower portion of a blade, just above the hilt.

koshi zori (waist curve) A curve that deepens distinctly at the *koshi* of the sword, found on most swords of the late Heian to middle Kamakura periods, some Muromachi-period swords and some *shinshintō* blades.

koshigatana (waist sword) An early term for a short sword or dagger.

koshihi (waist groove) A short groove carved along the *shinogi ji* near the *koshi*.

kotō (old swords) Swords made before the start of the Keichō era (1596), cf. *shintō*.

kozuka (small hilt) The rectangular hilt of the small knife kept in a pocket at the side of the scabbard.

kuchi kanamono (mouth metal piece) The collar fitting at the mouth of a *tachi* scabbard.

kuichigai/kuichigaiba Discontinuous sections of overlapping *hamon*.

kuidashi (eaten away) Short *wakizashi* under 30 cm in length.

kurijiri (chestnut base) Gently rounded tip of a tang.

kurikara Emblem carved on the blade of some swords in the form of a dragon coiled around a *ken*-type sword, representing the sword and rope of the deity Fudō Myō-ō. The style of sculpture is described as *shin* (true) carved roundly in *ukibori*, *gyō* (going) carved in outline, and *sō* (grass) carved as a negative impression.

kurikata (chestnut shape) The small protrusion on the side of *uchigatana* mountings pierced with a hole to take the *sageo* cord.

kuwagata (hoe shape) The horn-like crests often mounted at the front of the helmet, and also a *horimono* on sword blades.

kyō sukashi A school of pierced-iron *tsuba* makers associated with Kyoto during the Momoyama and Edo periods.

machi The boundary between the tang and cutting edge (*hamachi*), and that between the tang and back of the blade (*munemachi*).

machibori (town carvers) The studios of decorative sword-fitting makers, who became established around the end of the seventeenth century in the towns independently of the *iebori* tradition.

makie (sprinkled illustration) A method of decoration by sprinkling gold or other metallic dust onto lacquer before it sets hard.

martensite The hardest structure in quench-hardened steel, formed of an iron super-saturated with carbon.

marumune A *mune* that is rounded in cross-section.

masame A parallel longitudinal grain.

masu Box used to measure volumes of rice, and other grain and liquids.

matsukawa (pine bark) A distinctive form of *hada* similar to *hijiki hada*, characteristic of the work of the Nambokuchō-period smith Norishige of Etchū Province.

mekugi The peg that passes through the hilt and a hole (*mekugi ana*) in the tang to secure the blade in the hilt.

menuki Ornamental metal pieces positioned either side of the hilt.

mete zashi (horse-hand sword) A dagger worn at the right side of the waist with the cutting edge forward, and used to cut upwards under the armour.

midare komaru A *bōshi* that undulates away from the edge on a *komaru* return.

midare komi A *bōshi* that undulates away from the edge.

midare utsuri An undulating irregular form of *utsuri* of varying width.

midareba A *hamon* of wild or uncontrolled form.

midokoro-mono (things of three places) Matching set of *kōgai*, *kozuka* and *menuki*.

mihaba Blade width, as measured from the back to the cutting edge.

mitsumune A *mune* of truncated triangular form, also sometimes known as *shin no mune*

mizukage A crystalline formation similar to *utsuri* appearing at about 45 degrees to the edge of the blade around the *hamachi* on blades of certain schools and on blades that have been heat-treated at some time after

their original manufacture, when the original hardness has been lost due to fire or excessive wear (see *saiba*).

mokkō A quatrefoil *tsuba* shape deriving from the shape of the quince.

mokume (wood grain) A grain formed of masses of concentric loops.

mon A family crest, used on clothing, arms, furniture and other accessories.

monouchi (hitting part) The part of the cutting edge of a long sword that is about a quarter of the way down from the *kissaki* of an *uchigatana* and is regarded as the most efficient place to cut.

moroha A double-edged blade.

mune The back of the blade.

muneyaki Patches of hardened steel along the *mune* of the blade.

mura nashiji (thicket *nashiji*) *Nashiji* in which the gold filings fall together in distinct thickets.

nagamaki A long-bladed, single-edged pole-arm similar to a *naginata* and used particularly during the Nambokuchō and Muromachi periods.

naginata A glaive-like pole-arm with a single-edged blade that swells and curves deeply towards the point.

naginata hi A particular form of *hi* found on *naginata*, shorter than *bōhi* and often accompanied by a *soehi*.

naginata naoshi A sword fashioned from a *naginata* by cutting away the deeply curved back of the upper part of the blade and shortening the tang.

namazu hada (catfish *hada*) Dark splashes of *nie* on the *hira ji*, a distinctive form of *jifu*.

nanako (fish roe) The raised stippled effect on metalwork produced by a hollow-ended punch.

nashiji (pear skin) A grain of close-packed *mokume*. Also an effect obtained by sprinkling gold or other powder onto lacquer.

nie A metallurgical structure on a blade in which the crystals are individually visible to the naked eye, traditionally described as having the appearance of frost on grass or a cluster of stars on a clear night.

nijūba (double *hamon*) A *hamon*, usually *suguha*, forming a double line in places.

nioi A metallurgical structure whereby the steel crystals are not individually discernible with the naked eye but appear as a visible white line, traditionally likened to the appearance of the Milky Way, morning mist or the colour of blossoms on distant trees.

nioiguchi The line defining the edge of the *hamon* on a blade.

nodachi (moor sword) A very long sword favoured during the Nambokuchō period, also known as a *seoi dachi* .

notare (undulating) Wavy form of *hamon*.

nunome zōgan (textile inlay) A variety of inlay whereby gold or silver is thinly hammered onto a ground that has been hatched to give the appearance of woven textile.

ōitame Large *itame* grain on a blade.

ōmaru Large round return of the *bōshi* on a blade.

omodaka A water plant with three-petalled flowers, as seen represented on *mon*.

omote Side of a sword or *tsuba* that is visible when the sword is worn; cf. *ura*.

origane A form of *kurikata* made of metal.

oroshi mune A blade cross-section that narrows from the *shinogi* towards the *mune*, developed during the Muromachi period.

ōseppa (large *seppa*) Additional spacer fitted between the *seppa* and the *tsuba* on *tachi* mountings.

ōsujigai Deeply sloping file marks on a tang.

ōsuriage Substantial *suriage*, where the whole of the original tang has been removed.

rōnin (wave man) A masterless samurai.

sageo A braided cord used to tie the *uchigatana* in place at the belt.

saiba/saiha A blade that has been re-hardened by heat treatment some time after its original manufacture due to having lost its temper in a fire or through having been severely reshaped.

saka chōji (reverse *chōji*) A sloping *chōji hamon*.

sakagakari gunome A form of slanted *gunome hamon*, though not as vivid as *kataochi*.

saki zori A curve that deepens in the upper part of the blade, developed during the Muromachi period.

sambon sugi (three cryptomerias) A *hamon* resembling a row of three grouped cryptomeria treetops.

sampin bōshi A shape of *bōshi* found on work of the Sampin, or Mishina family.

satetsu (sand iron) An iron sand ore.

semegane Reinforcing metal bands on a *tachi* scabbard.

sensuki Marks on a tang made with a shaving tool or chisel rather than with a file.

seoi dachi (sword carried on the back) Very long swords of the Nambokuchō period, otherwise called *nodachi*.

seppa Oval copper spacers fitted either side of the *tsuba*.

seppuku Ritual suicide by cutting open the abdomen, also known as *hara-kiri*.

shaku Traditional unit of linear measurement equivalent to 30.3 cm.

shakudō An alloy of copper that has a few per cent of gold and traces of other elements found in *yamagane*, and can be patinated to a range of lustrous blacks and purple blacks.

shibuichi (one part in four) An alloy of three-quarters copper and one-quarter silver that was used by the *machibori* artists, and can be patinated to produce a range of colours from silver, through grey, to a variety of browns.

shinchū A form of brass.

shingane (heart steel) Inner core of resilient steel in a composite blade.

shinobi ana An additional peg hole on the tang, located near the tang tip.

shinogi The longitudinal line dividing the parallel-sided portion (*shinogi ji*) of the blade from the *hira ji*.

shinogi ji Flat surface of steel on a sword occupying the region between the *shinogi* and *mune*.

shinshintō (new, new swords) Swords of the late Edo period made in conscious revival of early styles.

shintō (new swords) Swords made after the Muromachi period, and by convention after the beginning of the Keichō era (1596), as opposed to *kotō*, made before then.

Shintō The indigenous religion of deities of nature and creation.

shirake (whiteness) A white cloudy mark along the blade resembling *utsuri*, but not in any distinct form. Found on many early blades of the Kyūshū schools and on Seki blades of the Muromachi period.

shirasaya (white scabbard) Plain wooden hilt and scabbard to preserve the blade when not mounted for use. Also called *yasumizaya* (resting scabbard).

shishi Leonine beasts from Chinese art.

shishiai-bori Carving in sunken relief.

shōjō Red-haired drunken sprites.

Shugendō The 'mountain religion' containing elements from Buddhism and Shintō and numbering many swordsmiths among its adherents during the *kotō* era.

sō no kurikara See *kurikara*.

soehi (accompanying groove) A narrow groove carved immediately under a *bōhi* along the length of a sword.

sōhei Buddhist warrior monks.

sokutō (bundled swords) Mass-produced blades made during the Period of the Warring Provinces, also called *kazu uchi mono*.

sōryū (twin dragon) The motif of a pair of dragons, as found on *horimono* of some blades.

sudareba A form of layered *hamon* resembling a *sudare*, a hanging screen of horizontal bamboo strips.

sue (late) Applied to the later generations of a swordmaking tradition.

suguha A straight *hamon*.

sujigai Angled file marks on a tang.

suken The 'simple sword', motif of a double-edged sword used in outline in *horimono*.

sukidashi bori (scooped-out carving) Carving made by cutting the ground away to leave the design modelled on the remaining high parts.

sumi hada (charcoal *hada*) Dark patches of steel that appear to be sunk into the jihada.

sun Unit of linear measurement equal to one tenth of a *shaku*, equivalent to 3.03 cm.

sunagashi (drifting sand) Lines of *nie* crystals forming thick longitudinal lines within the *hamon*.

sunnobi (extended in length) Usually applied to a *tantō* more than one *shaku* (30.3cm) in length.

suriage Practice of cutting down very long swords to a more convenient length.

tachi A general term for a long sword, but applied specifically to swords made to be suspended loosely from the belt with the cutting edge downwards.

taka no ha (hawk's feather) File marks on a tang that slant away from the *shinogi* in opposite directions, like a feather.

takamakie *Makie* lacquer designs applied and sculpted in high relief.

tameshi-giri (trial cuts) Cutting tests that were designed to prove the quality of swords and were conducted during the early Edo period on straw bundles, armour components or the bodies of condemned criminals.

tanago bara (bitterling belly). A tang shape resembling the belly of the bitterling fish, found on swords made by the smith Muramasa of Ise.

tantō (short sword) A dagger.

tawara byō The characteristic *tawara* (rice bale) shape of the heads of pins used to fix the tang into the hilt on Heian-period *tachi*, surviving as purely symbolic decorative pieces on some later *tachi*.

teishitsu gigei-in (imperial craftsman) A system instituted in 1890, whereby selected artists and craftsmen were designated Imperial Craftsmen under the patronage of the imperial household.

tobiyaki (flying *hamon*) Closed, rounded formations seen on the *ji* of a blade, away from the *hamon*, but of the same quality of crystalline steel as the *hamon*.

togariba (pointed *hamon*) A form of *gunome* with pointed crests.

togidashi makie (polished-out *makie*) Form of *makie* in which a design laid upon lacquer is covered by further layers of lacquer, which are then partly polished away to reveal the design on an even surface.

tomoe Comma-shaped motif, occurring usually in twos or threes and linked within a circular outline.

tōramba (billowing) *Hamon* resembling sea waves.

tsuba Guard of a sword.

tsuba katana General name used in the Edo period for those short swords with a *tsuba*, also known as *chisa katana*, that had previously been known as *koshigatana*.

tsuishu Style of lacquerwork that originated in China, whereby alternating layers of coloured lacquer (usually red and black, sometimes also green and yellow) have been applied and cut through in the outline of a design, usually floral, to reveal the laminated underlying layers.

tsuki ni kumo (clouds beneath a moon) *Tobiyaki* formation sometimes found on *bōshi*.

ubuha (original blade) A sword that has been polished only once or a few times, so that a few centimetres of original blunt edge remain close to the *hamachi*.

uchi noke Small upward-pointing, crescent-shaped formations along the *hamon* of a blade.

uchi zori (inner curve) A slight downward curve in a blade, found mainly on daggers of the middle Kamakura period.

uchigatana (hitting sword) A sword meant for making strong cuts on foot, as opposed to the wheeling cuts of the cavalryman's *tachi*.

ude nuke ana Two holes pierced through a *tsuba* to carry a cord that retains the blade in the scabbard.

ukibori Carving in sunken relief.

uma no ha gunome (horse-tooth *gunome*) A form of abruptly undulating *hamon* resembling a row of horse's teeth, also called *hako gunome*.

umabari (horse needle) Broad, double-edged steel implement, sometimes kept in the pocket of a scabbard in place of a *kōgai*. Its special function was to do minor emergency surgery on horses' legs.

u-no-kubi (cormorant's neck) A dagger of shape similar to that of a *kammuri otoshi*.

ura The side of a sword or *tsuba* that is opposite to the *omote* and not visible when the sword is worn.

utsuri (reflection) A distinct white shadow along the *ji*, sometimes of a regular, wavy, continuous form, like a reflection of the *hamon*.

vajra Pronged implement of esoteric Buddhist imagery representing aspects of the Buddhist law.

wakizashi (side/companion sword) Shorter of a *daishō* pair of swords.

wari-kōgai *Kōgai* split longitudinally into two pieces to form chopsticks, or tongs.

'whale's beard' Bristles extracted from the baleen of certain whales and used for binding the hilts of swords.

yaguragane Triangular metal pieces to which the suspending cords of a *tachi* are fitted.

yakidashi Lower end of a complex *hamon* that straightens into *suguha* on *shintō* blades of some Edo schools and slopes down to the *hamachi* on *shintō* blades of some Ōsaka schools.

yakiire Operation of quenching a heated blade in water to harden the edge, producing the *hamon*.

yakitsume A form of *bōshi* in which the *hamon* ends at the *mune* without turning back.

yamabushi An adherent of the Shugendō sect.

yamagane (mountain metal) A crude copper containing small amounts of impurities, which are responsible both for the characteristic patina that develops on *yamagane* and the alloy *shakudō*.

yari A pike or spear used to cut and thrust, but never thrown.

yasurime File marks on the tang.

yō (leaves) Discrete patches within the *hamon*, similar to *ashi* but separate from the line of the *hamon*.

yō sukashi Pierced work in positive silhouette.

yokote On a sword, the line perpendicular to the *mune* defining the boundary of the *hira ji* and the triangular *kissaki* sections.

yoroi dōshi (armour piercer) A thick-bladed *hira zukuri* dagger.

yozakura (evening cherry) Minutely raised designs on lacquer or metal, which are so faint that they can only be seen in strong light.

zukuri (make or form) For example, *shinogi zukuri* – a blade having a *shinogi*.

Further Reading

This list covers books in English only.

DOBRÉE, A., *Japanese Sword Blades*, Edgware, 1967 (reprinted from *The Archaeological Journal*, vol. XLII, 1905)

EARLE, J. (trans.), *The Japanese Sword*, Tokyo, 1983 (translation of K. Satō, *Tōken*, Nihon no Bijutsu Series No. 6, Tokyo, 1966)

HARRIS, V. and N. OGASAWARA, *Swords of the Samurai*, London, 1990

HAWLEY, W. H., *Japanese Swordsmiths*, California, 1966

INAMI, H., *Nippon-Tō, the Japanese Sword*, Tokyo, 1948

IRVINE, G. *The Japanese Sword: The Soul of the Samurai*, London, 2000

JOLY, H. L. and H. INADA, *Sword and Samé*, London, 1913

MISHINA, K. (trans.), *The Connoisseur's Book of Japanese Swords*, Tokyo, New York and London, 1997 (translation of K. Nagayama, *Tōken Kantei Tokubon*, Tokyo, 1995)

OGASAWARA, N., *Japanese Swords*, Osaka, 1970

OGAWA, M., *Nippon-Tō: Art Swords of Japan*, New York, 1976

OGAWA, M., *Japanese Swords and Sword Furniture in the Museum of Fine Arts, Boston*, Tokyo, 1987

OGAWA, M., *Japanese Master Swordsmiths: The Gassan Tradition*, Museum of Fine Arts, Boston, 1989

ROBINSON, B.W., *The Arts of the Japanese Sword*, London, 1961

SINCLAIRE, C., *Samurai: The Weapons and Spirit of the Japanese Warrior*, London, 2001

YOSHIHARA, Y., L. KAPP and H. KAPP, *The Craft of the Japanese Sword*, Tokyo, New York and San Francisco, 1987

Place Names with their Present-Day Locations

Ashū (or Awa Province): Tokushima Prefecture

Awa Province (or Ashū): Tokushima Prefecture

Awataguchi (of Heian-kyō, in Yamashiro Province): Awataguchi of Kyoto City, Kyoto Prefecture

Bingo Province (in Bishū): eastern part of Hiroshima Prefecture

Bishū (Bingo, Bitchū and Bizen Provinces): eastern part of Hiroshima Prefecture and western and south-eastern parts of Okayama Prefecture

Bitchū Province (in Bishū): western part of Okayama Prefecture

Bizen Province (in Bishū): south-eastern part of Okayama Prefecture

Bungo Province (in Hōshū): southern part of Ōita Prefecture

Bushū (or Musashi Province): Tokyo, Saitama Prefecture and the eastern part of Kanagawa Prefecture

Buzen Province (in Hōshū): eastern part of Fukuoka Prefecture and northern part of Ōita Prefecture

Dewa Province (or Ushū): Akita and Yamagata Prefectures

Echizen Province (in Esshū): northern part of Fukui Prefecture

Edo (in Musashi Province, Bushū): Tokyo

Esshū (Echizen, Etchū and Echigo Provinces): northern part of Fukui Prefecture, Toyama Prefecture and mainland Niigata Prefecture

Etchū Province (in Esshū): Toyama Prefecture

Gashū (or Iga Province): western part of Mie Prefecture

Harima Province (or Banshū): south-western part of Hyōgo Prefecture

Heian-jō (or Heian-kyō, in Yamashiro Province): Kyoto City, in Kyoto Prefecture

Higo Province (in Hishū): Kumamoto Prefecture

Hishū (Higo and Hizen Provinces): Kumamoto and Nagasaki Prefectures

Hitachi Province (or Jōshū): western part of Ibaraki Prefecture and northern part of Chiba Prefecture

Hizen Province (in Hishū): Nagasaki and Saga Prefectures

Hōshū (Buzen and Bungo Provinces): eastern part of Fukuoka Prefecture and Ōita Prefecture

Hyūga Province (or Nisshū): Miyazaki Prefecture

Iga Province (or Gashū aka Ishū): western part of Mie Prefecture

Ise Province (or Seishū): northern and central part of Mie Prefecture

Iyo Province (or Yoshū): Ehime Prefecture

Izumi Province (or Senshū): south-western part of Osaka Prefecture

Izumo Province (or Unshū): eastern part of Shimane Prefecture

Kaga Province (or Kashū): southern part of Ishikawa Prefecture

Kawachi Province (or Kashū): eastern part of Osaka Prefecture

Kazusa Province (in Sōshū): northern part of Chiba Prefecture and western part of Ibaraki Prefecture

Kibi (Bizen, Bitchū, Bingo and Mimasaka Provinces): Okayama Prefecture and eastern part of Hiroshima Prefecture

Kii Province (or Kishū): Wakayama Prefecture and southern Mie Prefecture

Kōfu (or Edo): Tokyo

Kōzuke Province (or Jōshū): Gumma Prefecture

Mimasaka Province (or Sakushū): northern part of Okayama Prefecture

Mino Province (or Nōshū): southern part of Gifu Prefecture

Mito (in Hitachi Province): western part of Ibaraki Prefecture and northern part of Chiba Prefecture

Musashi Province (or Bushū): Tokyo, Saitama Prefecture and the eastern part of Kanagawa Prefecture

Mutsu Province (or Ōshū): Aomori, Iwate, Miyagi and Fukushima Prefectures

Nōshū (or Mino Province): southern part of Gifu Prefecture

Ōgaki (in Mino Province): Ōgaki, in the south-western part of Gifu Prefecture

Oki (island): Oki, off mainland Shimane Prefecture

Ōmi Province (or Gōshū): Shiga Prefecture

Osafune (in Bizen Province): Osafune, in the south-eastern part of Okayama Prefecture

Owari Province (or Bishū): western part of Aichi Prefecture

Sagami Province (or Sōshū): central and western part of Kanagawa Prefecture

Satsuma Province (or Sasshū): western part of Kagoshima Prefecture

Seki (in Mino Province): Seki, in the southern part of Gifu Prefecture

Shinano Province (or Shinshū): Nagano Prefecture

Sōshū (or Sagami Province): central and western part of Kanagawa Prefecture

Tamba Province (in Tanshū): central part of Kyoto Prefecture and central eastern part of Hyōgo Prefecture

Tanshū (Tamba, Tango and Tajima Provinces): central and northern parts of Kyoto Prefecture and central eastern and northern parts of Hyōgo Prefecture

Tosa Province (or Doshū): Kōchi Prefecture

Tsukushi (Chikushū or Chikuzen and Chikugo Provinces): north-western and southern parts of Fukuoka Prefecture

Ushū (or Dewa Province): Akita and Yamagata Prefectures

Wakasa Province (or Jakushū): southern part of Fukui Prefecture

Yamashiro Province (or Yōshū): southern part of Kyoto Prefecture

Yamato Province (or Washū): Nara Prefecture